Transitions to democracy from authoritarian political systems have often occurred at times of economic crisis. The reforms required to transform the economic systems often cause severe material hardships for vast sectors of the population. Hence, new democracies forming under such circumstances confront a formidable challenge: to consolidate the nascent political institutions under conditions of economic hardship.

To identify the reform strategies that lead to resumed growth and strengthen democracy, the authors assess the experiences of economic reforms in Southern Europe, Latin America, and Eastern Europe. They argue that economic reforms must be explicitly oriented toward a resumption of growth, that they must protect the welfare of those hardest hit by reforms, and that they must make full use of representative institutions. A new democracy, they argue, must offer politically important groups incentives to process their demands within the representative institutional framework; otherwise support for the democratic system will be tenuous.

ECONOMIC REFORMS IN NEW DEMOCRACIES

Luiz Carlos Bresser Pereira
José María Maravall
Adam Przeworski

ECONOMIC REFORMS IN NEW DEMOCRACIES

A SOCIAL-DEMOCRATIC APPROACH

CAMBRIDGE
UNIVERSITY PRESS

Published by the Press Syndicate of the University of Cambridge
The Pitt Building, Trumpington Street, Cambridge CB2 1RP
40 West 20th Street, New York, NY 10011-4211, USA
10 Stamford Road, Oakleigh, Victoria 3166, Australia

First published 1993

Printed and bound in Canada

Library of Congress Cataloging-in-Publication Data
Bresser Pereira, Luiz Carlos.
Economic reforms in new democracies : a social-democratic approach /
Luiz Carlos Bresser Pereira, José María Maravall, Adam Przeworski.
p.   cm.
Includes index.
ISBN 0-521-43259-6. – ISBN 0-521-43845-4 (pbk.)
1. Latin America – Economic policy.   2. Mixed economy — Latin
America.   3. Democracy – Latin America.   4. Europe, Southern –
Economic policy.   5. Mixed economy – Europe, Southern.
6. Democracy – Europe, Southern.   7. Europe, Eastern – Economic
policy.   8. Post-communism – Europe, Eastern.   9. Democracy – Europe,
Eastern.   I. Maravall, José María.   II. Przeworski, Adam.
III. Title.
HC165.P46   1992
338.98 – dc20   92-17342
                                                            CIP

A catalog record for this book is available from the British Library.

ISBN 0-521-43259-6   hardback
ISBN 0-521-43845-4   paperback

ACKNOWLEDGMENT: This work is part of the project on East–South Systems Transformations supported by a grant from the John D. and Catherine T. MacArthur Foundation.

Contents

Introduction

The recent waves of transition to democracy began in Southern Europe in the mid 1970s, surged in Latin America in the mid 1980s, and swept Eastern Europe, including the Soviet Union, in 1989–90. The transitions often occurred when the respective economies faced serious difficulties or even profound crises.

In several countries the collapse of authoritarian regimes was accompanied by economic crisis, caused typically by the exhaustion of state-led and inward-oriented strategies of development. The state grew too much, regulated to excess, protected beyond reason: In Latin America the state was onerous; in Eastern Europe, overwhelming. Special interests of bureaucrats, managers of large firms, and private businessmen replaced the public interest. Populist practices, combined with inward-oriented developmentalist strategies, led to fiscal indiscipline and public deficits. The consequence, besides the increasing inefficiency of the entire economic system, was a fiscal crisis: In many countries, the state became bankrupt. Hence, even though the regimes were in various shades authoritarian, the state became economically impotent.

Since economic crises often coincide with transitions to democracy, many new democracies face a double challenge: how to resume growth and at the same time consolidate the nascent political institutions. Moreover, since the reforms necessary to restore the capacity to grow inevitably engender a transitional deterioration in the material conditions of many groups, the consolidation of democratic institutions can easily be undermined under such conditions. The question thus arises whether there is any reform strategy that will lead to resumed growth and strengthen democracy.

Posing the question in this way does not assume that new democracies are less capable of managing economic crises than established democracies or authoritarian regimes. According to some arguments, the capacity of new democracies to undertake stabilization programs and to implement structural reforms is hampered by the vast expectations of economic improvement they generate and by their vulnerability to popular pressure and to interest-group influence, while electoral cycles and pluralist competition undermine their ability to plan for the long term (Stallings and Kaufman 1989; Marer 1991). Yet new democracies appear to have been no less able to impose economic discipline in hard times. Comparative studies of economic reforms in the less developed countries have shown no systematic differences among regimes in the choice of economic reform strategies (Nelson 1990) and in economic performance (Remmer 1986, 1990; Haggard, Kaufman, Shariff, and Webb 1990). And even if it were true that authoritarian regimes are more capable of imposing and persevering with economic reforms, we would not be willing to treat democracy as an instrumental value to be judged by its consequences for economic performance. The question we pose is not how regimes affect the success of economic reforms but whether there are ways to resume growth under democratic conditions.

The ultimate economic criterion for evaluating the success of reforms can only be whether a country resumed growth at stable and moderate levels of inflation. Economic reforms comprise various mixes of measures designed to stabilize the economy, steps taken to change its structure, and, at times, sales of public assets. The central purpose of stabilization is to slow down inflation and improve the financial position of the state. The central goal of structural reforms is to increase the efficiency of resource allocation. The aim of privatization is less clear, since the ostensible reasons for the sale of public assets are not always the true ones.[1] Yet even if all these measures are successful in their own terms, their effect on growth is not immediately apparent. Stabilization entails a reduction of demand, structural reforms engender closings of inefficient firms, and privatization temporarily disorganizes the economy. While particular reform programs differ in scope and pace, stabilization and in particular structural reforms necessarily cause a temporary decline in consumption. To be sustained, stabilization must entail a transitional reduction of demand through a combination of reduced public spending, increased taxation, and high interest rates. Trade liberalization, antimonopoly measures, and reductions of subsidies to industries and for prices inevitably cause temporary unemployment of capital and labor. Privatization implies reorganization – again, a costly transition. Moreover, market-oriented reforms are often undertaken when the effects of the original shock are still present and while some important markets are still missing. Finally, architects of reforms make mistakes, and mistakes are costly. Hence, the effect of economic reforms on growth must be negative in the short run.[2] Indeed, for proponents of reforms, unemployment and firm closing constitute evidence that reforms are effective: If currently low unemployment failed to rise to between 8 and

10 percent in 1991, said the Czechoslovak economics minister, Vladimir Dlouhy, "it would be a sign that the reforms were not working" (*Financial Times*, 6 February 1991). Reform programs are thus caught between the faith of those who foresee their ultimate effects and the skepticism of those who experience only their immediate consequences.

This is why interim evaluations of reform programs tend to be highly inconstant and controversial. Given that market-oriented reforms inevitably entail a transitional decline in consumption, it is not apparent how to judge their success. There are three ways to think about success. The first, followed by Nelson (1990) and most of her collaborators, is to define it merely in terms of a continued implementation of reform measures, whatever they may be; they gave up on using economic criteria to evaluate the success of reforms and decided instead to explain "the degree to which policy decisions were carried out rather than economic outcomes of the measures taken." The second, implicit in most of the economics literature and in Haggard and Kaufman (1991), is to conceptualize success in terms of stabilization and liberalization. The third, to which we adhere, is to remain skeptical until an economy exhibits growth under democratic conditions.

The first conception is untenable, since it is based on the assumption that whatever measures have been introduced must be appropriate. This conception admits no possibility of policy mistakes; and – the point bears emphasis – such mistakes are frequent and perhaps inevitable. The choice of the anchor (the nominal quantity on which the stabilization program rests), the sequencing of deregulatory measures (capital account versus trade first), the method and timing of devaluations, and the distribution of cuts in public expenditures are not obvious. There is no such thing as *the* sound economic blueprint, only alternative hypotheses to be tested in practice and at a cost. Indeed, the sequencing of reform strategies evokes sharp disagreements, and, as the Chilean debacle of 1982 demonstrates, wrong decisions lead to costly mistakes.

The second conception is safer but still based on the conjecture that stability and efficiency are sufficient to generate growth – a conjecture we believe to be false. This posture assumes that partial steps will eventually lead to growth and prosperity. Proponents of reforms argue as if they had a Last Judgment archetype of the world: a general model of economic dynamics that allows evaluation of the ultimate consequences of all the partial steps. Yet this model is but a conjecture. Inflation may be arrested by a sufficient dose of recession, but the evidence that successful stabilization leads to restored growth is weak. Opening the economy and increasing exports may result in improved creditworthiness of a country, but the beneficiaries may be only the foreign creditors.

The sale of public firms may fill state coffers, but the revenues may be stolen or squandered. Thus, the causal links between the particular reform measures and their ultimate goal remain flimsy. As Remmer (1986) reported with regard to the IMF standby programs, there is "only a moderate correlation between the implementation of IMF prescriptions and the achievement of desired economic results."

If the ostensible purpose of market-oriented reforms is to increase material welfare, then these reforms must be evaluated by their success in generating economic growth. Anything short of this criterion is just a restatement of the neo-liberal hypothesis, not its test. Given that the reform process entails intertemporal trade-offs, conjectures about distant consequences cannot be avoided. Yet unless we insist on thinking in terms of growth, we risk suffering through a long period of tension and deprivation only to discover that the strategy that brought them about was wrong. Having cited several instances in which stabilization policies undermined the capacity for growth, Tanzi (1989: 30) concluded:

In all these examples, the *supply* has been reduced, thus creating imbalances that, in time, have manifested themselves as excessive demand. In these cases, demand-management policies alone would have reduced the symptoms of these imbalances but would not have eliminated the causes. Thus, stabilization programs might succeed stabilization programs without bringing about a durable adjustment.

The argument that the worse, the better cannot be maintained indefinitely; at some time things must get better. Resumed growth is the only reliable criterion of economic success.

While economic reforms have been pursued by some authoritarian regimes and by some well-established democracies, newly established democratic regimes face simultaneously an urgent need to overcome an economic crisis and to consolidate the nascent institutions. Hence, the second criterion of successful reforms must be the consolidation of democracy. And if reforms are to proceed under democratic conditions, distributional conflicts must be institutionalized: All groups must channel their demands through the democratic institutions and abjure other tactics. Regardless of how pressing their needs may be, political forces must be willing to subject their interests to the verdict of democratic institutions. They must be willing to accept defeats and to wait, confident that these institutions will continue to offer opportunities the next time around. They must adopt the institutional calendar as the temporal horizon of their actions, thinking in terms of forthcoming elections, contract negotiations, or at least fiscal years. They must assume the stance put forth by John McGurk, chairman of the British Labour Party, in 1919:

We are either constitutionalists or we are not constitutionalists. If we are constitutionalists, if we believe in the efficacy of the political weapon (and we do, or why do we have a Labour Party?) then it is both unwise and undemocratic because we fail to get a majority at the polls to turn around and demand that we should substitute industrial action. (Cited in Miliband 1975: 69)

Hence, democratic institutions can be consolidated only if they offer the politically relevant groups incentives to process their demands within the institutional framework. But economic reforms inevitably engender at least a transitional decline in consumption. This is, then, the source of the dilemma faced by new democracies: how to create incentives for political forces to process their interests within democratic institutions when material conditions must decline in the foreseeable future.

Our purpose is to investigate whether there is a space between these two constraints: a strategy that will lead to resumed growth under democratic conditions. Like everyone else who plunges into these opaque waters, we rely on historical experience, arguments from first principles, and conjectures.

Our argument is based on three interrelated hypotheses: (1) The reforms that constitute the currently standard recommendation are necessary but not sufficient to restore the capacity to grow unless they are accompanied by active state coordination of the allocation process. (2) Since any reform package must consist of discrete steps taken over an extended period, political conditions for the continuation of reforms become eroded without a social policy that protects at least those whose subsistence is threatened by the reforms. (3) If democracy is not to be undermined by the reform process – that is, if political conflicts are to be processed through the democratic institutions – the representative institutions must play a real role in shaping and implementing the reform policies.

In the 1950s, the recognition of economic policy as a powerful tool for promoting industrialization or for achieving full employment led to a successful wave of state interventions in both the developed and underdeveloped countries. In the latter group of countries, development economics, based on the "big push" hypothesis, was the theoretical tool; industrialization was the main objective; import substitution, the basic strategy; the World Bank, the fundamental financial and advisory institution at the international level.[3] Since the 1970s, however, this picture has changed radically. The Keynesian consensus collapsed in the developed economies, and command economies of the Soviet type stagnated. By the 1980s, the monetary policies of developed countries had become stricter, the direction of net capital flows had been inverted, and credits to debtor countries had been made conditional on accepting stabilization and trade-liberalization programs. High foreign indebtedness, usually related to ambitious import substitution and inward-oriented industrial projects, brought many developing countries to fiscal crisis, balance-of-payments crisis, economic stagnation, and high rates of inflation. Concomitantly, neo-liberal thought conquered universities, governments, and multilateral agencies in the First World. Development economics lost ground, and market-oriented economic reforms became the strategy offered by the First World to developing countries. While autarkic industrialization was the blueprint for joining the developed world in the past, economic liberalization is now the panacea offered to the less developed countries, even though in the successful Far Eastern countries and among the OECD countries state intervention, including a large dose of protectionism, in fact continues to play a decisive role.

The neo-liberal policies – the "Washington consensus" (Williamson 1990) – are based on the assumption that an exclusive reliance on markets will of itself bring a massive reallocation of resources across sectors and processes (see, for example, Lipton and Sachs 1990). This assumption is but an article of faith, for the state played a major role in all cases of successful development, including Western Europe and the Far East, by mobilizing savings, providing infrastructure, shaping sectoral priorities, and in many cases forcing individual agents to engage in market-oriented activities through taxation. Stabilization, as well as measures designed to increase foreign and domestic competition, may thus be necessary in many countries, but they are not sufficient to engender growth. Hence, we must think of reforms in terms broader than those usually adopted. Markets may successfully orient individual agents to allocate resources efficiently, but they are not sufficient to coordinate individual actions toward intertemporal efficiency and other normatively desirable and politically desired goals.[4] *Market orientation* is not sufficient to generate *market coordination* toward collective prosperity.

To justify this assertion would call for a lengthy excursion into economic theory. The bare bones of our argument are the following: Those who expect the market to coordinate economic activities toward intertemporally efficient allocations of resources argue as if they could justify the proposition that competitive markets are sufficient to generate efficiency, at least in the absence of public goods, externalities, or increasing returns. But this proposition is based on the assumption that markets are complete; that is, that there is a market for every contingent state of nature. But, following Arrow (1964) and Greenwald and Stiglitz (1986), this assumption is no longer tenable. And when some markets are missing, labor markets, capital markets, and goods markets do not clear, and the resulting allocation can be improved upon.[5] Clearly, as the debate concerning public goods has shown, the mere fact that the market does not do it does not yet imply that the state would do it better. We still need to rethink the role of the state in a decentralized economy in which some markets and some information are inevitably missing. Having reviewed the inefficiencies caused by different types of market incompleteness, Newbery (1989) came to the conclusion that the scope for government intervention is limited. Yet the notion that, if it is only left alone, the market will efficiently coordinate the allocation of scarce resources is purely hortatory. In the words of Murell's (1991: 73) conclusion to his devastating critique of reforms based on the neo-classical model, "blanket prescriptions . . . surely do not deserve a place in the debates between economists."

There is overwhelming evidence (Nelson 1990) that stabilization efforts are normally undertaken as a result of a state's fiscal crisis. By "fiscal crisis" we mean not only that the public deficit is chronic or the public debt excessive but that the state has lost the capacity to finance its debt in noninflationary terms. The erosion of public savings deprives the state of the ability to pursue any kind of development policies. And when the state hovers on the verge of bankruptcy and is unable to borrow, all governments, regardless of their social base, the ideology they profess, or the campaign promises they have made, end up undertaking the measures that are necessary to restore their creditworthiness.

Yet if growth is to be resumed, the goal of reform measures must be not only to reduce inflation and to increase competition but to restore the capacity of the state to mobilize savings and to pursue development-oriented policies. State intervention in allocating resources across sectors and activities, judicious and carefully targeted, is a condition necessary to resume growth.[6] Having examined the characteristics of financial markets in most developing countries, Blejer and Cheasty (1989) concluded that they do not efficiently allocate investments.[7] The state must acquire the capacity to mobilize savings. According to Blejer and Cheasty (1989: 45–7), the government should

aim to set its total tax revenues and its total expenditures (both current and capital) at levels that would yield an overall surplus, which could then be made available, on a competitive and nonconcessionary basis, to the private sector as well as to public enterprises. This would provide the government with a powerful and flexible tool that would facilitate . . . the efficient allocation of investment. [Moreover, they argue] the government could increase domestic savings by undertaking actions which increase the perceived rate of return on private sector investments. One way of doing this would be to invest directly in projects which would result in positive externalities to the private sector.

Public savings are essential to stimulate private investment and to allocate it more efficiently, to permit the state to pursue industrial policies, to promote technological development, to protect the environment, and to pursue social policies.

Economic reforms are inevitably a protracted process, and they necessarily induce a temporary reduction of consumption for an important part of the population. If such reforms are to proceed under democratic conditions, they must enjoy continued political support through the democratic process. The typical argument of economists – that the economic blueprint is "sound" and only irresponsible "populists" undermine it – is just bad economics. A sound economic strategy is a strategy that addresses itself explicitly to the issue of whether reforms will be supported as the costs set in. At the least, reforms must be credible (Calvo 1989): It must be in the best interest of politicians to pursue the measures they announce once they obtain support for these measures.[8] But the difficulty is more profound: how to persuade people to have confidence in the reform process when this process temporarily induces increased material deprivation.

If people are to make intertemporal trade-offs, if they are to accept a transitional reduction of consumption and be impervious to populist appeals, they must have confidence that the temporary sacrifices will lead to an eventual improvement of their own material conditions. The policy style, about which more is said below, is an important factor in shaping this confidence. But even more important is that the imminent danger they face not threaten their livelihood: People whose physical survival is imperiled cannot think about the future. They have no intertemporal trade-offs to make.

Citizens of new democracies expect them to grant social as well as political rights. Demands for the satisfaction of "social citizenship" – in T. H. Marshall's (1964: 76) words, "a kind of basic human equality associated with the concept of full membership of a Community" – require that security and opportunity be shared by all. Social policies respond to these demands through the provision of health and education and through income maintenance. This provision is generally limited when new democracies venture on the path of economic reform; this is why the short-term effects of stabilization and liberalization threaten the basic livelihood of those most adversely affected by steps toward a market economy. The question is whether or not these steps will be continued as a verdict of the democratic process.

Finally, what is at stake is not only continued political support for the reform process, itself a condition necessary to avoid the stop-and-go character of most economic reform programs, but democratic institutions themselves.

Reforms can progress under two polar conditions regarding the organization of political forces: The forces have to be strong and support the reform program, or they have to be weak and unable to oppose it effectively. Reforms are least likely to advance when political forces, in particular opposition parties and unions, are strong enough to be able to sabotage them and not large enough to internalize the cost of arresting them. As Haggard and Kaufman (1989: 269) put it, "The greatest difficulty comes in intermediate cases where labor is capable of defensive mobilization, but uncertain about its longer-term place in the political system." To put it bluntly, reform-oriented governments face a choice of either cooperating with opposition parties and unions, as did the Spanish governments from 1977 onward, or destroying them, as did the Bolivian government of Paz Estensoro with unions.

The generic dilemma facing governments that embark on the path of reform is that broad consultation with diverse political forces may lead to inertia, while reforms imposed from above may be impossible to implement in the face of political resistance and economic incredulity. Faced with this dilemma, governments can adopt different policy styles. At one extreme, the executive rules by decree, imposing reforms without any public consultation, often by surprise and against popular resistance. In other cases, policy alternatives are discussed during the election campaign, but the winning majority interprets its victory as a mandate to proceed by legislative fiat without any further discussion or consultation. In yet other cases, governments consult and compromise with opposition parties as the policy is being formulated and implemented. Finally, at the other extreme, the design and implementation of reform policies are a result of formal concertation with extraparliamentary organizations, notably employers' associations and trade unions.

Yet since the neo-liberal strategy entails significant social costs and hence political opposition, reforms tend to be initiated from above and launched by surprise, independent of public opinion and without the participation of such organized political forces as there may be. They tend to be adopted by decree or rammed through legislatures without modifications to reflect the divergence of interests and opinions. The political style of implementation tends to be autocratic; a government seeks to demobilize its supporters rather than compromise its program by public consultation. In the end, the society is taught that it can vote but not choose; legislatures are trained to think that they have no role to play in policy elaboration; the nascent political parties, trade unions, and other organizations are taught that their voices do not count. Hence, the autocratic policy style characteristic of Washington-style reforms tends to undermine representative institutions, to personalize politics, and to generate a climate in which politics becomes reduced to fixes, to a search for redemption. Even if neo-liberal reform packages make good economics, they are likely to generate voodoo politics.

These consequences are not inevitable. Indeed, the reason why the entire pattern of stop–go reforms sets in is that democracy is incomplete to begin with. In a country with constitutional provisions that force the executive to seek legislative approval for policies before they are launched, with effective representative institutions, and with widespread political participation, a government cannot set out on the path of reforms independently of the support it can muster. Reforms would have to emerge from consultations channeled through the representative institutions. The Spanish Socialist government did proceed in this fashion and succeeded in conducting the country through a painful program of industrial reconversion with widespread support.[9] If democracy is not to be undermined as a consequence of economic reforms, the representative organizations and institutions must participate actively in the formulation and implementation of the reform program, even if this participation weakens the logic of the economic program or increases its cost. And it is precisely the strength of democratic institutions, not exhortations by technocrats, that reduces the political space for the pursuit of immediate particularistic interests; that is, for populism. Populism is an endogenous product of technocratic policy styles.

Our argument thus adds up to three recommendations: (1) Stabilization and structural adjustment policies should be conceived as means for restoring the fiscal health of the state and its capacity to pursue active development policies; (2) any reform strategy should include from the onset a net of social protection for those who suffer the most dire consequences of these reforms; and (3) the reform strategy itself must be a product not of technocratic blueprints but of a widespread deliberation through the representative institutions.

A note is needed to introduce the structure of what follows. While each of the following three chapters is based on evidence from a different region, the structure of the chapters is not intended to be parallel. In the first chapter, Luiz Carlos Bresser Pereira examines the evidence derived from Latin America to focus on the relationship of stabilization, liberalization, and growth. In the second chapter, José María Maravall uses the experience of Southern Europe to examine the importance of social policies for the political dynamics of reforms. Finally, in the third chapter, Adam Przeworski explores the evidence derived from Eastern Europe, mainly Poland, to highlight the impact of reforms on democratic institutions. Our intent is not to provide comparable inductive evidence for each of these points; given the paucity of historical experience, such an attempt is simply not feasible at the present. Nor is it to develop a blueprint for a policy that could be applied everywhere; reform strategies must trade off conflicting objectives to meet constraints that are specific to each situation. All we seek is to expose the tacit assumptions that underlie the current neo-liberal model of economic reforms and to demonstrate that only a strategy that combines an emphasis on growth, income security, and democratic institutions can produce successful reforms.

Notes

1. While the ostensible purpose of privatization is most often to enhance efficiency or to increase fiscal discipline (Lipton and Sachs 1990), the more likely reason is often the desperate need to fill state coffers or to infuse new investment.
2. For a detailed argument that market-oriented reforms necessarily cause a transitional decline of consumption, see Przeworski 1991: ch. 4 and Blanchard et al. 1991: 10–11.
3. We now tend to forget that this strategy seemed highly successful at the time. From 1960 to 1980, the gross domestic product of Latin American countries grew at an unweighted average of 5.2 percent, and in Eastern Europe the rate of growth of net material product exceeded 6.0 percent. Several countries experienced periods when industrial production grew at a double-digit rate. This growth simply collapsed in the late 1970s. Between 1980 and 1985, the average rate of growth of GDP in Latin America was 0.0, and during these years the three Eastern European countries that furnished data to the IMF – Hungary, Poland, and Yugoslavia – had an average growth rate of 1.0 percent.

   Moreover, Murell (1991) has shown that while it seems prima facie apparent that the command economies were less efficient than the more developed market economies, this claim is not supported by empirical evidence based on the neo-classical model. Indeed, the question why Poles massively rejected their economic system while Argentines did not remains wide open.
4. On the static bias of the neo-classical theory, see Fanelli, Frenkel, and Rozenwurcel 1990.
5. As Newbery and Stiglitz (1981: 209) put it, "With an incomplete set of markets, the marginal rate of substitution of different individuals between different states of nature will differ; farmers (or producers in general), in choosing their production technique, look only at the price distribution and their own marginal rates of substitution, which may differ markedly from those of other farmers and consumers. When they all do this, equilibrium which results may not be Pareto efficient; there is some alternative choice of technique and redistribution of income which could make all individuals better off."
6. New arguments in favor of state intervention arise from endogenous growth theories (Lucas 1988; Romer 1990). In these theories either physical or human capital gives rise to positive externalities that generate increasing returns to scale not captured

by individual agents. And although Benhabib and Jovanovic (1991) failed to find increasing returns to physical capital, school enrollment ratios are the only robust predictor of economic growth in a number of recent statistical investigations (Meyer, Hannan, Rubinson, and Thomas 1979; Marsh 1988; Levine and Renelt 1991; Persson and Tabellini 1991).

Another source of arguments in favor of state intervention is the theory of international trade that exchanges the traditional Walrasian environment for an imperfectly competitive one. But even within the competitive framework, industrial policies are justified in a number of cases, in particular when an industry shows increasing returns due to learning. (For a judicious review of arguments for and against industrial policies, see Grossman 1990.)

7. They cite three reasons: (1) The capital market is undiversified and fragmented, (2) financial returns to savings or investment are insufficient, and (3) financial assets bear uncompensated risks.
8. Suppose that at time $t = 0$, a government promises to A at time $t = 2$ if it wins the election at time $t = 1$. A strategy is credible if A is the maximizing strategy of the government at $t = 1$. If a government says, "Reelect us and we will reduce unemployment" when it is clear that anyone elected must reduce public spending, such a strategy is not credible.
9. Note that when the Italian Communist Party decided in 1976 to support the government's austerity policy, it processed a million workers through evening economics schools that explained the necessity of austerity.

References

Arrow, Kenneth J. 1964. "The Role of Securities in the Optimal Allocation of Risk Bearing." *Review of Economic Studies* 31: 91–6.

Benhabib, Jess, and Jovanovic, Boyan. 1991. "Externalities and Growth Accounting." *American Economic Review* 81: 82–114.

Blanchard, Oliver, Dornbusch, Rüdiger, Krugman, Paul, Layard, Richard, and Summers, Lawrence. 1991. *Economic Reform in the East*. Cambridge, Mass.: MIT Press.

Blejer, Mario I., and Cheasty, Adrienne. 1989. "Fiscal Policy and Mobilization of Savings for Growth." In Mario I. Blejer and Ke-young Chu (eds.), *Fiscal Policy, Stabilization, and Growth in Developing Countries*. Washington, D.C.: IMF.

Calvo, Guillermo A. 1989. "Incredible Reforms." In Guillermo Calvo, Ronald Findley, Pentti Kouri, and Jorge Braga de Macedo (eds.), *Debt, Stabilization and Development: Essays in Memory of Carlos Diáz-Alejandro*. London: Blackwell Publisher.

Fanelli, J., Frenkel, R., and Rozenwurcel, G. 1990. "Growth and Structural Reform in Latin America: Where We Stand." Report prepared for UNCTAD. Buenos Aires: CEDES, October.

Greenwald, Bruce, and Stiglitz, Joseph E. 1986. "Externalities in Economies with Imperfect Information and Incomplete Markets." *Quarterly Journal of Economics* 90: 229–64.

Grossman, Gene M. 1990. "Promoting New Industrial Activities: A Survey of Recent Arguments and Evidence." *OECD Economic Studies,* no. 14 (Spring).

Haggard, Stephan, and Kaufman, Robert. 1989. "The Politics of Stabilization and Structural Adjustment." In Jeffrey D. Sachs (ed.), *Developing Country Debt and the World Economy.* Chicago: University of Chicago Press.

————. 1991. "Economic Adjustment and the Prospects for Democracy." Paper presented at workshop "States, Markets and Democracy," University of São Paulo, July.

Haggard, Stephan, Kaufman, Robert, Shariff, Karim, and Webb, Steven B. 1990. "Politics, Inflation and Stabilization in Middle-Income Countries." Manuscript, World Bank, Washington, D.C.

Levine, Ross, and Renelt, David. 1991. "A Sensitivity Analysis of Cross-Country Growth Regressions." World Bank Working Paper WPS 609. Washington, D.C.

Lipton, David, and Sachs, Jeffrey. 1990. "Creating a Market Economy in Eastern Europe: The Case of Poland." *Brookings Papers on Economic Activity,* pp. 75–145.

Lucas, Robert E., Jr. 1988. "On the Mechanics of Economic Development." *Journal of Monetary Economics* 22: 3–42.

Marer, Paul. 1991. "The Transition to a Market Economy in Central and Eastern Europe." *OECD Observer,* no. 169 (April–May).

Marsh, Robert M. 1988. "Sociological Explanations of Economic Growth." *Studies in Comparative International Research* 13: 41–76.

Marshall, T. H. 1964. *Class, Citizenship and Social Development.* New York: Doubleday.

Meyer, John W., Hannan, Michael T., Rubinson, Richard, and Thomas, George M. 1979. "National Economic Development, 1950–70: Social and Political Factors." In John W. Meyer and Michael T. Hannan (eds.), *National Development and the World System.* Chicago: University of Chicago Press.

Miliband, Ralph. 1975. *Parliamentary Socialism: A Study in the Politics of Labour.* 2d ed. London: Merlin.

Murell, Peter. 1991. "Can Neoclassical Economics Underpin the Reform of Centrally Planned Economies?" *Journal of Economic Perspectives* 5: 59–76.

Nelson, Joan (ed.). 1990. *Economic Crisis and Policy Choice.* Princeton, N.J.: Princeton University Press.

Newbery, David M. 1989. "Missing Markets: Consequences and Remedies." In Frank Hahn (ed.), *The Economics of Missing Markets, Information and Games.* Oxford: Clarendon Press.

Newbery, David M., and Stiglitz, Joseph. 1981. *The Theory of Commodity Price Stabilization.* Oxford: Oxford University Press.

Persson, Torsten, and Tabellini, Guido. 1991. "Is Inequality Harmful for Growth? Theory and Evidence." Working Paper no. 91–155. Department of Economics, University of California at Berkeley.

Przeworski, Adam. 1991. *Democracy and the Market: Political and Economic Reforms in Eastern Europe and Latin America.* Cambridge: Cambridge University Press.

Remmer, Karen L. 1986. "The Politics of Economic Stabilization: IMF Standby Programs in Latin America, 1954–1984." *Comparative Politics* 19, 1 (October).

1990. "Democracy and Economic Crisis: The Latin American Experience." *World Politics* 42, 3 (April).

Romer, Paul M. 1990. "Endogenous Technical Change." *Journal of Political Economy* 98: S71–S103.

Stallings, Barbara, and Kaufman, Robert. 1989. "Debt and Democracy in the 1980s: The Latin American Experience." In Stallings and Kaufman (eds.), *Debt and Democracy in Latin America*. Boulder, Colo.: Westview.

Tanzi, Vito. 1989. "Fiscal Policy, Stabilization and Growth." In Mario I. Blejer and Ke-young Chu (eds.), *Fiscal Policy, Stabilization, and Growth in Developing Countries*. Washington, D.C.: IMF.

Williamson, John. 1990. "What Washington Means by Policy Reform." In Williamson (ed.), *Latin American Adjustment: How Much Has Happened?* Washington, D.C.: Institute of International Economics.

1. Economic reforms and economic growth: efficiency and politics in Latin America

LUIZ CARLOS BRESSER PEREIRA

> A pragmatist turns away from abstraction and insufficiency, from verbal solutions, from bad a priori reasons, from fixed principles, closed systems, and pretended absolutes and origins. . . . It means the open air and possibilities of nature, as against dogma, artificiality and the pretense of finality in truth.
>
> William James, "Pragmatism," in *Pragmatism and the Meaning of Truth* (Cambridge: Harvard University Press, 1975)

Introduction

Stabilization and other market-oriented economic reforms face a double challenge in new democracies: They have to be economically effective and politically feasible. Economists usually emphasize the former aspect and political scientists the latter, but the two are interdependent and equally important. It is an error to believe, as political scientists often do, that economists know how reforms are to be designed, and it is also mistaken to assume, as economists like to think, that all that is necessary for the success of reforms is a technically correct program. On the one hand, some economic programs are just wrong because they start from a false assessment of the problem to be solved or because they entail unnecessarily high economic and social costs. On the other hand, political obstacles, particularly populism and all kinds of dogmatism, repeatedly impede badly needed reforms. The recent Latin American crisis is eloquent on both counts. Political obstacles are particularly troublesome for new democracies, where the risk of populism is ever present, but it is important to remember that the present crisis is the heritage of authoritarianism.

In the 1980s Latin America faced the worst economic crisis in its history – a crisis defined by stagnation and high rates of inflation. In the midst of this crisis several countries turned to democracy, and ever since they have been striving to reform their economies. In the early 1990s some countries began to overcome the crisis, but it is premature to say whether a new wave of growth is under way. In 1991 growth in the region was negative; for 1992

Table 1.1. *Macroeconomic variables in the 1980s*

	1980	1985	1989	1990
GDP growth (index)	100.0	102.3	111.6	111.5
GDP per capita (index)	100.0	92.3	92.6	90.6
Investment/GDP	23.2	16.2	16.0	15.6
Resource transfers/GDP	− 5.9	2.7	3.2	2.5
Debt/exports	2.2	3.5	3.0	2.9
Inflation (%)	54.9	274.7	1,157.6	1,260.1

Sources: ECLA (Economic Commission for Latin America), *Panorama económico de América Latina 1990* and *1991*; World Bank, *World Development Report*, various issues; Interamerican Development Bank, *Economic and Social Progress in Latin America: 1990 Report.*

a modest GDP increment, inferior to population growth, is forecast by the multilateral agencies.

The crisis affected Latin America as a whole (see Table 1.1). The performance of individual countries, however, has not been uniform. Some were already growing. Others achieved price stability but did not resume growth. What prevails is stagnation, if not decline, of per capita incomes. Moreover, in the past few years several countries have entered an inflationary spiral recurrently interrupted by price freezes. In Bolivia (1985), Peru (1988–9), Nicaragua (1988–9), Argentina (1989–90), and Brazil (1990), the rate of inflation at some points exceeded 50 percent per month, thus reaching hyperinflation – an unprecedented phenomenon in Latin America.

Why was the crisis so profound? Why did per capita income in Latin America fall by 7.4 percent between 1980 and 1989? Why did inflation, which in 1980 averaged 54.9 percent, climb to 1,157.6 percent in 1989? Why did the share of investment in GDP plunge from 23.2 to 16.0 percent in the same period? Can a sufficient explanation be found just in the populist practices of politicians and in an immoderate state intervention, as we commonly hear? What is it necessary to do to overcome this crisis? For growth automatically to resume, is it enough to achieve stabilization, to privatize, and to liberalize?

To understand the crisis and to formulate solutions, two alternative interpretations can be distinguished: on the one hand, the neo-liberal, or Washington, approach and, on the other hand, a pragmatic approach that focuses on the fiscal crisis of the state. These approaches share several diagnoses and some recommendations. In particular, both are critical of the populism and national developmentalism that prevailed for so long in Latin America. Yet I believe that the pragmatic approach presents a more realistic view of the

Latin American crisis, that it is less dogmatic with regard to the policies to be followed, and that it is more efficient, since it promotes reforms at a smaller cost than the neo-liberal approach. Nevertheless, since the neo-liberal approach emanates from Washington – the dominant source of foreign political power for the region – future policy will most likely consist of a mixture of the two approaches.

Although the focus of this essay is on new democracies, I do not limit my analysis to them. I examine eight countries, of which five (Peru, Bolivia, Argentina, Brazil, and Chile) experienced a transition to democracy in the recent decade, two (Colombia and Venezuela) have been stable democracies for a long time, and one, Mexico, is a semiauthoritarian regime that has recently shown signs of democratization. In all these countries the transitional costs of adjustment and reform were high when the crisis broke out in 1982. One question I try to answer is if and in what way the new democracies reacted differently from the old ones, from the regime that remained authoritarian (Mexico), and from the country where the transition to democracy took place after the reforms were completed (Chile). This means that I discuss not only the economics of reforms – their effectiveness –but also the politics involved.

The chapter is divided into three parts. In Part 1, I review the Latin American economic crisis as seen from the perspective of the two approaches. In the first two sections, the neo-liberal approach to the Latin American crisis – the "Washington consensus" – and the pragmatic approach are defined; in the third and fourth sections, I analyze the Latin American fiscal crisis and its origins. The fifth section distinguishes *market orientation* and *market coordination,* and the sixth outlines appropriate reforms.

The reforms undertaken in eight Latin American countries are analyzed in Part 2. These country studies evaluate the usefulness of the two approaches.

Part 3 focuses on the politics of reforms and their effectiveness. The first section analyzes the dilemma between a frontal attack on the fiscal crisis and a confidence-building strategy, in which the more powerful sectors of society are spared the transitional costs involved in fiscal adjustment. The second section discusses the endemic populist threat to reforms, distinguishing populism in general and the "populist pact" from economic populism. In the third section, the compatibility of democracy with reform is discussed. This section questions the common assumption that economists know what must be done and that the only problem is to mobilize the required political inputs. In the fourth section, a model is built to discuss transitional costs at the moment reforms are undertaken; the costs of adjustment are compared with the costs of muddling through the crisis. The question in this part concerns the political power governments must acquire to reform the state and to recover confidence in the national currency guaranteed by the state.[1]

In the conclusion, besides summing up, I show that although the neo-liberal and pragmatic approaches coincide in several respects, focus on the fiscal crisis of the state leads to a number of distinct recommendations. Whereas the neo-liberal approach attributes the economic crisis in Latin America to the existence of a state too big and too strong, the pragmatic approach acknowledges that the state grew too much – and in a distorted way – but explains the crisis more by the weakness of a state hampered by fiscal crisis than by its excessive strength. The state was crippled by fiscal crisis and lost the ability to perform its role of complementing the market in coordinating the economy. The neo-liberal approach, adopted by the policy-making capital of the world, paradoxically limits economic policy to a negative role: that of reducing the state apparatus. Moreover, it ignores an essential characteristic of Latin American inflation since the 1970s: its inertial character. As a consequence, stabilization programs that follow the orthodox approach, when they are not simply ineffective, tend to generate high costs, and once stabilization is achieved, growth is slow to be resumed. This ineffectiveness is aggravated by the dependence of multilateral agencies upon the developed world and particularly the United States, whose interests do not always coincide with those of Latin American countries. This dependence became particularly clear in the soft approach to the debt crisis.[2] In contrast, the pragmatic approach emphasizes the need – presented by the gravity of the fiscal crisis – to reduce or cancel public debt, and it stresses the importance of recovering public savings. As a pragmatic approach, it emphasizes policy making, discarding the pessimistic neo-liberal view that state intervention is always promoted to the personal benefit of policy makers. It asserts the need for a broad and flexible development policy once stabilization is achieved: a strategy in which state coordination has a subsidiary but significant role and the national-interest criterion replaces nationalism.[3]

Neo-liberal or pragmatic approach?

The Washington approach

The Washington approach to the Latin American crisis has crystallized in the last ten years. John Williamson (1990a) recently published a paper in which he defined what he called the "Washington consensus" – and, though the word "consensus" may be too strong,[4] it is quite clear that some kind of concord on the Latin American crisis does exist in Washington and more broadly in the OECD countries.

The origins of this perspective are reasonably clear. Its roots rest in the collapse of the Keynesian consensus (Hicks 1974; Bleaney 1985) and in the crisis of development economics (Hirschman 1979). It is marked by the rise of a new right – neo-liberalism – that is represented in the domain of economics by the Austrian school (Hayek, von Mises), monetarists (Friedman), the new classics (Lucas, Sargent), the free traders (Krueger, Balassa), and the public-choice school (Buchanan, Olson, Tullock, Niskanen). These views, tempered by some degree of pragmatism, are espoused by multilateral agencies in Washington, the Federal Reserve, the U.S. Treasury, the finance ministries of the G–7 countries, and the chairmen of the twenty most important commercial banks.[5] They form the Washington consensus: the neo-liberal approach that, having Washington as its geographical origin, has a powerful influence over governments and elites in Latin America.

According to this approach, the causes of the Latin American economic crisis are basically two: (1) excessive state intervention, expressed in protectionism, overregulation, and an oversized public sector, and (2) economic populism, depicted as fiscal laxity: unwillingness to eliminate the budget deficit. Following this assessment, economic reforms should in the short run combat economic populism and control the budget deficit, and in the medium term should embrace a market-oriented strategy of growth: that is, reduce state intervention, liberalize trade, and promote exports.

In Williamson's (1990a: 8–17) version, the Washington consensus comprises ten measures: (1) Fiscal discipline should be imposed to eliminate the fiscal deficit, (2) priorities in state expenditures should be changed to eliminate subsidies and to enhance education and health expenditures, (3) a tax reform should be implemented, with increased rates if unavoidable but with the admonition that "the tax base should be broad and marginal tax rates should be moderate," (4) interest rates should be market-determined and positive, (5) the exchange rate should be market-determined, (6) trade should be liberalized and outward oriented (there is no priority for liberalization of international capital flows), (7) direct investment should suffer no restrictions, (8) state-owned enterprises should be privatized, (9) economic activities should be deregulated, and (10) property rights should be made more secure. Note that the first five reforms could be summarized by one: stabilization by orthodox fiscal and monetary policies, in IMF style, where the market performs a major role. The remaining five reforms constitute different ways of saying that the size and role of the state should be severely reduced. Thus, the implicit diagnosis is transparent: The Latin American crisis originated in fiscal laxity (populism) and statism (protectionism and nationalism).

It is worth noting that the Washington consensus says nothing about the foreign debt crisis and ignores the problem of public savings,[6] while economic populism and state intervention are not historically situated. The implicit suggestion is that these problems have always been serious handicaps for Latin America.

The Washington approach assumes that growth will automatically resume once macroeconomic stabilization, trade liberalization, and privatization are completed. There is no doubt about the priority of stabilization. Moreover, market-oriented reforms will probably improve resource allocation and increase the efficiency of the economic system. But in no Latin American country was the neo-liberal ideal of a minimum state reached. Even in Chile and Bolivia, where more was done in this direction, the economic role of the state remains crucial. In Colombia, no structural reforms were undertaken, and yet fiscal discipline was achieved, and in the 1980s the country presented the best economic performance of the group. In turn, countries that succeeded in stabilizing and that are implementing liberal structural reforms, Bolivia and Mexico, present unsatisfactory rates of growth (Table 1.2). Both Williamson and Rüdiger Dornbusch (1989) analyzed this fact, while Pedro Malan (1990) noticed that this situation was provoking a clear malaise in Washington.

The fiscal-crisis, or pragmatic, approach

The assumption that it is enough to stabilize and to reduce state intervention for growth to follow is false. While liberalizing reforms do foster market coordination and improve resource allocation, making the economic system more efficient is not enough for growth. If growth is to resume, it is necessary to combat the fiscal crisis, to recover a capacity for public savings, and to define a new strategic role for the state, so that total savings are increased and technological progress can be promoted.

The fiscal-crisis, or pragmatic, approach relates Latin American economic difficulties to the debt problem as much as to economic populism.[7] Both have as a consequence a fiscal crisis of the state that expresses itself in high rates of inflation. As prices and wages tend to be informally indexed, this high inflation has a chronic, or inertial, character. In the light of this approach, stabilization programs, besides adopting orthodox fiscal and monetary policies, should include incomes policies and should reduce the outstanding public

Table 1.2. *Latin America: Per capita GDP growth and inflation in the 1980s in selected countries (percentages)*

	Per capita GDP			Inflation		
	1985–9	1989	1990	1985–9	1989	1990
Argentina	−2.1	−5.6	−1.8	468.6	4923.8	1344.4
Bolivia	−1.8	−0.1	−0.2	192.8	16.6	18.0
Brazil	2.2	1.2	−5.9	489.4	2337.6	1585.2
Chile	4.4	8.0	0.3	19.8	21.4	27.3
Colombia	2.7	1.5	2.1	24.5	26.1	32.4
Mexico	−1.3	0.9	1.7	73.8	19.7	29.9
Peru	−2.6	−13.2	−6.8	443.2	2775.8	7649.7
Venezuela	−1.1	−10.1	3.2	32.5	81.0	36.5

Source: ECLA, *Panorama económico de América Latina 1990*, and *1991*.

debt. Once stabilization is achieved, market-oriented reforms should ensue, but the state that emerges from these reforms, while smaller and reorganized, should have not only a political and a welfare role but also an economic role, particularly in the area of targeted industrial policy oriented to export promotion.

The pragmatic approach has as its antecedent the dependency approach that was dominant in the late 1960s and throughout the 1970s. The major difference lies in the fact that the dependency approach took the causes of underdevelopment to be structural, whereas the pragmatic approach assumes that they are to some extent strategic. Yet both are concerned with the importance of international variables – at this point the debt crisis – and both are critical of diagnoses and recipes that ignore the specifics of Latin American countries.[8]

Since the onset of the debt crisis, the adjustment programs sponsored by Washington have called for balancing budgets through reductions in both current expenditure and investment. The alternative of eliminating the budget deficit through an increase in taxes and reduction of the public debt has received less attention.[9] In practical terms, balance-of-payments and price adjustments are regarded as so important that the quality of fiscal adjustment is not taken into account. Fiscal adjustment that hurts investment is considered as good as adjustment that cuts current expenditures. Expenditure cuts are treated as superior to tax increases, ignoring the fact that expenditure cuts will usually be regressive while tax increases can be a tool for income distribution.[10] Debt reduction is systematically left aside as a last resource. And the idea that recovery of public savings is an essential part of reforms is usually disregarded.

In contrast, the fiscal-crisis approach starts from the hypothesis that growth does not automatically resume after stabilization, either because stabilization is achieved at the cost of public investment or because reform does not tackle the question of public savings. This approach asserts that growth will be resumed only if stabilization and market-oriented reforms are complemented by recovery of the capacity for public savings and by policies that define a new strategic role for the state. For the fiscal crisis means not only that the state has no credit, being unable to finance its activities, but also that it has lost the capacity to invest and push forward long-term policies oriented to industrial, agricultural, and technological development. Once the fiscal crisis is overcome, public savings will have to be restored in order to finance a growth strategy.[11]

The neo-liberal approach assumes that private savings and investment will substitute for public investment. True, historically this has been the trend. While the state performed a decisive role in Germany and in Japan at the end of the nineteenth century, directly investing in industry, since then this role has been reduced and transformed. Yet it is not realistic to expect that such a transformation would take place abruptly. The substitution of private investment for investment directly undertaken or induced by the state must necessarily be a gradual process. The state, particularly at the present stage of development in Latin America, performs a supplementary but nevertheless strategic role in coordinating the economy and promoting economic growth. When the state is paralyzed because of a fiscal crisis, the whole economy tends to be immobilized.

The pragmatic approach supports trade liberalization, but not as a magic formula. As Colin I. Bradford, Jr., observes (1991: 88), the recent literature on development strategies presents alternatives for achieving international competitiveness: (1) "structural reform of the national economy for domestic competitiveness which results in dynamic growth and an increased supply of exports" or (2) "trade policy reform for international competitiveness which allows the economy to respond to external demand." The second alternative is characteristic of the Washington approach. Its representatives enumerate several prerequisites for a successful outward-oriented strategy (Krueger 1985), but it is quite clear that the essential prerequisite in their view is to liberalize trade and open the economy to foreign investment. The first alternative is preferable under the pragmatic approach.[12] While trade liberalization alone may be an appropriate strategy for a small country like Singapore, Hong Kong, or Uruguay, for the large countries of Latin America trade liberalization should be just one ingredient in a development strategy encompassing public savings and investment in education and technology as well as export promotion. The import-substitution strategy, having a long time ago exhausted its potential, has been given up; it does not assure international competitiveness. But it makes little sense to believe that it is enough for the state to stabilize, to liberalize trade, and to promote public education for growth automatically to resume. In the words of Bradford (1991: 93):

The export-led growth [neo-liberal] idea is based on the notion that if conditions are right, exports will occur, but the theory does not specify the agents of dynamic export growth beyond the efficiency gains from the static allocative effects of getting prices right. The growth-led export [pragmatic] idea is based on a richer range of elements which activate the growth process. These focus on knowledge generation process both domestically through education, training, literacy, R&D support and the like as well as the crucial absorption of technologies from abroad through open economic policies.

The pragmatic approach should not be viewed as a rejection of but as an alternative to the Washington consensus, with which it shares many views. Both are opposed to the "nationalist–populist" posture that still exists in Latin America, although with progressively less credibility and support.[13] The pragmatic approach accepts the need to reduce the size of the state, which has grown exorbitantly in the last fifty years, and agrees that this expansion generated serious distortions, since the state tended to be captured by the special interests of rent seekers. Our approach emphasizes, however, that the crisis of the Latin American state is due to exhaustion of the form of state intervention – the import-substitution strategy of industrialization – rather than to the sheer size of the state. It does not accept the neo-liberal axiom that says, "Since state failures are worse than market failures, the solution is to reduce state intervention to a minimum." Though state failures may be as bad as market failures, economic reforms and, more broadly, economic policies represent an attempt to limit and overcome these failures. Sometimes reforms imply less state intervention, but sometimes more.

Hence, with these caveats, the pragmatic approach supports the liberalizing, state-reducing reforms embodied in the neo-liberal posture. Yet the neo-liberal assessment of the causes of the crisis is incomplete and partially mistaken, particularly since it confuses a deep fiscal crisis with a voluntaristic conception of fiscal "indiscipline." As a result, the reforms entailed in the Washington consensus are insufficient.

The neo-liberal diagnosis of the origins of the Latin American crisis of the 1980s is historically inaccurate. This crisis cannot be attributed solely to economic populism, for populism always existed in Latin America. It cannot be ascribed to an import-substitution strategy, since for many years this strategy yielded excellent economic results. It cannot be attributed to the intrinsically mistaken character of state intervention, because for many years this intervention was successful. Latin American economic development between 1930 and 1980 never would have been so intense had it not been for the active role of the state.

According to the pragmatic approach, the Latin American crisis can be explained by the cumulative distortions provoked by years of populism and national developmentalism, by the excessive and distorted growth of the state, by the exhaustion of the import-substitution strategy, and by the central consequence of all these accumulated trends: the financial crisis of the state – a crisis that immobilizes the state, transforming it into an obstacle rather than an effective agent of growth.

The concept of the fiscal crisis of the state should be clearly distinguished from mere fiscal laxity or budget deficits. The fiscal crisis is a structural phenomenon, not a short-run, circumstantial one. Persistent public deficits certainly engender a fiscal crisis, but once the deficits are eliminated the country confronts a more serious problem. James O'Connor (1973) introduced the concept of the fiscal crisis of the state,[14] explaining this crisis by the increasing incapacity of the state to cope with the growing demands of several sectors of the economy and corresponding social groups.

In the 1980s the fiscal crisis of the state in Latin America had five ingredients: (1) a budget deficit, (2) negative or very small public savings, (3) excessive foreign and domestic debt, (4) poor creditworthiness of the state, expressed in lack of confidence in the national money and in the short-term maturity of the domestic debt (e.g., the Brazilian overnight market for Treasury bonds),[15] and (5) the government's lack of credibility.

A public deficit and public savings insufficiency are flow characteristics of the fiscal crisis; the size of the public debt – be it internal or external – is a stock property. The lack of credit and credibility are sociopsychological phenomena directly related to the real characteristics, but with some autonomy in relation to them. A country may have a large public deficit and also a large public debt, but the state need not lose credit or its government credibility. This is the present case in the United States and Italy, where in spite of the deficit and the debt, there is no fiscal crisis, or at least one much milder than the crises prevailing in Latin America. The loss of credit by the state – its inability to finance itself except through seigniorage (creation of money) – is the quintessential characteristic of fiscal crises. There is thus a direct relation between a fiscal crisis and the hyperinflationary regime that tends to prevail as its consequence.

Most characteristics of the fiscal crisis are self-explanatory. But I believe that it is important to stress the issue of insufficiency of public savings. Particularly in a developing country, this factor has a fundamental strategic role. Negative public savings tend to be a direct cause of low investment rates and the stagnation of per capita income. Public savings, S_G, are equal to current revenue, T, less current expenditure, C_G, where interest is included:[16]

$$S_G = T - C_G.$$

Public savings are a concept distinct from the public deficit, D_G, which is equal to current state revenue less all expenditures including investments, I_G, and corresponds to the increase in the public debt:

$$-D_G = T - C_G - I_G.$$

Given these definitions, and not considering real seigniorage, public investment is financed either by public savings or by the public deficit:

$$I_G = S_G + D_G.$$

These distinctions are important. They are part of the standard national accounts system but with a shortcoming: State-owned enterprises are excluded from the calculation of public savings. Few economists include public savings among their tools.[17] Under the fiscal and monetary adjustment approach adopted by the IMF, the stabilization literature refers almost exclusively to the public deficit. Yet to analyze the economy of any country, public savings are a concept at least as important as the concept of the public deficit.

Public savings will be a particularly important tool if we adopt a broad concept of public investment. According to this concept, public investment covers, on one side, (1) investment proper, which includes (a) investments in projects in which the private sector has not shown interest (infrastructure), (b) social investments (education, health), and (c) investments in security (police, prisons), and, on the other side, (2) subsidies or incentives to private investment (agricultural and industrial policy).

When public savings are near zero, the state will have only one alternative if it wants to invest: to finance projects through the public deficit. However, if the objective is to reduce the public deficit – an intrinsic part of any program to resolve a fiscal crisis – a likely outcome will be a cut in public investment.

If the state invests, its indebtedness will be increasing and its credit diminishing; if the public deficit is eliminated, investment will be cut. And if public savings are negative, the state will have a deficit even if public investment is zero. The deficit will finance current expenditure, most of it typically interest. In any event, the state will be paralyzed and unable to formulate or implement policies that promote growth. And this paralysis, more than anything, reveals the relation between fiscal crises and economic stagnation.

The fiscal crisis in Latin America

Since the early 1980s, when the foreign debt crisis erupted, Latin American countries have engaged in adjustment and reform strategies in accord with the neo-liberal approach. The results in terms of stabilization are modest; in terms of growth, with the exception of Chile, practically none. The proponents of the neo-liberal approach will certainly say that these efforts are not enough: Fiscal adjustment should be more rigid, monetary policy firmer, the interest rate higher. I accept that it is impossible to stabilize without incurring costs. But the efforts must have a return. Yet in many cases these efforts, particularly the stabilization initiatives, have proved to be perverse, self-defeating, since they did not attack the core of the crisis: the fiscal crisis and consequent immobilization of the state (Bresser Pereira 1989). And the other core of the crisis – the exhaustion of the import-substitution strategy – was also not solved, because the state was paralyzed.

Governments in Latin America, which between the 1930s and the 1970s performed a major role in structuring national self-interest and in promoting economic growth through the appropriation and utilization of forced public savings, were hurt by the fiscal crisis and eventually immobilized. Table 1.3 gives figures for eight Latin American countries. In spite of its deficiencies, the table is quite clear on the fiscal crisis.[18] In most countries public investment was kept at least at the level of the early 1980s; in the cases of Mexico and Peru, it fell sharply. The data on public savings are impressive. In 1980, among the eight selected countries, only Bolivia presented negative public savings; in 1988, only Chile and Colombia (precisely the two countries that do not face a fiscal crisis) exhibited positive public savings. The public deficit was reduced in practically all the countries, but it remains high. The only exception is Chile, which has presented a surplus since the beginning of the decade. The deficit in Colombia is small. Mexico, which in this table still shows a deficit, was finally able to control its public finances by achieving an extraordinarily high primary surplus.[19]

Table 1.3. *Latin America: Investment, savings, and public deficits in selected countries*

	Public investment (% GDP)[a]		Public savings (% GDP)[a]		Public deficit (% GDP)[b]	
	1980	1988	1980	1988	1980	1988
Argentina	8.9	7.9	2.3	−2.2	7.6	8.6
Bolivia	1.2	2.7	−6.7	−2.0	9.1	5.5
Brazil	2.4	3.0	1.1	−2.6	6.7	4.8
Chile	2.6	3.5	6.4	11.4	−5.4	0.5
Colombia	6.6	7.7	0.7	1.1	2.5	2.2
Mexico	9.6	4.4	1.5	−0.9	3.8	3.5
Peru	3.0	0.5	2.0	−3.6	3.9	7.6
Venezuela	1.3	3.2	7.3	−0.4	−4.0	8.6

[a]Bolivia, Peru, and Venezuela: Central government only; Chile: central government, decentralized entities, and municipalities; Brazil: state-owned enterprises not included. Argentina, Bolivia, Chile, and Venezuela: Public investment does not include capital transfers.
[b]Bolivia: 1980, central government only.
Sources: Interamerican Development Bank, *Economic and Social Progress in Latin America: 1990 Report;* ECLA, *Panorama económico de América Latina 1990* and *1991*. For the public deficit (PSBR) also Central Bank of Brazil and Bank of Mexico.

Table 1.4 presents some data related to the foreign accounts of the eight selected countries: debt/export ratio, debt/GDP ratio, and interest burden on the central government (external and internal).[20] The table clearly shows that the debt ratios remain very high except in Colombia and Chile. In all countries the debt/export ratio deteriorated between 1980 and 1988. Transfers of real resources continue to be, on average, very high. When they are small (Peru) or even negative (Venezuela in 1988), this may just denote a bad performance of the trade and real services balance and a significant current-account deficit. Data relative to interest payments are not fully trustworthy. Interest paid by the Mexican central government seems to be excessive, but it is consistent with a primary surplus of 7 percent of GDP and a public deficit (PSBR) of 5 percent of GDP.

Origins of the fiscal crisis

As the data in Tables 1.3 and 1.4 indicate, the efforts to adjust the Latin American economies during the 1980s were impressive. Yet they were basically self-defeating. The only country able to adjust and overcome the fiscal

Table 1.4. *Public external debt ratios in Latin America (selected countries)*

	Debt/export ratio			Resource transfers (% GDP)		
	1980	1988	1989	1980	1988	1989
Argentina	2.8	5.3	5.4	−2.2	5.2	6.4
Bolivia	2.3	6.1	4.0	5.4	8.3	−3.3
Brazil	3.2	3.1	3.1	−3.3	6.2	4.9
Chile	1.9	2.1	1.7	−4.2	5.6	4.0
Colombia	1.3	2.4	2.2	0.6	6.7	3.0
Mexico	2.4	3.5	2.9	−2.3	8.4	0.9
Peru	2.1	4.5	3.7	0.0	1.9	3.2
Venezuela	1.5	3.0	2.3	7.0	−4.8	4.4

Sources: ECLA, *Panorama económico de América Latina 1990* and *1991*; Interamerican Development Bank, *Economic and Social Progress in Latin America: 1990 Report.*

crisis was Chile, and this had happened earlier, in the 1970s. Moreover, during the 1980s Latin American countries strove not only to adjust, but also to implement structural reforms. But the results in terms of growth were again unsatisfactory except again in Chile and perhaps recently Mexico. These two countries are being offered as showcases for the Washington approach. For Chile this may be true, but even this country has not followed strictly neo-liberal recipes since 1983. As for Mexico, it is important to remember that stabilization was achieved through a combination of fiscal policy and a heterodox shock and that industrial policy remains on the government's agenda. In any case, Mexico is usually viewed as nearer to the Washington than to the fiscal-crisis approach, particularly because the Mexican government was the first to sign a debt agreement under the Brady Plan.

The fiscal crisis of the state in Latin America was the result of two factors: on one hand, the excessive foreign indebtedness of the 1970s; on the other, the delay in replacing the import-substitution strategy of industrialization with one export-led. The two origins may be reduced to one if we note that the high indebtedness of the 1970s was the vicious way Latin American governments and business enterprises found to artificially prolong a strategy of development that was already worn down in the 1960s. Fanelli, Frenkel, and Rozenwurcel (1990: 1), in their critique of the Washington consensus, observed that the Latin American crisis

did not originate in the weaknesses of the import substitution strategy but rather in the dynamics of the adjustment to the external shock that took place in the beginning of the 1980s. In fact we consider that the principal constraints to growth today originate in the long-lasting features of the external and fiscal imbalances induced by the debt crisis that has still not reversed after ten years of adjustment.

These three Argentinean economists underestimate the exhaustion of the import-substitution strategy, but their definition of the origins and nature of the crisis is an excellent example of the fiscal-crisis approach.[21]

Secondly, the political origins of this crisis are not primarily in economic populism, as is usually thought in Washington.[22] Populist economic policies undoubtedly play a role, but populism always existed in Latin America, and before the 1980s it did not represent an impediment to reasonable price stability and growth. The new historical fact that led the Latin American economies to a fiscal crisis never experienced before was a nonpopulist decision taken in the 1970s, mostly by military regimes, to underwrite an enormous foreign debt and subsequently to have it nationalized. Populism is blamed by the neo-liberal approach for something that was not primarily its fault (Bresser Pereira and Dall'Acqua 1989; Cardoso and Helwege 1990). It was not by chance that the only country in Latin America that presented satisfactory rates of growth in the 1980s was the one that had not previously compiled a large foreign debt: Colombia.

Inability to finance the state through taxes, particularly income taxes, is an essential feature of the Latin American countries in fiscal crisis. Wealthy people do not pay taxes in Latin America. The tax burden tends to be systematically low, not only compared with developed countries but also with Asian countries at about the same level of development (Kagami 1989). Most taxes in Latin America are indirect, so the tax systems tend to be regressive. The state in Latin America was originally financed by export taxes. In the second phase, when rents from primary products exports were reduced, it was financed by indirect taxes and by taxes geared to the setting up of special investment funds. In the third phase, in the 1970s, when these sources of revenue for the state were exhausted or demonstrated to be insufficient, foreign debt proved an easy alternative. When this source was suspended, inflationary taxes increased their role in financing the state. Income taxes always represented a minor fraction of tax collections.[23]

As Przeworski observes, "The crucial question is whether the particular state is capable, politically and administratively, of collecting tax revenue from those who can afford it: in several Latin American countries, Argentina notably, the state is so bankrupt that the only way it can survive day-to-day is by borrowing money from those who could be tax-payers" (1990a: 20–1).

This feature could be attributed to populism, but I would rather identify it with the authoritarian character of the Latin American capitalist state, which entails subjection of the state to the rich.

The fact that governments in Latin America usually tax insufficiently while incurring budget deficits, initially financed by borrowing and later by inflationary taxes, may have an explanation besides populism and authoritarian rule. Some authors, involved in a "new political economy," relate the phenomenon to political instability and political polarization. The perspective of political alternation (instability) and the highly conflicting social systems (polarization) existing in Latin America as a consequence of an extremely uneven distribution of income induce governments to incur deficits today that will be paid in the future by another government probably representing other interest groups (Alesina and Tabellini 1988; Alesina and Edwards 1989; Edwards and Tabellini 1990).

"Market-oriented" reforms

If the pragmatic approach embodies a more correct assessment of the causes and nature of the Latin American economic crisis than the neo-liberal view, the economic reforms that are necessary are also somewhat different. It is not enough to fight populism and to reduce the state. While fiscal discipline is an essential goal, as is a smaller state, state intervention is not intrinsically bad.

The state did turn into an obstacle to growth in Latin America, but in an earlier phase it was a strategic agent of this same growth; the distortions of this intervention strategy eventually exceeded its benefits. The resulting inefficiency of state action plus persistent budget deficits and the consequent public debt led Latin American economies to fiscal crisis. Hence, the fundamental economic reform is to solve the fiscal crisis; that is, to reduce the public debt and recover the savings capacity of the state. This is the condition that will allow the Latin American countries to reestablish confidence in the national currency and stabilize prices in the short run and to replace the import-substitution strategy by a new, export-led and market-oriented industrial policy in the medium term.

Reforms should be "market-oriented" – but this concept needs to be reexamined. In the 1980s the expression "market-oriented" became a magic formula. This fact is expressed in statements like "Economies, to be successful, should be market-oriented"; "only market-oriented economies, like Japan, Korea, and Germany are able to sustain high rates of economic and technological growth''; ''market-oriented economies are economies controlled by a self-regulating market.'' Particularly in Asia, policy makers, who in fact practice state intervention, often use ''market-oriented'' to conceal these same practices, knowing, as they do know, that these practices are not accepted in international forums. Ask a Japanese, a Korean, or a Singapore policy maker how he or she would define their respective economies, and the answer will be, promptly: ''A market-oriented economy.'' Yet when they say this, they are obviously not thinking of an economy controlled by a self-regulating market. As is well known, the state had in the past and still has a major role in the development of East and Southeast Asian countries.[24] In saying that their economies are market-oriented, they are stating something that is true – they are indeed outward-market-oriented – while pragmatically avoiding ideological discussion.

But what is a market-oriented economy? Is it synonymous with an economy coordinated by the market, where the state has practically no economic role? Certainly not. In order to clarify this question, with minimal ideological interference, the concepts of market orientation and market coordination should be distinguished. Market orientation and market coordination are different phenomena.

Capitalist economies are, by definition, market-oriented. They can be inward-oriented, as they were in Latin America during the period of the import-substitution strategy of industrialization, or outward-oriented, as the East Asian ''tigers'' have been since the 1960s. Only statist economies, like the former Soviet Union, are not market-oriented. The state enterprises in these economies do not produce primarily for the market, but for the plan. Capitalist economies, however, are coordinated not only by the market but also by the state: by policy, by some form of planning.[25] Every capitalist economy is a result of mixed market and state coordination.[26] These ideas are organized in Table 1.5.

Since the 1940s, when development economics began to be formulated, the basic development strategy was based on state intervention. The ''big push'' strategy, the theory of unbalanced growth, the surplus theory of labor, the theory of uneven exchange, the two-gap model, and the import-substitution strategy were all based on some form of state intervention. These academic theories were widely pursued by developing countries. Washington adopted them and used the World Bank, an institution that was supposed to lend only to governments, as its main instrument to promote growth. For at least a quarter of a century (1945–70), the developing countries and the World Bank successfully challenged the old international liberal order. But in the 1960s

Table 1.5. *Some countries classified according to market-orientation and market-coordination criteria*

		Market orientation	
		Inward	Outward
Market coordination	Mixed	Latin America	Korea Japan France/Germany
	Market		England United States

some Asian countries realized that the import-substitution part of the overall strategy was exhausted, and they abandoned it. They decided to copy the Japanese model of intervention based on case-by-case industrial policy rather than on protectionism. But the role of the state in promoting growth remained crucial.

In the 1970s, at the very moment when development economics and the Keynesian consensus collapsed, the developing countries launched the New International Order movement, a systematic political attempt to challenge the liberal international system. It was a wrong moment. By that time, several forms of state intervention had gone too far, had provoked increasing distortions, and had facilitated the rise of neo-liberalism.[27] The failure of the New International Order movement is a good indication that times had changed. And around 1970 the academic wave of neo-liberalism was beginning, a wave that in the 1980s would be put into practice by politicians and policy makers.

In the early 1970s the expansion phase of the state that began in the 1930s was over, and a new phase of state reduction was beginning. The cyclical and ever-changing pattern of state intervention once more manifested itself (Bresser Pereira 1988a). The distortions provoked by the excessive and disorganized growth of the state provoked a fiscal crisis, indicating that it was time for debt restructuring and debt reduction, privatization, deregulation, and trade liberalization.

The neo-liberal wave, however, has obvious limits. The attempt to exclude the state from the economy proved to be more rhetorical than real in the industrialized countries. Protectionism increased while neo-liberalism was preached. In Britain, where the neo-liberal rhetoric was particularly loud, some privatization was achieved, but the economic role of the state remained important. The European Community, controlled by a bureaucracy based in Brussels, is a contemporary case of successful state intervention. In East and Southeast Asia, while some liberalization has taken place, the role of the state continues to be fundamental. These economies are outward-market-oriented but not market-coordinated.

Thus, economic reforms in Latin America do not necessarily have to be exclusively neo-liberal, purely market-coordinated. Certainly they will have to be market-oriented. More specifically, given the exhaustion of the import-substitution strategy, they will have to be outward-market-oriented. But their coordination should be mixed, as all the more recent successful strategies of growth are. The condition for success is that reforms must overcome the fiscal crisis of the state so that it recovers its capacity to intervene, plan, and implement policy.

The same is true for Eastern Europe, including the former Soviet Union. The year 1989 was the year of the democratic revolution. It was also the year when it became dramatically evident that statist social formations, where a technobureaucratic mode of production is dominant and where the economy is centrally commanded rather than centrally planned, are unable to coordinate the economy in the long run. What was not clear is that this is particularly true if the state is bankrupt, a victim of fiscal crisis. This is the case in the former communist states of Eastern Europe.[28] Now, after Eastern Europe has had its democratic revolution, stabilization and liberalization are certainly a must. But a priority will be, in addition to reducing the state apparatus, to overcome the fiscal crisis in order to empower the state to assume a positive role in development. The next few years will be years of hardship. If statism is inefficient and socialism infeasible, capitalism is irrational (Przeworski 1989).[29] Markets do not function out of nothing. They are institutions that depend on other institutions, particularly on a strong state and a respected government.

The appropriate reforms

Thus, the appropriate economic reforms are not only those suggested by the Washington approach: (1) to stabilize and (2) to reduce the role of the state. According to the pragmatic approach, it is necessary to add two other directions: (3) to overcome the fiscal crisis, and (4) to define a new (although reduced) strategy of growth, that is, a new pattern of state intervention.

To stabilize the economy is to control inflation and the balance of payments.

The essential requirement is fiscal discipline. The basic tools are macroeconomic: fiscal policy, monetary policy, and incomes policy (wage and price policy).

To reduce the state apparatus is to reduce its size and the intensity of its intervention. The basic tools are privatization, trade liberalization, and deregulation. Privatization is necessary not only because state-owned enterprises grow too much and prove to be vulnerable to external (to the enterprise) political and internal technobureaucratic interests, and not only because they do not respond fast enough to market stimuli, but also because their sale may help to solve the public debt problem. Leslie Armijo (1991: 34), after studying the privatization process in Argentina, Brazil, Mexico, and India, admits that this last consideration is the real motive for privatization, but she adds that the four countries acted on privatization under strong pressure from the Washington consensus. This last motivation is obviously perverse.

Trade liberalization is not a panacea, but protectionism was so strong in Latin America that a movement in the opposite direction was necessary. Besides, experiences of trade liberalization have proved generally positive.[30] This positive result, however, should be attributed not only to the intrinsic advantages of free trade – after all, free trade is not effectively in practice among developed countries – but also to the fact that these experiences are a response to earlier excessive protectionism. The same argument holds for deregulation.

To overcome the fiscal crisis of the state means not only to generate a budget surplus (or a much smaller public deficit) but also to reduce the public debt (internal and foreign), to recuperate the credit of the state and the credibility of the government, and to recover public savings. The basic reform is to restructure the internal and the foreign public debt and their respective interest payments, reducing the total amounts and lengthening maturities.

Given the objective of rebuilding the state's ability to formulate and implement a growth strategy, a restoration of public savings is an essential part of economic reform. In addition to reducing the public debt, tax reform that aims at increasing the tax burden (together with improving tax collections) is the basic strategy to be followed. Internal and external resistance to these measures will be great. The standard argument against debt reduction, which can be achieved internally through a capital levy and externally through some kind of unilateral decision, is that such measures will harm the state's credit. The argument against tax reform is that increasing taxes will hurt investment.

Undoubtedly, state expenditures and subsidies must also be reduced. There are expenditures that just feed a corrupt bureaucracy and privileged business sectors, particularly suppliers to the state. But the limits – economic and political – on reduction of state expenditures are quite strict. Salaries and wages in the public sector are usually very low. Excess personnel in some departments are counterbalanced by shortages of public officers in others. Besides its classic law-and-order role and its social and economic promotion functions, the state in Latin America has always performed the role of sustaining a middle class of bureaucrats. This bureaucracy, usually protected by constitutional rights, is far from idle. Administrative reforms should organize and utilize this bureaucracy more rationally. But this is a long-term reform rather than a short-term measure to overcome the present crisis.

Once public savings have recovered, an essential reform is to define a new pattern of state intervention. The old pattern was based on trade protection, direct investment in state-owned enterprises, and subsidies to private investment. The new pattern will probably exclude direct investment and trade protection, as it relies on privatization and trade liberalization. But it will not ban subsidies of all kinds. The major coordinating role will be performed by the market, but the state will have its part. In the words of the 1990 report of the Inter-American Dialogue: "The objective, in short, should not be to strip the state of its economic role. The challenge instead is to redesign and improve that role and to expand and strengthen the contribution of the private sector and the market at the same time" (1990: 29). Public savings will be used primarily to stimulate strategic private investments and technological developments, to protect the environment, and to ensure health and education standards.

The neo-liberal paradigm dismisses industrial policy. Yet not only successful past experiences in Latin America but also the current performance in Asia and even in the OECD countries show that no government, even Thatcher's government in Britain, can afford not to pursue such policies. Industrial policy, while often disguised, is part of everyday practice in the developed world, particularly in connection with high-technology industry. And an increasing number of studies show the need for industrial policy when markets are not perfect, as is the rule in high-technology industries, where there are large fixed costs of entry, substantial economies of scale, steep learning curves, potential spillovers across firms due to externalities, and asymmetry of information between suppliers and buyers.[31]

Industrial and technological policy will not be based on generalized protection and subsidies, but on a case-by-case analysis of projects, aiming at international competitiveness. Following a market-oriented strategy, subsidies will be targeted to export promotion and directly tied to the export performance of individual firms. As Amsden (1991: 185–6) shows,

> The East Asian evidence suggested that in subsidy-dependent industrialization, growth will be faster the greater the degree to which the subsidy allocation process is disciplined and tied to performance standards – exports possibly being the most efficient monitoring device. . . . The Taiwanese and South Korean states only became developmental pragmatically. Once they began not just to subsidize business but to impose performance standards on it (not least of all export targets), then growth increased.

In sum, although essentially organized by the price system, resource allocation will continue to be influenced by the state. In particular, a subsidized interest rate for financing priority projects will have to be considered. The market interest rate that is required to attract capital flows or to prevent capital flight in Latin America is substantially higher than the prevailing rates in the developed countries. The spreads required by the local banks to cover operating costs are also substantially higher than in the developed countries. The resulting market interest rates for loans are consistent only with extremely high rates of return on investments, rates that could be achieved only through an enormous and probably infeasible wage compression. The alternative is to limit these high market interest rates to the financing of working capital and to nonpriority investments, while overtly subsidizing interest rates of priority investments.[32]

Country studies

Introduction

In the perspective of the two approaches to the Latin American crisis, I now examine what is actually happening in eight major countries. Have they been victims of a fiscal crisis? Which reforms did they undertake – only the Washington reforms or also reforms based on the pragmatic approach? What has been their performance?

Up to 1990, and considering only its eight major countries,[33] Latin America has remained basically stagnant. Income per capita is not growing. The exceptions are Chile, Colombia, and possibly Mexico.[34] On the other hand, Brazil, Argentina, and Peru faced hyperinflation and continue to confront high rates of inflation. The obvious question is, then, whether the countries

Table 1.6. *Chile: Macroeconomic variables in the 1980s*

	1980–4	1985–8	1989	1990
GDP growth	0.1	5.3	9.8	2.0
GDP per capita	−1.3	3.5	8.0	0.3
Investment/GDP	15.3	14.3	16.9	17.7
Wages (1980 = 100)	102.4	96.1	102.9	104.8
Resource transfers/GDP	−0.7	7.0	4.0	2.2
Debt/exports	3.4	3.5	1.7	1.7
Budget deficit/GDP[a]	3.0	1.5	−1.2	−0.5
Inflation	22.1	19.4	21.4	27.3

[a]Minus indicates surplus.
Sources: See Table 1.1.

that have achieved stabilization and growth did previously undertake the four relevant reforms, whereas the countries that have not been successful failed to pursue these reforms. A separate question is why some countries were able to undertake the necessary reforms and others were not.

Chile and Colombia

In the case of Chile, the answer to the first question is positive: The economy was stabilized, the fiscal crisis overcome, the state apparatus reduced, and trade liberalized. It is only not clear what the new pattern of state intervention is. Chile is not a model of a liberal, market-coordinated economy. According to one estimate, during the period 1982–7 subsidies to private enterprises financed by the Central Bank amounted to 4.3 percent of GDP (Oliveira 1991). Codelco, the state-owned enterprise that exploits the copper mines and remains responsible for 50 percent of Chilean exports, was not privatized. It was restructured and made much more efficient and today is an example of successful state administration.

Fiscal adjustment and liberalizing reforms were imposed by an authoritarian regime that for many years counted on the political support of the middle class and capitalist sectors. These reforms were successful. Inflation has been under control for several years. As for economic growth, 1990 was a bad year for the Chilean economy. But between 1985 and 1988 per capita GDP growth averaged 3.3 percent, and in 1989 it reached 7.5 percent (Table 1.6).[35]

Up to 1983 the transition costs were very high. In 1974/5 income per capita fell 26 percent; in 1982/3, 16 percent. Unemployment hovered above

Table 1.7. *Colombia: Macroeconomic variables in the 1980s*

	1980–4	1985–8	1989	1990
GDP growth	2.6	5.1	3.5	4.1
GDP per capita	0.5	3.0	1.5	2.1
Investment/GDP	18.0	15.7	15.4	14.6
Wages (1980 = 100)	106.8	117.9	119.4	115.9
Resource transfers/GDP	−1.4	5.2	3.0	2.2
Debt/exports	2.2	2.6	2.2	2.1
Budget deficit/GDP	6.1	1.7	2.4	N.A.
Inflation	22.2	24.0	26.1	32.4

Sources: See Table 1.1.

15 percent between 1975 and 1985; in 1983 it reached 30 percent. Workers thus paid a heavy toll. Income concentration deepened. Income per capita and real wages in 1988 were not much higher than in 1973. The Chilean society probably would not have tolerated these transitional costs if the regime had been democratic.

Zhiyuan Cui (1991), commenting on an earlier draft of this work, observed that "it is necessary to divide the reform history of Chile into pre–1982 and post–1982 period." Quoting Sebastian and Alejandra Edwards (1987: 215), according to whom the "automatic adjustment macroeconomic policy of the early Chicago boys helped unleash the 1982 crisis," and using information from their book, Cui concludes that "the Chilean success in the late 1980s is due to active state policy in macroeconomic management, promoting investment and conversion schemes. So Chile case actually shed some doubts on 'Washington consensus.' " Cui's observation is consistent with the evidence cited above that after 1982 the Chilean reforms were not as neo-liberal as is usually thought.

The situation of Colombia is different. First, in spite of drug and terrorist problems, Colombia has been a stable democracy for many years. No political transition took place in the 1980s. Second, since Colombia did not suffer from a fiscal crisis, adjustment was not necessary. Inflation was never high. When the budget deficit threatened to get out of control in the early 1980s, it was reduced. The foreign debt is the smallest in Latin America: Colombia faced the suspension of voluntary loans in 1982 only because it is in Latin America, not because its debt ratio justified suspension. Like Chile, Colombia did not want to take advantage of the Brady Plan, feeling that this would undermine its creditworthiness (Bacha 1991). It was the only Latin American

Table 1.8. *Bolivia: Macroeconomic variables in the 1980s*

	1980–4	1985–8	1989	1990
GDP growth	−1.9	0.5	2.7	2.6
GDP per capita	−4.5	−2.2	−0.1	−0.2
Investment/GDP	12.5	13.3	13.7	12.7
Wages (1980 = 100)	105.9	66.0	78.7	N.A.
Resource transfers/GDP	6.2	4.3	−3.3	−3.6
Debt/exports	3.2	5.6	4.0	3.9
Budget deficit/GDP[a]	13.0	6.6	4.2	2.6
Inflation	272.1	268.6	16.6	18.0

[a]Includes central government only until 1985.
Sources: See Table 1.1.

country to avoid debt rescheduling. It is true that the investment rate fell during the decade and that the per capita rate of growth was moderate. Yet it was consistently positive (Table 1.7). What was never clearly defined was the long-term industrialization strategy; basically, an import-substitution strategy was maintained. Liberalization and privatization, although taking place, are very limited in Colombia.

Bolivia

Bolivia is a new democracy that has almost fully adopted the orthodox neo-liberal approach. The only major deviation in the 1985 stabilization program was a foreign debt moratorium.

The 1985 hyperinflation was the result of a fiscal crisis. Current revenues of the Bolivian state fell from 13.1 percent of GDP in 1980 to 4.6 in 1984, whereas current expenditure increased from 16.5 to 25.4 percent. The state was literally bankrupt. Inflation reached 11,750 percent in 1985. In September of that year, the consumer price index increased 56.5 percent.

According to Williamson (1990b: 381), "Bolivia is perhaps the most extreme case of adoption of the policies that constitute the 'Washington consensus.' " The stabilization program was an orthodox fiscal shock. Government expenditures were strongly curtailed, the budget deficit was controlled, the interest rate turned positive, state-owned tin mines were closed, subsidies were eliminated, trade was liberalized (a flat 10 percent tariff was introduced), and the tax system was simplified and made less progressive.

Inflation has remained under control since then. In 1989 and 1990 it averaged 17 percent. Nevertheless, the economy remained stagnant. Income per capita continued to decline in the aftermath of the neo-liberal reforms. Most probably this lack of growth can be explained by the fact that the fiscal crisis was not overcome nor a new strategy of growth defined. The very low rate of investment, around 10 percent of GDP, is an indication that public savings did not recover. The high debt/export ratio provides another signal that the fiscal crisis is still there.

Mexico

The heritage of the populist Echeverria government and the middle-of-the-road López Portillo government was onerous. But after 1983, under President de la Madrid, Mexico began to adjust, and since 1985 has implemented market-oriented reforms. A stable and capable group of economists has run the economic policy of the country since then. When one of them, Salinas de Gotari, was elected president at the end of 1988, the worst part of the job had been completed. Strong fiscal adjustment was under way, public investment and social expenditures were severely reduced, a primary budget surplus was achieved,[36] tax reform was undertaken, trade was fully liberalized (at a flat 10 percent tariff), regulations restricting foreign investment were eliminated, and in December 1987 a heterodox shock, the Pacto de Solidaridad, freezing prices and wages, stabilized the economy.

With the new president, privatization was extended, an agreement with the commercial banks conforming to the Brady Plan was signed, and in 1990 Mexico applied to be admitted into the North American Free Trade Agreement. At the same time, an elaborate social program was introduced, administered directly by the president, who devotes one day a week to it. An innovative feature of the program was its official connection with the privatization program: A fixed and substantial percentage of the revenue the government receives from each privatized firm is reserved for previously specified expenditures on the social program. As a consequence of the good economic results and probably of this program, the government party obtained a landslide victory in the 1991 provincial elections.

What were the results of these reforms? Mexico is being presented today as a showcase of the Washington consensus, an example Washington offers to the rest of Latin America.[37] And indeed the actual results are positive. They are positive because the fiscal adjustment was enormous, because market-oriented reforms were implemented, and because stabilization was

Table 1.9. *Mexico: Macroeconomic variables in the 1980s*

	1980–5	1986–8	1989	1990
GDP growth	3.0	−0.2	3.1	3.9
GDP per capita	0.5	−2.4	0.9	1.7
Investment/GDP	21.1	16.4	17.3	18.9
Wages (1980 = 100)	89.7	72.4	75.4	72.5
Resource transfers/GDP	4.2	9.5	0.9	0.5
Debt/exports	3.2	3.9	2.9	2.6
Budget deficit/GDP	3.0	1.3	1.8	0.0
Inflation	58.1	100.7	19.7	29.9

Sources: ECLA, *Panorama económico de América Latina 1990* and *1991*; World Bank, *World Development Report*, various issues; Interamerican Development Bank, *Economic and Social Progress in Latin America: 1990 Report*; Central Bank of Mexico, *The Mexican Economy 1990.*

achieved through a heterodox shock. The first two reforms are advocated by the neo-liberal as well as the pragmatic approach; the last is specific to the pragmatic approach. Yet results are far from spectacular, basically because the debt reduction obtained under the Brady Plan was modest and the debt remains a heavy burden on the Mexican economy.

Between 1986 and 1988 per capita GDP growth was negative; in 1989 and 1990, slightly positive (Table 1.9). For 1991, predictions were again for a growth rate around 4 percent. Real wages were reduced by 40 percent between 1982 and 1988 and since then have increased only slightly. The fiscal situation was very much improved. A large primary surplus, around 7 percent of GDP, was obtained, but, because of enormous interest payments, the budget deficit (PSBR concept) was not transformed into a surplus but in 1990 neared zero. Inflation, which was blocked in December 1987 by a heterodox shock and a social agreement, neared 30 percent in 1990 but in 1991 was expected to go down to 22 percent. The peso has undergone continuous revaluation since the December 1987 stabilization plan. As a consequence of this fact and of radical trade liberalization, the trade surplus was transformed into a deficit that in 1991 was expected to reach around $9 billion (American billion). The current account is strongly negative, but a large capital inflow (foreign investment and repatriation of capital) is attracted by high rates of interest and a new confidence in the economy. Reserves, which reached $15 billion in 1987, were around $10 billion in 1991.

Mexico is a case of confidence-building, where complying as much as possible with the Washington approach – sometimes only rhetorically – including in particular accepting the Brady scheme to restructure the foreign debt, played a decisive role. Yet this confidence is not based on solid foundations. The debt agreement was clearly unsatisfactory, involving only a minor effective debt reduction.[38] The public debt and the corresponding interest paid by the Mexican government remain very high. The budget deficit is under control only because of a very high primary surplus. Public savings have not recovered. The balance-of-payments situation continues to be fragile, being heavily dependent on capital inflows. In other words, the fiscal crisis of the Mexican state was only partially resolved. The fiscal adjustment was indeed severe, but the Brady debt agreement allowed for debt reduction clearly below Mexico's needs.[39] It is usually believed that the major benefit the debt agreement brought to Mexico was international confidence. But it is important to remember that first Mexico adjusted its economy, stabilized and implemented structural reforms and only later, after the fundamentals were under control, signed the debt agreement.

In any event, this agreement helped to recover international and internal confidence. The question now is whether the confidence-building strategy will be a sufficient substitute for a more direct attack on the foreign debt problem and more generally on the fiscal crisis of the state. In the limited term, if foreign direct investment and capital repatriation continue to be strongly positive, this may happen. But confidence must be based on solid facts. In Mexico, fiscal adjustment, trade liberalization, and privatization are solid facts, but the public debt continues to be very high. And, in the words of the *Economist* (14 December 1991),

For Mexico, external confidence is everything. If there is one thing that keeps economists awake at night, it is the knowledge that about 75% of the inflow of capital is going into easily liquidated portfolio investment, not into new factories, and that the lion's share of that comes from flight-capital repatriated by Mexicans. One thing is certain about this money: it is hot. If there is a shock of confidence, the inflow could quickly go into reverse.

Venezuela

Venezuela also suffered from a fiscal crisis. In the early 1980s it underwent a severe adjustment, and between 1985 and 1988 it resumed growth with reasonable price stability. Reforms, however, were not undertaken, nor was the fiscal problem resolved. At the end of the decade Venezuela was again in trouble, with inflation rising and the economy stagnant. Yet, as in Colombia, the fiscal crisis was never deep in Venezuela, nor was hyperinflation a

Table 1.10. *Venezuela: Macroeconomic variables in the 1980s*

	1980–4	1985–8	1989	1990
GDP growth	−2.4	4.0	−7.8	5.8
GDP per capita	−5.3	1.2	−10.1	3.2
Investment/GDP	24.0	19.2	15.7	14.4
Wages (1980 = 100)	83.1	60.9	38.0	36.3
Resource transfers/GDP	4.8	5.7	4.4	12.1
Debt/exports	1.8	2.9	2.3	1.6
Budget deficit/GDP[a]	0.7	3.5	1.1	−0.8
Inflation	12.9	22.6	81.0	36.5

[a]Minus indicates surplus.
Sources: See Table 1.1.

real threat. Venezuela is so rich in natural resources, particularly oil, that reasonable macroeconomic management will do the job of stabilizing the economy and promoting renewed growth.

In 1989, after a new president, Carlos Andrés Pérez, took office, the decision was taken to adopt the full neo-liberal approach, including a Brady Plan agreement similar to the Mexican one and an IMF-style adjustment program. Like de la Madrid in Mexico, Pérez offered a criticism of the long-term Latin American development strategy. To a certain extent, it was self-criticism, for he had been president of Venezuela earlier.[40] The immediate consequences of the adjustment process were social upheaval, a decline in GDP of 10.4 percent, and a rise in inflation to 81 percent. Indications are, however, that these may be considered transitional costs of a classic adjustment process. In 1990 inflation went down and growth resumed. Obviously, the oil price rise helped the recovery. In 1991, in spite of the decline in oil prices, GDP growth was expected to remain high. Inflation, however, was again accelerating.

Peru

The democratic transition in Peru took place in 1980, when Bellaunde came back to the presidency, but the crucial political and economic event was the election of the APRA candidate, Alan García. After his inauguration in July 1985, his government decided to adopt a typical package of populist–nationalist measures. Inflation was controlled by overvaluing the local currency; the balance of payments, by using a multiple-exchange-rate system. At the same time, the government increased wages and public expenditures, worsening

Table 1.11. *Peru: Macroeconomic variables in the 1980s*

	1980–5	1986–8	1989	1990
GDP growth	0.5	2.5	− 11.4	− 4.9
GDP per capita	− 1.9	0.3	− 13.2	− 6.8
Investment/GDP	22.4	17.9	16.1	17.7
Wages (1980 = 100)	95.0	91.6	41.5	39.4
Resource transfers/GDP	1.9	2.5	3.2	− 0.7
Debt/exports	3.0	4.4	3.7	4.2
Budget deficit/GDP	6.0	6.4	6.2	3.0
Inflation	97.3	299.3	2,775.8	7,649.7

Sources: See Table 1.1.

the budget deficit, while it limited the payment of interest on the foreign debt to 10 percent of export revenues. In the first two years, the economy grew, inflation declined, and wages and consumption increased, as classically happens in populist cycles (Diáz-Alejandro 1981; Sachs 1988). But after this honeymoon the devaluation of the inti became unavoidable, inflation returned, and by 1989 Peru faced economic chaos and hyperinflation. Table 1.11 is self-explanatory about the national tragedy this country is facing: a sharply declining per capita GDP and hyperinflation.

Peru is the bad example Washington usually presents to contrast with its views. Yet this rhetoric ignores the fact that the real alternative to neoliberalism is not nationalist populism but rather the approach that centers on the fiscal crisis. Up to 1989 Peru had not implemented either the Washington reforms or those based on the pragmatic approach; Alan García's government was a model of populism.

The election of a new president, Alberto Fujimori, in 1990, renewed hopes. The new president, like President Collor in Brazil, did not have a political party and a political tradition behind him. Yet in spite of his populist origins, he immediately adopted the Washington reforms. It is too early to draw conclusions from the plans and real achievements of the Fujimori government. By early 1991 the Peruvian economy was showing some signs of recovery (with prospects of 2.5 percent growth), and inflation had come down to 400 percent annually.

Argentina

The Argentinian crisis is probably the most serious in Latin America. The country is an extreme example of fiscal crisis. Argentina was a rich country,

Table 1.12. *Argentina: Macroeconomic variables in the 1980s before and after the democratic transition (1983)*

	1980–3	1984–8	1989	1990
GDP growth	−2.1	0.6	−4.4	−0.5
GDP per capita	−4.2	−0.8	−5.6	−1.8
Investment GDP	17.5	12.0	8.7	7.5
Wages (1980 = 100)	92.5	108.9	83.3	78.7
Resource transfers/GDP	1.0	4.1	6.4	6.7
Debt/exports	3.9	5.7	5.4	5.0
Budget deficit/GDP	12.5	7.9	7.2	4.9
Inflation	191.2	292.6	4,923.8	1,344.4

Sources: See Table 1.1.

but it has turned into a poorer one every year. After Perón assumed power, decadence began. The military, in and out of government several times since the first Perón government, were not able to face the economic problems and modernize the economy. Throughout most of this period, Perón and the Peronists represented the inward-oriented industrial bourgeoisie and urban workers, whereas the military was allied with the meat and cereals export-oriented oligarchy (the ''burguesía pampeana'') and the great bourgeoisie (O'Donnell 1977). Peronists were populist; the military, conservative and orthodox as to economic policy. At the end of the 1970s, under the ministry of Martínez de Hoz, the military tried to follow the neo-liberal approach, combining trade liberalization, fiscal discipline, and a preannounced exchange-rate devaluation. The failure of these policies, plus defeat in the Malvinas war, demoralized the military and opened the way for a democratic transition; Raúl Alfonsín was elected president at the end of 1983.

The Alfonsín government was not populist. Its defeat in the 1987 parliamentary elections is a good indication of this fact. The government did not bow to the demands of the diverse groups and classes that form the Argentinian society. The team of economists who conducted economic policy for five of the six years of the Alfonsín government was very competent. The importance of the state's fiscal crisis was probably not clear to them when they took office in 1984, but the day-to-day management of the economy led them to identify the origin of the crisis in the foreign debt and in the state's fiscal situation.[41] Argentina was the first country in Latin America to combine conventional fiscal and monetary policies with a freeze – the Austral Plan. The failure of this heterodox shock to stabilize the economy cannot be attributed to populism (as in the Brazilian 1986 Cruzado Plan), nor to its emergency and provisional character (as in the 1987 Bresser Plan and Collor Plan I), nor to lack of skill (as in the 1989 Summer Plan and Collor Plan II).

The Alfonsín government was not, however, able to control inertial, or chronic, inflation or "chronic dollarization," an economic phenomenon peculiar to Argentina.[42] It was unable to solve the debt crisis and to overcome the fiscal crisis. This failure is puzzling, for it was not caused either by incompetence or populism; enormous effort was put into reducing the budget deficit, agreements were reached with the IMF about stabilization and with the World Bank about structural reforms, and trade liberalization and privatization were initiated. The neo-liberal approach would probably answer that the Alfonsín government lacked sufficient determination and leadership. The fiscal-crisis approach would add that this lack of strength was particularly clear in two areas: inability to reduce the foreign debt and inability to tax the proprietary classes. The Alfonsín government was not able to establish a consensus among the dominant classes about the gravity of the fiscal crisis, nor was it able to impose its leadership over these classes. Years and years of economic deterioration had weakened the sense of and concern for the national interest in Argentina. The huge capital flight is an indication of this fact. The Alfonsín government, because of its political and personal limitations, and owing to lack of foreign support (the national interest of the creditors represented by the neo-liberal approach was contrary to the Argentinian national interest), was unable to change this situation.

The Alfonsín government ended with hyperinflation. The new president, Carlos Menem, elected by the populist Peronist Party, surprised the world and particularly Washington by its immediate and full compliance with the neo-liberal approach. An economy minister fully identified with the neo-liberal approach and the internationalized bourgeoisie was appointed. Liberalization and privatization were given absolute priority. Tax reform was initiated. For a few months applause in the First World was widespread and warm. But as the fiscal crisis had not been effectively attacked, nor had inertial inflation and chronic dollarization been tackled adequately, four months later, in December 1989, a second episode of hyperinflation erupted, and two months later, a third. The neo-liberal approach suffered a serious setback. Reforms based on liberalization and fiscal discipline continued to be enforced, but the economy did not show indications of recovery. In 1990 inflation hovered most of the time above 10 percent a month, whereas industrial production, which had fallen by 4.9 percent in 1987 and 7.5 percent in 1989, was forecast to fall by 7.0 percent in 1990.

In early 1991 a new stabilization plan – the Cavallo Plan – attempted to control inflation. Since the economy was chronically and almost fully dollarized, the simple idea was to fix the exchange rate to the dollar by law and to reach an agreement with business enterprises about prices. A full freeze was not necessary, because in a dollarized economy an exchange-rate anchor is enough. This plan was wrongly called a dollarization plan. What is actually being attempted is a kind of gold standard: a dollar standard. The Argentinian government committed itself to exchange australes for dollars at a fixed exchange rate. In this way the government also tried to commit itself to absolute fiscal discipline. The dollar standard favors the plan, and so do two other factors: the reduction of internal debt and the consolidation that was achieved through several unilateral measures plus the society's willingness to accept higher transitional costs. Prospects for the Cavallo Plan are not, however, good. The exchange rate was probably set at an overvalued level, and fiscal problems are not solved. Inflation is currently very low, but it takes place mostly in nontradables, every month aggravating the overvaluation problem. Only an enormous surge of confidence, national and international, will save the Cavallo Plan.

Brazil

Brazil was one of the wonders of the world in the 1970s. In the 1980s it was a stagnant country, and in early 1990 it had an episode of hyperinflation. As Brazil is the strongest and most highly industrialized economy in Latin America, the debt crisis was initially interpreted as a short-term problem, one that fiscal adjustment combined with additional finance would solve. This view coincided with the initial diagnosis in Washington: the so-called muddling-through approach to the debt crisis. Playing down the debt crisis was widespread. The authoritarian Brazilian government and the Brazilian elites shared this view with the creditors.

A huge adjustment effort was undertaken in 1981 (before the Mexican 1982 moratoriums), and another in 1983. The current account was balanced, but inflation averaged 200 percent yearly in 1984 and 1985. The democratic transition took place in early 1985. Wrong information published by the Central Bank at the end of 1984 and the beginning of 1985 led the new democratic government to believe falsely that the budget deficit had been transformed into a surplus.[43] Moreover, the large trade surplus in 1984 and some recovery of growth in 1984 and 1985 led most economists to conclude

Table 1.13. *Brazil: Macroeconomic variables in the 1980s before and after the democratic transition (1985)*

	1980–4	1985–8	1989	1990
GDP growth	1.3	4.7	3.3	−4.0
GDP per capita	−0.9	2.5	1.2	−5.9
Investment/GDP	19.3	17.5	16.7	16.0
Wages (1980 = 100)	106.0	112.5	116.0	106.0
Resource transfers/GDP	0.7	4.4	4.9	2.8
Debt/exports	3.7	4.0	3.1	3.5
Budget deficit/GDP[a]	5.4	4.6	6.9	−1.2
Inflation	131.5	313.3	2,337.6	1,585.2

[a]Minus indicates surplus.
Sources: Banco Central do Brasil, *Brazil: Economic Program*, various issues; ECLA, *Panorama económico de América Latina 1990* and *1991*.

that the crisis was over and the country ready to grow again. Inflation, which remained high, would be only inertial or autonomous.

The Cruzado Plan was the result of these optimistic views. Its failure may be explained by its poor (populist) administration. The democratic social pact, led by the Partido do Movimento Democrático Brasileiro (PMDB), which led Tancredo Neves to win the presidency and José Sarney to assume it, was in the end a classic populist pact: an encompassing compromise among social classes based on the belief that democracy and the "right" expansionist economic policies would solve all of Brazil's problems.

But populism, which dominated the first two years of the Sarney government (1985–6), is only part of the story.[44] The basic reason why the Cruzado Plan failed was lack of a correct assessment of the fiscal crisis. The idea of a fiscal crisis did not exist in Brazil at that time. Economists – except for the populist ones – recognized the fiscal deficit as a major problem but believed that its elimination would be a relatively easy job, provided the government was not populist.

In the aftermath of the Cruzado Plan, during the first half of 1987 inflation lost its relatively stable and dominantly inertial character. A hyperinflationary process was beginning. The Bresser Plan was an emergency attempt to stop it. But it was clear to the new economic team that the Brazilian crisis was much more serious than previously thought: that it was not enough to stop inertial inflation and to eliminate the budget deficit, since the economic crisis was basically a fiscal crisis of the state, which had its origin in foreign indebtedness and the increase of internal debt. The Macroeconomic Control Plan was the first consistent official diagnosis of these facts (Finance Ministry of Brazil 1987). This diagnosis distinguished a stock component – foreign and domestic public debt that had to be reduced – from a flow problem – the need to recover the state's savings capacity. The authors, however, did not find political support for their diagnosis and strategy. They left government in December 1987 when inflation was already 14 percent a month and showed a moderate but persistent tendency to grow.

For one year, inflation continued its ascending course. The government tried unsuccessfully to control it through conventional fiscal and monetary policies. In 1988 a conventional agreement with foreign banks was concluded. The agreement was so bad for Brazil that the Brazilian debt was further discounted in the secondary market. Brazil was now experimenting with a hyperinflationary regime. A new freeze, the Summer Plan (January 1989), combined with extremely high interest rates,[45] only aggravated the situation. Instead of helping to control inflation, the high interest rate perversely indicated to economic agents that the state – the great debtor – was bankrupt and in the end would not honor its bonds. Consequently inflation accelerated explosively after the Summer Plan. Artificially holding down public prices and overvaluing the exchange rate did not help, for these were perceived as additional indications of the weakness and disorientation of the departing government. This process culminated in March 1990 when monthly inflation reached 84 percent.

The Sarney government, which left office that month, lacked determination and courage to face the Brazilian fiscal crisis. Fundamentally, it was a populist government – in the first two years, fully; in the last three, hesitantly. And the society was not yet ready for a consensus about how to solve the fiscal crisis. Yet since 1987 some progress in this direction had been achieved: The public deficit had come to be viewed as a major evil. The need for a substantial reduction of the debt – domestic and foreign – is now accepted as much more natural.

The new government that took office on 15 March 1990 profited from this increasing consensus to initiate the next day a new radical stabilization plan: the Collor Plan. The new freeze and the blockage of 70 percent of all financial assets were bold measures, strengthening the impression that the new president had the determination and courage his predecessor lacked. His firm position in relation to the foreign debt provided the same positive signal. His decisions to liberalize trade and to speed up the privatization process were in the right direction. The fiscal adjustment undertaken was very firm: The Treasury had cash surpluses throughout the year, and the public deficit was transformed into a surplus of 1.2 percent in operational, real, terms. A capital levy, which took several forms, reduced internal debt substantially. The foreign debt remained without solution.

The problem, however, is that determination and courage are not sufficient; what is also required are vision and political ability. Vision was needed to make a correct assessment of the crisis, and political ability, to obtain support for them. Neither was present in the first year of the Collor presidency. By May it had become clear that the plan had failed. Still, up to September or October local and international confidence remained high. Only in December, when inflation reached almost 20 percent, did the government acknowledge failure. In January a new freeze was adopted, without adequate preparation and without any political negotiation. From the outset it was clear that this plan would also fail to control inflation. The days of the incumbent minister of the economy were numbered. Her aggressiveness in fighting the public deficit and in reducing the public debt,[46] coupled with her failure to control inflation, made the internal and foreign elites demand her resignation. In May 1991 a new economic team took office. The heroic and often wrong-headed times of Collor and Zélia were over (Bresser Pereira 1991). President Collor ceased confronting society and began negotiating and compromising. He adopted a more relaxed and softer policy style. Nevertheless, in mid 1991 Brazil was still far from stabilization and the resumption of growth.

Frontal attack versus confidence building

Given the accounts just presented, it is now possible to examine the two approaches to the Latin American crisis according to two criteria: (1) the trade-off between the decision to unilaterally or quasi-unilaterally reduce the debt and the strategy of direct confidence building and (2) the trade-off between political support for adjustment and reforms and the transitional costs involved (bearing in mind that they are not a given but also a variable).

Among the eight countries discussed, only in Chile has the full range of reforms been implemented, and even there to a lesser extent than is usually supposed. Colombia did not need fiscal adjustment, since it had not acquired a large debt. Among the remaining countries – all of them victims of fiscal crisis – we have two cases: countries that adjusted in fiscal terms, stabilized, and have been implementing liberalizing economic reforms for some time but have not resumed sustained growth (Mexico, Bolivia, and perhaps Venezuela) and countries that have more recently been trying to implement reforms but have not yet stabilized (Brazil, Argentina, and Peru).

We have seen why the countries that stabilized did not resume growth: All elements of the fiscal crisis were not effectively eliminated, and no new strategy of growth replaced import substitution. Moreover, stabilization programs and reforms were only partially able to re-create confidence in the economy.

A central objective of reform is to recover economic agents' confidence (1) in the national currency, which since abandonment of the gold standard depends on the state's credit, and (2) in the country's economy, which is coordinated and regulated not only by the market but also by the state. Confidence in money means stabilization; confidence in the country's economy, new investment and resumption of growth. Both depend on confidence in the state. How can this confidence be recovered?

Two possible strategies may lead to reestablishing confidence. One is to attack the causes of the crisis directly, reducing public debt unilaterally or quasi-unilaterally and increasing taxes, and consequently facing resistance from the powerful sectors of society that will have to pay the bill. It is to act on the fundamentals. The other strategy is to win the support of creditors and local capitalists while compromising on debt reduction and tax increases. In the first case, the fiscal crisis will be eliminated, and the costs of adjustment will be distributed among all groups: creditors, who will have their loans reduced; technobureaucrats, who will have their salaries and the number of posts at their disposal diminished; capitalists, who will pay higher taxes and will have their loans to the state partially canceled; workers, whose wages will temporarily fall. In the second case, the fiscal crisis will be reduced but not eliminated, since those best equipped to foot the bill – the foreign creditors and the local capitalists – will be spared the burden.

Mexico clearly adopted the second alternative. Brazil and Argentina, facing hyperinflation, had no other choice but the first in dealing with the internal public debt. But the debt reduction was incomplete. There was not, in either case, a complete cancellation of the debt, as happened in other programs of monetary reform,[47] and taxes were not increased as much as necessary. In other words, Machiavelli's advice forgotten, "evil" was not fully done. The fiscal crisis was not fully eliminated, meaning that full recovery of confidence was impossible. On the contrary, as the state broke the law – in effect, confiscating bank deposits – confidence was reduced.

This dilemma – either to act aggressively in connection with the fiscal crisis but risk the reaction of the powerful sectors or to act much less aggressively while trying to be gentle and a reliable partner for the capitalist class – is a classic one. Keynes, for instance, perceived it clearly. In *A Tract on Monetary Reform*, he started from the assumption that a central task of governments is to preserve confidence in money. Yet in the preface to the French edition, he observed that in France, where the situation was not so bad, this task was possible without the government's resorting to extreme measures, whereas in Russia, Austria, and Germany, "the problem of balancing the budget was, during the earlier phases, a virtual impossibility. The initial impulse to collapse was, therefore, also a continuing impulse" (1923: xix–xx). Clearly having in mind this perverse situation, Keynes emphasized that

When the piled-up debt demands more than a tolerable proportion, relief has usually been sought in one or other of two out of three possible methods. The first is repudiation. . . . The second method is currency depreciation. . . . The remaining, the scientific, expedient, the capital levy. [But, he added] there is a respectable and influential body of opinion which, repudiating with vehemence the adoption of either expedient, fulminate alike against devaluations and levies, on the ground that they infringe the untouchable sacredness of contract. . . . Yet such persons, by overlooking the fundamental distinction between the right of the individual to repudiate contract and the right of the state to control vested interest, are the worst enemies of what they seek to preserve. (pp. 54–6)

The problem is to know before the collapse – not afterward – if there is an alternative to breaking contracts. If there is not, or if this alternative is highly unjust, the government will have to consider some type of shock treatment. Yet if contracts are to be broken, it is better to do it in a straightforward way once and for all and, if possible, preceded by some negotiation. Thus, the act is not unilateral but quasi-unilateral: preceded and followed by negotiations.

Mexico was able to adjust in fiscal terms starting in 1985, and in 1987, when inflation had fallen below 200 percent a year, the government was able to control it through a heterodox shock coupled with a social agreement. In this way, Mexico was able to limit violations of contracts. No monetary reform, no capital levy, no quasi-unilateral reduction was undertaken. The only violence was a price freeze. As a trade-off, Mexico had no alternative but to impose high costs on its people.

Perhaps this strategy was possible because Mexico never faced hyperinflation and because it counted on an authoritarian political regime. Just the reverse was the case in Brazil and Argentina, countries that after the democratic transition were unable to adjust, faced hyperinflation, neared or reached collapse, and eventually had no alternative but to reduce the internal debt unilaterally. But this reduction was conducted in such an incomplete and awkward way that stabilization was not achieved and confidence has not recovered.

The politics of economic reform in Latin America

Populism

The Washington consensus and the pragmatic approach agree that it is essential to adjust and to implement market-oriented reforms. Why is adjustment not achieved? Why are these reforms not completed? What are the obstacles the Latin American policy makers confront? In particular, what are the political obstacles? Are they only internal? Is politics only a matter of populism, or should a broader understanding of political obstacles be sought?[48] Are Latin American countries doomed to undertake fiscal adjustment and economic reforms only when the crisis reaches the bottom of the well, when hyperinflation and economic chaos prevail, or will they be able to start reforming before this point?

According to the Washington consensus, the central political obstacle is internal: economic populism. Populist politicians, who control Latin American parliaments and often the executive branch, constitute the main reason why neither is the public deficit eliminated nor inflation controlled. But though economic populism is part of the problem, it is not the essential part. Economic populism is just another name for fiscal indiscipline. It is the willingness to satisfy excessive and inconsistent demands of all sectors of society while ignoring savings, fiscal, and foreign-exchange constraints and to postpone adjustment when imbalances arise. The question is why economic populism is so common in Latin America.

To answer this question it is necessary to distinguish populism in general, the ''populist pact,'' and economic populism. Populism as a political practice is a strategy adopted by politicians to establish a direct relation with the people, using a discourse that emphasizes the national interest, economic growth, and income distribution. As a political practice, populism is reinforced by the existence throughout Latin America of presidentialist regimes and direct presidential elections. Industrialization in Latin America from the 1930s to the 1960s was usually undertaken under the leadership of populist politicians.

They formed "populist pacts": broad coalitions of industrialists, urban work-ers, military and civilian technobureaucrats, and sectors of the old agrarian oligarchy that promoted growth and promised income distribution through state intervention and import substitution. These coalitions ended in the 1960s, replaced by new authoritarian technobureaucratic–capitalist coalitions that excluded workers, giving rise to what O'Donnell (1973) called "bureaucratic–authoritarian regimes."[49] But in most Latin American countries the devel-opmentalist and populist economic policies based on state intervention were maintained by the new military regimes. Foreign debt and foreign direct investment were the new sources of financing for this second wave of import substitution. When this source was also closed in the early 1980s, states in Latin America were bankrupt and the crisis erupted.

Thus, there is a clear distinction among populism in general, the "populist pact" that prevailed between the 1930s and the 1960s, and economic po-pulism. Actually, in these countries, economic populism and orthodox policies tend to follow a cyclical pattern.[50] At some point a populist regime adopts policies that hold down inflation while increasing aggregate demand and growth. The basic tool is exchange-rate overvaluation. Bolstering nominal and real wages and raising government expenditures complete the populist strategy. For some time the results are wonderful; inflation seems under control and the economy healthy. When balance-of-payments difficulties emerge, import controls are strengthened. When demand inflation starts, price controls are enhanced. But these ad hoc remedies do not have a lasting effect. Soon, as exports go down and imports up, the country faces a full-fledged balance-of-payments crisis. Foreign reserves are exhausted, and since the government is forced to devalue the local currency, inflation rises again. When the eco-nomic crisis breaks out, a political crisis usually follows. In the past this was the moment for a military coup, supported by the capitalist class. Populism is over for the time being. By this stage, the crisis is so serious that it is not enough for the new government to devalue. It adopts a full "orthodox" package of economic policies: price liberalization, trade liberalization, ex-penditure cuts, tax increases. Some of these reforms are necessary; others, ill-suited to the economic and social realities of the country. The transitional costs are high and the results not always bright. Sometimes, as in Argentina in 1979 and Chile in 1980–1, they may be disastrous. In any event, as long as economic policies are purely orthodox, growth tends to be modest, eco-nomic inequalities increase, and popular unrest rises. In other words, a new populist cycle is under way.

Economic populism is a consequence of democratic politics in countries where the electoral body is formed of an enormous mass of people poorly educated and economically deprived. Sachs (1988), noting that in Asia economic populism is much less frequent, attributed the problem to the high degree of income concentration prevailing in Latin America. As a matter of fact, some degree of populism is part of the democratic experience in Latin America. It is a problem of political underdevelopment with deep economic and cultural roots. The alternative to populism is, ideally, modern democracy, but in practical terms it has often been authoritarian regimes. Probably a more realistic approach is to live with some degree of political populism while strongly criticizing economic populism. After all, the phenomena are not necessarily correlated. In Brazil, the Vargas regime (1930–45 and 1951–4) was politically populist; economically, it was not. A classic episode of economic populism took place in Brazil under a military, nonpopulist government (1979–80). As Faucher (1991: 1–2) remarks, "populism is not associated with any specific economic policy or program. . . . Populism uses economic levers to satisfy political ends. . . . Populist governments do not always adopt 'popular' economic policies." Menem in Argentina, Collor in Brazil, Fujimori in Peru were elected after classic populist political campaigns, and once in government they adopted orthodox economic antipopulist policies.

Democracy and reforms

If populism is viewed as a perverted manifestation of democracy in underdeveloped societies, the temptation is to ascribe economic reforms and economic efficiency to authoritarian regimes. These regimes will be "a necessary step" not only between underdevelopment and development but also between traditional oligarchic political regimes and modern democracy.

During long years when authoritarian regimes were backed by Washington as a barrier to communism, they were also seen as pursuing sound economic policies. The alternatives were presented as between "modern" authoritarian regimes able to stabilize and populist regimes unable to do so. This view was expressed in Thomas Skidmore's 1977 paper on stabilization efforts in the 1950s and 1960s in Argentina, Brazil, and Mexico. According to Skidmore, "governments in competitive political systems find it *extremely* difficult to reduce inflation, once it has exceeded 10 percent. . . . All the cases of successful stabilization have been carried out by authoritarian (or one-party) governments" (p. 181).

Hence, it would seem that under authoritarian regimes and in two-party systems like the one in Colombia, where it is difficult to distinguish democratic from authoritarian rule, the adoption of long-term adjustment efforts is more feasible than in democratic regimes (Haggard and Kaufman 1991). Yet the same authors, plus Webb, having found support for the hypothesis that "authoritarian regimes may be more likely to stabilize when inflation and social conflict are high," add that their "findings provide no evidence for the general proposition that authoritarian governments have lower inflation than democracies or are more likely to stabilize" (Haggard, Kaufman, and Webb 1990: 4, 23, 27). One reason is that populist–developmentalist practices were pursued by many Latin American authoritarian regimes.

The perception of the economic superiority of authoritarianism was challenged in the 1980s when, on the one hand, the United States changed its policy toward authoritarian regimes in Latin America, and, on the other hand, these regimes became the object of severe criticism on the part of Latin American elites. Since authoritarian regimes failed to implement market-oriented reforms in the 1960s and 1970s and finally drove their economies to an enormous crisis in the 1980s,[51] the new assumption, shared – for different reasons – by U.S. and Latin American elites, was that the new democracies would be able to stabilize and implement reforms. This assumption is confirmed in several new studies. Karen Remmer studied IMF standby programs in Latin America between 1954 and 1984 and came to the conclusion that authoritarianism is not a condition for economic stabilization. She added: "Authoritarian regimes may inspire greater outside investor confidence or otherwise surpass their democratic counterparts in economic management, but they are no more likely to initiate stabilization programs or to survive their political reverberations" (1986: 20). In another paper, where she reported on a study of twenty-one competitive elections in Latin America between 1982 and 1990, she concluded (after noting "the paradox" that transitions to democracy took place in the midst of severe economic crisis) that the new democracies are more stable than is usually thought: "The so-called 'new' democracies do not stand out as a distinctive group that can be characterized as unusually vulnerable to economic reversals. . . . Latin American experience of the 1980s suggests that economic crisis should be described less as a threat to democracy than a challenge posing opportunities as well as risks" (1991: 28–9).

Remmer is probably too optimistic about democracy when she adds that "the assumption that political leaders in new democracies will be peculiarly predisposed to succumb to the temptations of economic populism thus seems inappropriate" (p. 30). Badly needed economic reforms were delayed in the new Latin American democracies, particularly in Argentina, Brazil, and Peru.

When populist leaders in Argentina, Bolivia, Venezuela, Peru, and Brazil adopted nonpopulist policies, it was because the crisis in these countries was so deep that even the short-term costs of sticking to populist policies became higher than the costs of adjustment. When there is no alternative to undertaking reforms, they are undertaken independently of the authoritarian or democratic character of the regime. And indeed a democratic regime is not necessarily less able than an authoritarian one to introduce them.

The political power of a government is derived in large measure from the support it receives from civil society at large and from the country's elites. In democratic regimes, this support tends to surge at special moments, particularly after elections. At such moments, newly elected governments have enough popular support to impose transitional costs on the population. If the economic crisis is particularly acute, the political power of the new government is greater. In Brazil the inauguration of the Collor government (March 1991), and in Argentina the inauguration of the Menem government (August 1989) coincided with bursts of hyperinflation. In both cases the government was very powerful at that moment and adopted strong reform initiatives. Yet both failed. Authoritarian regimes may have more stable power, but only as long as they receive the support from elites. When they lose this endorsement, they are especially weak.

Efficiency of reforms

The frequent failure of fiscal-adjustment and reform efforts poses the question whether or not these efforts are effective and efficient. This is both an economic and a political problem. Political scientists, when analyzing constraints on economic policies, usually accept as a given that economists (or the World Bank or the IMF) *know* which policies are to be adopted. Starting from this assumption, they ask if governments will win the political support or will mobilize the required political inputs to implement the reforms.[52] This question, discussed above, is undoubtedly relevant; indeed, both democratic and authoritarian regimes usually fail to introduce reforms because they are not able to assemble the political inputs required to implement them. But, particularly with regard to stabilization programs, they commonly fail – or engender excessive transitional costs – not for lack of political power but because the reforms are poorly designed.

Stabilization in Chile in the 1970s is a typical case that was successful but inefficient, given the exorbitant transitional costs.[53] In turn, Collor Plan I (March to December 1990) is a paradigmatic example of an ineffective policy.

Its failure cannot be attributed to lack of political power or insufficient political will. It failed because it was poorly designed; because in its second phase, from May to December, the Brazilian government adopted a strictly monetarist strategy, ignoring the fact that the inertial component of inflation was very high.[54] The first phase of Collor Plan I, between March 16 and May 15, was a heterodox shock phase. It consisted of monetary reform that included a capital levy, blockage of 70 percent of all financial assets in the economy, and a freeze. It acknowledged the inertial, or autonomous, character of inflation. After May, however, when it became clear that inertial inflation was back, a second, strictly monetarist, phase began. Ignoring the informal indexation of the economy and the endogeneity of money supply in these circumstances, an infeasible monetary target was defined (a 9 percent increase in the monetary base in the second half of 1990), and everything was subordinated to the attainment of this target. In August an IMF mission visited Brazil and wrote a letter of intent fully supporting the stabilization program, which the Brazilian government signed. This agreement was not approved by the IMF's board, but only because Brazil was in arrears and the commercial banks were pressing for settlement. For seven months, from May to November, mainstream orthodox economists were projecting a fall of inflation "next month," given the abandonment of any kind of formal indexation, the consequent reduction in real wages, the severity of the fiscal policy, the rigor of the monetary policy, the high interest rates, and the consequent recession. When in December inflation reached almost 20 percent and the Central Bank lost control of the monetary base, the prediction of the neo-structuralist theory of inertial, or autonomous, inflation was confirmed. Yet monetarist economists resorted to their classic explanation when their sponsored programs failed, arguing that fiscal and monetary measures were not severe enough. They were. Collor Plan I failed not over a weak fiscal or monetary policy but because, ignoring the inertial character of inflation and the hyperinflationary regime prevailing since the failure of the Cruzado Plan, it did not use an incomes policy and a nominal anchor (the exchange rate) – the two tools essential to control this type of inflation.

In general, stabilization plans that follow the Washington approach tend to fail if inflation is high and chronic with a strong inertial component and thus autonomous in relation to demand. This type of inflation, situated between the moderate inflation existing everywhere and hyperinflation, has been variously called "autonomous," "inertial," "high," and "chronic."[55] When inflation is chronically over 5 percent a month, a series of informal and formal indexation systems are bound to appear as a result of economic agents' struggle to protect their relative share of income. As economic agents index their prices to some index of past inflation, raising them in a phased way, it becomes difficult to curb inflation. Relative prices are continually being balanced and unbalanced, given the lack of coordination of price increases. Informal indexation makes inflation rigid, autonomous of demand, inertial.

To control this kind of inflation, conventional fiscal and monetary policies are not enough. Since the ultimate cause of inflation is the fiscal crisis of the state, a fiscal shock will be necessary. And given the inertial component, an incomes policy, some kind of freeze, is required. This fact, which became clear to Latin American structuralist, and probably also to Israeli economists in the early 1980s, is being increasingly acknowledged. In the introduction to a recent book called *Lessons of Recent Economic Stabilization and Its Aftermath,* Michael Bruno (1991: 2) sums up the findings of a group of economists on this intermediate species of inflation that has become so common in recent times:

Given inflationary inertia, the orthodox cure is necessary but not sufficient. The correction of fundamentals does not by itself remove inflationary inertia, as the most recent Mexican example has shown. Supplementary direct intervention in the nominal process, such as a temporary freeze of wages, prices, and the exchange rate, can substantially reduce the initial cost of disinflation.[56]

This type of inflation is typical in Latin America, particularly in Brazil and Argentina. The Washington consensus, given its monetarist foundations, has enormous difficulty in understanding it. IMF theoretical analysis and the ensuing stabilization programs ignore autonomous, or inertial, inflation. The consequence is inefficient, if not ineffective, stabilization policies.

Transitional costs and consensus

Since adjustment and reforms involve transitional costs, the more general reason why they are postponed is the absence of a minimum political consensus on what must be done. Questioning begins with the meaning of adjustment and reform. The broad objectives – stabilization, growth, distribution – are generally accepted, but from that it does not follow that fiscal adjustment, balance-of-payments adjustment, and trade liberalization should be adopted. It is true that, as populist policies are increasingly discredited, fiscal discipline and market orientation are increasingly included in the consensus. But the consensus usually stops here. Even economists have very different views on how to stabilize and reform. Is it already time for reform? How to share the

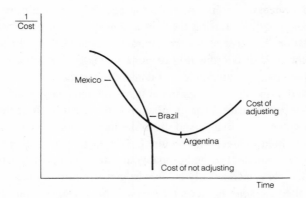

Figure 1.1. The costs of reforming and of muddling through.

transitional costs among social classes? Which groups or sectors of society should pay the bill? Should the sacrifices be endured only internally or shared with foreign creditors?

These questions have no simple answers. Politicians are always under pressure from the constituencies they represent. The rational economic behavior consistent with a relatively high preference for future consumption would be to correct any distortion, particularly any acceleration of inflation, as soon as it happens. But this posture represents some form of anticipation of the transitional costs. In Latin America, entrenched populist beliefs make economic agents accept sacrifices only when the crisis becomes unbearable. But even then nothing guarantees that the consensus will be achieved. Usually economic agents will try to pass the required sacrifices on to others.

The decision to adjust as soon as distortions appear implies a trade-off between the short-term costs, which are in some way anticipated, and the medium-term benefits from reform. Transitional costs are anticipated in the sense that, at this early moment, the costs of reforming are higher than the costs of muddling through, of not reforming. The concept of transitional cost is based on this anticipation. Yet if reform is not undertaken and the crisis continues to get worse, sooner or later the costs of muddling through become equal to and eventually higher than the costs of adjusting and reforming. At this point it is no longer appropriate to speak of transitional costs as an opportunity cost, since not to reform costs more than to reform.

This phenomenon may be seen more easily with the help of Figure 1.1. On the vertical axis we have the inverse of the cost: both of reforms and of muddling through (1/cost).[57] The curve of the cost of muddling through declines at an increasing rate. When it becomes vertical, or perfectly inelastic in relation to time, this means that the economy has arrived at economic disorder or chaos, usually made visible by hyperinflation. The curve of the cost of reform has a U shape. It declines for a while at a declining rate and then inflects and moves upward as the benefits of adjustment increase.

The vertical distance between the curves, where the cost of adjustment is to the left of the cost of immobility, represents the net transitional cost, the anticipated cost of initiating reforms. Net transitional costs are the difference between the costs of adjusting and of muddling through.

While the cost of muddling through is given and retrospective, the cost of adjustment is prospective; that is, it will materialize only if adjustment is implemented. In the graph this cost depends on the time when the decision is made. For Mexico, for instance, the adjustment curve would be upward and to the left. Thus, there is a curve of adjustment for each country, depending on the point at which it decides to reform. But if this is so, which cost-of-adjustment curve appears in Figure 1.1? The curve plotted is "the limit" curve of adjustment – the limit because it is the curve whose bottom point corresponds horizontally to the moment the curve of immobility becomes vertical; that is, to the point where the costs of not having adjusted may increase infinitely. The limit curve corresponds to the last moment reform may be undertaken before economic chaos. It is also the curve that envelops all the possible adjustment curves that could be plotted for any country, depending on the specific moment when it decides to adjust.

From this figure it is possible to derive a rational "bottom of the well" concept. In practical terms, there is no bottom of the well for a crisis. It can go on forever. But we can also define the bottom as the point where the curves cross. At this intersection, the curve of nonadjustment becomes vertical, and net transitional costs are zero. After that first point, it is irrational, even to short-term thinkers, to postpone reforms. Reform is imperative. And probably it will be as chaotic as the crisis it tries to cure.

We can locate on this figure the moment when Mexico and Argentina introduced reforms. Mexico did it at an early stage. Thus, the transitional costs were high. In compensation, the cost-of-adjustment curve soon turned up. This curve is not plotted in the figure, but it can easily be imagined. In contrast, Argentina postponed reforms as long as possible. It initiated reforms several times after the assumption of the Alfonsín government, but it was not able to see them through. Only after several episodes of hyperinflation and after the two curves had crossed were reforms finally implemented: initially in 1990 in a chaotic form, and subsequently in 1991 in a more orderly way with the Cavallo Plan. Brazil is between these two countries. At the end of 1990 it was probably at the point where the two curves cross. Yet, given the experience of Argentina, there was no assurance that reforms would finally be firm and successful. The consensus required to follow through was still to be achieved.

Rational collective economic behavior implies that reforms are undertaken as soon as distortions arise. It requires that consensus on what is to be done be reached as early as possible. Democratic politics is, essentially, a process of negotiation and persuasion that drives society to this consensus. But it is a time-consuming process. And it may be very costly if the required measures are postponed for a long time. The crisis may linger for years while one waits for the consensus.

Leadership matters. A statesman endowed with Machiavellian *virtù*, with vision and courage, may be able to anticipate the consensus. Support will emerge a posteriori, given the success that reforms eventually achieve.[58] The courageous ways in which Mario Soares in Portugal and de la Madrid in Mexico faced the crises in their respective countries exemplify such leadership. But statesmen are a product of chance. In their absence, a country may wait for hyperinflation and chaos before political and economic elites are persuaded that there is no alternative but to adopt a program of reforms.

Conclusion

Two basic alternatives are left in Latin America to overcome the fiscal crisis. The first is to attack it directly, reducing internal and foreign public debt and increasing taxes. The second is to spare the dominant sectors of the economy from sacrifice while adjusting in fiscal terms and implementing reforms. The first alternative is risky. If the attack is not well designed and strong enough, chances are great that the ensuing situation will be worse than before. The second alternative is politically easier, since little is demanded from the most powerful groups, on whom stabilization and the resumption of growth depend. The flow of fiscal measures, the reforms, and an agreement with banks according to the Brady Plan will work toward confidence building. Yet, as it will probably be infeasible to make the workers and the middle class accept all the necessary sacrifices – as the cases of Venezuela and Peru underline – the fiscal crisis will not be completely solved. For some time the threat of the collapse of the whole system will be present.

Mexico is quite consistently following this second alternative. Up to this point the results are mixed. The Mexican economy remained stagnant until recently, and while there is now some per capita growth, it remains modest. Mexico is far from having solved all its problems. Yet it is possible that the fiscal crisis will eventually be overcome through new investment and the repatriation of capital. The debt agreement under the Brady Plan called for an unsatisfactory debt reduction, but it contributed positively to the confidence-building process. Mexico is following this strategy on a razor's edge. International reserves are stable. The current-account deficit is being compensated for by large capital inflows. Oil price increases were a great help in 1990. If the price of oil remains high and if foreign direct investment and capital inflow are maintained, the negative trade and current accounts may be neutralized. And in the medium term productivity increases may bring the exchange rate back into balance.

Argentina, Venezuela, and Peru try to follow the Mexican example – for the moment, without clear success. In 1991 the three countries were being presented by Washington as successful examples. But the deep political crisis in Venezuela, following an abortive military coup in February 1992, and President Fujimori's coup in Peru in April showed that the internal costs of economic reform were very high and that democracy was as yet feeble and unstable. Brazil, as long as it confronted foreign creditors and local capitalists with Collor Plan I, seemed to have chosen the first alternative of distributing among all sectors of society the sacrifices required to overcome the fiscal crisis. But the failure of the orthodox stabilization program that in May 1990 followed the heterodox shock of March left the Brazilian economy in a difficult situation. Washington, having supported this stabilization program, now blames only Brasilia for its failure. In May 1991 a new finance minister, identified with Washington, took office. One year later, however, inflation remained at over 20 percent per month, and the economy was still stagnating.

Latin America is still mired in economic crisis. Colombia, committed to fiscal discipline, was the only country to avoid the fiscal crisis. Two authoritarian governments, Chile's and more recently Mexico's, overcame or are overcoming it. But the transitional costs have been very high. The Bolivian economy remains stabilized but has not resumed growth. Venezuela engaged in a severe fiscal adjustment in 1989 and is so rich that it is resuming growth in spite of the limited debt reduction derived from the Brady Plan agreement on the foreign debt. Peru's and Argentina's crises went so far and so deep, and the hyperinflation episodes and the fall in income were so distressing, that at present the costs of not facing the crisis are higher than the costs of adjusting, including the costs of canceling a part of the internal public debt.

The Brazilian economy, much more powerful, in 1991 had not yet reached the point where a crisis becomes unbearable to society. Most sectors still believed either that the transitional costs of fiscal adjustment were greater than the costs of immobility, or that there exists some magic formula to avoid the transitional costs, or that these costs should and could be transferred to other sectors of the economy.

The neo-liberal approach to the Latin American crisis involves international pressure. This pressure entails formal conditions on the part of the multilateral agencies and informal ones on the part of the governments of the advanced industrial countries and the international business community. I have criticized this approach on several counts: because it does not sufficiently acknowledge the gravity of the fiscal crisis, compromises excessively with internal and foreign creditors, does not provide for reasonable burden sharing, is based on a misguided assessment of the nature of inflation, proposes stabilization programs that are too costly, and, most important, because even if it succeeds in stabilizing, it does not offer effective strategies to recover public savings and promote the resumption of growth.

Yet the Washington consensus, if it is coupled with internal pressure coming from the well-informed and modern sectors of society, if it is identified with the national interest, and if it is determined to cope with the fiscal crisis, to implement market-oriented reforms, and to define a new strategy of growth, may be effective. As it discards populism and nationalism, internal pressure, while rejecting naive internationalism and foreign subordination, may be bolstered by external influences, provided that local governments preserve a critical assessment of the neo-liberal assumptions behind the Washington consensus and that governments, multilateral agencies, and civil society in advanced countries, particularly in the United States, are less doctrinaire and more pragmatic.

Politics is the art of compromise – compromise that in Latin America has to be achieved not only internally but also in international relations. Neo-liberalism is rhetoric rather than an effective practice in the advanced countries. It is usually doctrinaire rhetoric. But it is rhetoric that has to be taken into consideration, particularly when it argues for badly needed fiscal discipline and market-oriented reforms.

The fundamental challenge faced by Latin America is its fiscal crisis. Stabilization as well as the resumption of growth depend on overcoming the insolvency of the state and on recovering public savings. Washington, while pressing for the elimination of the public deficit, pays much less attention to the recovery of public savings. The structural reforms it insists on have an essentially negative character. They must lead to a new development strategy where the market will play the major role but a reorganized and reduced state has an orienting task.

Latin America is a dependent region. The national interest of each of its countries has much in common with the national interest of advanced countries, particularly the United States. But there are also conflicts of interests and of views. Compromise will have to be achieved on a variety of issues – compromise that acknowledges differences but does not overestimate them.

Notes

1. I do not use the words "government" and "state" as synonyms, as is usual in Anglo-Saxon countries. In this chapter they are distinct concepts. The *government* is the body that runs the state (the presidency and its ministers, the legislature, the supreme court). The *state* is the bureaucratic organization, the apparatus, that has the exclusive power to legislate and to tax the population living in a given territory. Thus, the state is a larger entity of which the government is an essential part. Still larger is the concept of the *nation-state,* the sovereign country or nation, which should not be confused with the state.

2. Washington, although dominated by neo-liberal ideas, remains very much worried by income and wealth concentrations in Latin America. It knows that inequality is not just a major social problem but also a crucial obstacle to effective modernization in the region.

3. On the pragmatic aspect of the approach I am proposing, see my paper "A Pragmatic Approach to State Intervention" (1990), where I analyze the pragmatic approach East and Southeast Asian economists use to deal with their problems.

4. The "Washington approach" is the dominant approach in Washington and more broadly in the industrialized countries, but it is not necessarily a consensual one. Richard Feinberg, commenting on Williamson's paper, left it clear that although there is a movement toward a "centrist consensus" in Washington, there are many doubts: "An example, the role of the state. We agreed that there should be some trimming and streamlining. But do we want the final product to be a sleek high performance Jaguar or a minimalist Yugo?" (1990: 22).

5. In relation to the management of the foreign debt crisis, this group forms what Susan George called the "system" (1988). This system is commanded by the Treasury and has as basic arms the Fund for International Development and the World Bank. The finance ministers of the other G–7 countries, on one side, and the chairmen of the most important international banks (around twenty), on the other, complete the system. In the early phase of the debt crisis, the Federal Reserve Bank, then governed by Paul Volcker, represented the U.S. government. After the announcement of the Baker Plan (1985), the influence of the Fed began to diminish and practically disappeared after Volcker left its governorship in 1987.

6. This omission of foreign debt is not casual. Although Washington recognizes the

existence of a debt crisis – or rather a debt "problem" – the current position is that this problem has been grossly overestimated.

7. It is not as easy as in the case of the Washington approach to define the sponsors of what I am calling, for lack of an established name, the fiscal-crisis, or pragmatic, approach: "fiscal crisis" to underline the basic cause of the Latin American crisis, "pragmatic" to disallow any kind of dogmatism. As direct predecessors of the present chapter I should cite Sachs 1987; Dornbusch 1989; Fanelli, Frenkel, and Rozenwurcel 1990; and my essay "A Pragmatic Approach to State Intervention" (Bresser Pereira 1990). Here I will quote several economists, not only in Latin America and Asia, but also in the USA and Europe, who share the basic tenets of this approach. Among the economists quoted in this essay, besides the other two coauthors of this book, Adam Przeworski and José María Maravall, I would indicate as sharing my espousal of the fiscal-crisis, or pragmatic, approach Adolfo Canitrot, Albert Hirschman, Alice Amsden, Andre Lara Resende, Edmar Bacha, Colin I. Bradford, Jr., Elhanan Helpman, Eliana Cardoso, Felipe Passos, Fernando Fajnzylber, Gene Grossman, Guillermo Rozenwurcel, Jeffrey Sachs, José María Fanelli, Joseph Ramos, Michael Bruno, Miguel Kiguel, Mitsuhiro Kagami, Nora Lustig, Paul Beckerman, Paul Krugman, Pedro Malan, Persio Arida, Richard Feinberg, Roberto Frenkel, Rogério Werneck, Rüdiger Dornbusch, Sebastian Edwards, Werner Baer, and Yoshiaki Nakano.

8. Barbara Stallings (1991: 3) pointed out recently that "the older ideas about external influence have been too quickly abandoned. Ironically, just as international variables became specially important in the 1980s, they disappeared as a key factor from theories of development."

9. This is not consensual in Washington. The World Bank has recently been stressing the importance of increasing taxes to balance budgets and also to finance antipoverty programs that would make fiscal adjustment and structural reforms compatible with democracy. The IMF is increasingly worried about how to achieve stabilization with growth. See particularly Vito Tanzi's paper (1989) in the IMF book edited by Mario Blejer and Ke-young Chu, *Fiscal Policy, Stabilization and Growth in Developing Countries* (1989).

10. This critique was originally Sachs's (1987).

11. There is obviously an alternative: to finance growth with foreign savings, particularly with foreign direct investment. This is in part the route being followed by Mexico. Foreign investment and capital repatriation have permitted Mexico to overcome stagnation and start economic recovery.

12. It is present, for instance, in Fajnzylber 1990.

13. The populist and nationalist approach shuns any type of adjustment, assumes that fiscal deficits and higher wages are functional in invigorating aggregate demand and growth, and denies that state intervention was too great and that the protectionist import-substitution strategy is exhausted. The number of proponents of these ideas in Latin America has been drastically reduced in recent years. The corresponding practices, however, continue to be widespread.

14. There is a redundancy in this expression; a fiscal crisis is always a crisis of the state. "Financial crisis of the state" is an alternative expression with the same meaning. "Fiscal crisis of the state," however, serves to stress that the state is in a crisis.

15. The state in Brazil is internally financed by the overnight market. Every day economic agents transform their deposit accounts in the banks into loans to the state with a maturity of one day. In this way, financial assets are indexed and protected from inflation, and the state is financed with a bond that is quasi-money. Collor Plan I (March 1990) was an attempt to cope with this problem (Bresser Pereira and Nakano 1990).

16. We could exclude from current revenue and expenditure the state-owned enterprises. In such a case, the simplest way to consider their savings (or dissavings) is to add to each identity the profits (savings) or deduct the losses (dissavings).

17. I have no knowledge of any study of public savings in Latin American countries. For Brazil, the information exists but, as everywhere, excludes the state-owned enterprises. An economist who used the public savings concept in a pioneering way was Rogério Werneck in his study of the economy of the Brazilian state (1987).

18. As the notes to Table 1.3 state, the criteria are not the same for all countries. For some countries, state-owned enterprises are included; for others, they are not.

19. In Mexico the public deficit increased up to 1982, when it reached 8.3 percent of GDP, and then decreased because of a particularly strong fiscal adjustment. In 1989 the Mexican public deficit fell to 1.8 percent. In 1990 it reached zero. However, data about the operational public deficit (PSBR – public sector borrowing requirement in real terms) are not usually mentioned by the proponents of the Washington consensus when they refer to Mexico. They normally use the concept of primary deficit (public deficit minus interest), which in 1980 was 3.1 percent of GDP and increased to 7.4 percent in 1982 but since 1983 has been greatly reduced, changing into a primary surplus of 8.0 percent of GDP in 1988 and 7.8 percent in 1989. The primary surplus shows, undubitably, the great effort undertaken by Mexico. But the permanence of a considerable public deficit, which only in 1990 reached zero, is an indication that the public debt problem – particularly the foreign public debt – was not solved, which constrains the Mexican government to pay an enormous sum in interest.

20. These ratios, together with the data in Table 1.3, particularly the public savings ratio, are excellent indicators of the fiscal crisis. An additional and important piece of information would be total public indebtedness (internal and external, including state-owned enterprises), but I have not been able to find these data for the eight countries. The interest burden on the central government gives an indication.

21. On the fiscal character of the crisis, see also Sachs 1987; Bresser Pereira 1987, 1988b; Reisen and Trotsenburg 1988; Fanelli and Frenkel 1989.

22. Economic populism has some classic contributions: Canitrot 1975, O'Donnell 1977, and Diáz-Alejandro 1981. These papers plus recent contributions by Sachs (1988), Dornbusch and Edwards (1989), Cardoso and Helwege (1990), and myself, alone (1988c) and with Fernando Dall'Acqua (1989), were put together in a book, *Populismo econômico,* ed. Bresser Pereira (São Paulo: Nobel, 1991).

23. The average revenue from income taxes in Latin America in 1988 was only 23 percent of total government revenues. And this figure is inflated because of oil producers like Ecuador and Mexico (Cheibub 1991).

24. Proponents of the Washington approach try insistently to use the Asian NICs (New Industrializing Countries) to support their views, which does not make sense in view of the role of the state. The definitive book on this subject was written by Alice Amsden (1989).

25. Robert Heilbroner (1990: 98) observes: "Capitalism is thus intimately entangled with planning as is the market. Its entanglement is called not planning but economic policy, and I need hardly add that economic policy is very different from central planning. It is planning nonetheless – that is, a deliberate effort to bring about some outcome different from that would otherwise emerge from the market process."

26. Sachs (1987), criticizing the Washington approach, showed that the economic success of Japan, Korea, and Taiwan cannot be attributed to trade liberalization, given the mixed character of these economies, where the state continues to play a decisive role.

27. Stephen Krasner (1985: 7) observes that "the demands associated with proposals for the New International Order, which assumed their greatest saliency in the mid–1970s, are the clearest manifestation of the Third World efforts to restructure market oriented international regimes."

28. I examined statist social formations and the technobureaucratic mode of production in my 1981a.

29. According to Przeworski, "capitalism is irrational in the sense that under this system we cannot use full productive potential without rewarding those who control the productive endowments." In turn, socialism, which he defines "as synonymous with centralized command over resource allocation," is infeasible, while "in the real world people starve" (1989: 3, 16, 28).

30. See especially the study by Michaely, Papageorgiou, and Choksi (1991).

31. For a survey of these studies, see Grossman 1990. Among the works surveyed are Grossman and Helpman 1986, Pack and Westphal 1986, Krugman 1987, Flam and Staiger 1989, and Helpman and Krugman 1989.

32. Real interest for investors in the developed countries is around 4 percent. The spread is 2 percent. Thus, the real interest rate for loans will be around 6 percent, consistent with a reasonable rate of return on investments of around 12 percent. In Latin America the real interest rate that would attract capital is around 10 percent and the spread required by the banks around 5 percent. Thus, the real interest rate on loans – 15 percent – will be consistent only with an average rate of return on investment of around 25 percent. Such a high rate of return would only be possible with additional concentration of incomes in a region where this is already a major economic and political problem.

33. Brazil, Mexico, Argentina, Chile, Venezuela, Colombia, Peru, and Bolivia.

34. Mexico's per capita rates of growth in 1989 and 1990 were respectively 0.8 and 0.4 percent.

35. It is important to note that a substantial part of the high rates of growth may be explained by the increase in copper prices in the international market since 1985. This increase was fully captured by Codelco, whereas in Peru, for instance, the same did not happen. I owe this observation to Roberto Frenkel.

36. Primary budget surplus (or deficit) is equal to budget deficit minus interest on internal and foreign debt.

37. David Goldman, for instance, wrote in *Forbes* magazine (9 July 1990): "Mexico's stock market index has approximately doubled since July 1989. . . . Under President Carlos Salinas de Gotari, Mexico is set to repeat the success story of South Korea but on a far grander scale."

38. Debt reduction in net cash-flow terms, taking into account the new loans that had to be offered as collateral to the banks, was around 10 percent, when a reasonable reduction would be 60 percent (see Lustig 1990). According to Bacha (1991: 9), the reduction in net annual interest due was 19 percent. But he used a Libor of 9.125 percent. "If the calculations were done with the much lower Libor rates observed in 1990–91, the interest savings would be correspondingly reduced."

39. Obviously, assessment of the Mexican debt agreement is the subject of controversy. Wijnbergen (1991: 41), for instance, believes that "the package meets Mexico's financing needs as currently projected and is compatible with a gradual recovery of growth in Mexico over the next six years." A different view is held by Islam (1990), according to whom the Brady Plan missed the opportunity to give breathing room for growth. I think that Mexico's positive performance is better accounted for by sounder policies and higher oil prices.

40. President Pérez (1990) declared to a Brazilian journalist that "there was a basic mistake in the Latin American development process. . . . Governments developed a series of defensive strategies against abusive practices of international capital, which we then called imperialism. This brought excessive state intervention and an artificially protected economy."

41. Mario Brodersohn, who was responsible for negotiations on the foreign debt in the Alfonsín government, says: "There is today a broad political consensus in Argentina that the public sector faces a deep structural crisis" (1989: 1). This consensus did not exist in 1984 when Juan Sourrouille's economic team took office. The same thing happened in Brazil. Only in 1987, after the failure of the Cruzado Plan, did it become clear that a fiscal crisis was the origin of the Brazilian crisis.

42. On this subject, see Bresser Pereira and Ferrer 1991. True dollarization took place in several countries for a short period, together with hyperinflation. In Argentina, however, there was true or effective dollarization of the economy for several years before, during, and after hyperinflation. This fact poses additional difficulties for the stabilization of the economy.

43. See Central Bank of Brazil 1985: 25.

44. An analysis of the populist character of the first years of the Sarney government may be found, for instance, in Bresser Pereira 1988c, Sachs 1988, and Beckerman 1990.

45. In the first month the real interest rate was 16 percent a month.

46. Internally, Zélia Cardoso de Mello was successful in reducing the public debt. Around 50 percent ($30 billion) was canceled. She was just beginning to negotiate externally when she left the ministry.

47. For instance, the monetary reform in West Germany in 1948.

48. My first systematic attempt to answer this question is in Bresser Pereira 1988c.

49. I prefer to use the expression "technobureaucratic–capitalist authoritarian regime" to define this political coalition, emphasizing that it was based on a fundamental agreement between the bureaucrats, particularly the military, and capitalists. O'Donnell's expression, however, has been generally adopted and is very useful to define a type of coalition that was dominant for about twenty years in Latin America, at first with the support of Washington.

50. On this subject, see Canitrot 1975, O'Donnell 1977, Diáz-Alejandro 1981, and Sachs 1988.

51. Mexico and particularly Chile represent exceptions to this general rule.

52. This attitude is present, for instance, in a book edited by Joan Nelson, *Economic Crisis and Policy Choice* (1990).

53. See on this subject Diáz-Alejandro 1981, Foxley 1983, Ramos 1986, and Edwards and Edwards 1987, among others.

54. See on this subject Bresser Pereira and Nakano 1990 and, for the definition and analysis of the two phases, Bresser Pereira 1991.

55. The theory of inertial inflation was developed in the early 1980s. Passos, who wrote a pioneering book on the subject (1972), calls it "chronic inflation." Initially I called it "autonomous inflation" (1981b). Roberto Frenkel (1979) uses the expression "high inflation," but the dominant expression came to be "inertial inflation," a misleading expression because it is inconsistent with the acceleration that usually comes along with it. For a survey of the subject, see Bresser Pereira and Nakano 1987 and Baer 1987.

56. A similar kind of analysis can be seen in Kiguel and Liviatan 1988 and Beckerman 1990. It is Washington adopting the pragmatic approach.

57. I got the idea of constructing a curve of the costs of transition from Przeworski 1990b. I added the curve of "unadjustment," of not implementing the required reforms. I used the inverse of the cost in order to indicate graphically a fall to the bottom of the well as costs go up.

58. Fernandez and Rodrik (1991) specify some conditions in which this may be true. Suppose that, if implemented, reforms generate a low price for many people and a large loss for a few but that individuals do not know a priori whether they will gain or lose. Then the expected value of reforms is negative, but once they are introduced the winners outnumber the losers.

References

Alesina, A., and Edwards, S. 1989. "External Debt, Capital Flights and Political Risk." *Journal of International Economics* 27, 3–4 (November).

Alesina, A., and Tabellini, G. 1988. "Credibility and Politics." *European Economic Review* 32.

Amsden, Alice H. 1989. *Asia's Next Giant.* New York: Oxford University Press.
1991. "The Diffusion of Development: The Late Industrialization Model and Greater East Asia." *American Economic Review* 81, 2 (May).

Arendt, Hannah. 1960. "On Humanity in Dark Times: Thoughts about Lessing" (1960). Published in Arendt, *Men in Dark Times.* New York: Harcourt Brace Jovanovich, 1968.

Arida, P., and Resende, A. L. 1985. "Inertial Inflation and Monetary Reform." In Williamson (ed.) 1985.

Armijo, Leslie Elliot. 1991. "Private Capital for the Public Good or Surrender of National Patrimony? Debating Privatization in Four Semi-industrial Countries and the Washington Policy Community." Paper presented at Congress of the Latin American Studies Association, Washington, 4–7 April.

Bacha, Edmar L. 1991. "The Brady Plan and Beyond: New Debt Management Options for Latin America." Working Paper no. 257, May. Department of Economics of the Catholic University (PUC), Rio de Janeiro.

Baer, Werner. 1987. "The Resurgence of Inflation in Brazil: 1974–1986." *World Development* 15, 8 (August).

Bates, Robert (ed.). 1988. *Toward a Political Economy of Development.* Berkeley and Los Angeles: University of California Press.

Beckerman, Paul. 1990. "Recent 'Heterodox' Stabilization Experience." Paper presented at seminar "The Economic Crisis in Latin America in the 1980s and the Opportunities of the 1990s," University of Illinois, Urbana-Champaign, September. Published in *Quarterly Review of Economics and Business* 31, 3 (Fall 1991).

Bleaney, Michael. 1985. *The Rise and Fall of Keynesian Economics.* London: Macmillan.

Blejer, M., and Chu, K. (eds.). 1989. *Fiscal Policy, Stabilization and Growth in Developing Countries.* Washington, D.C.: IMF.

Bradford, Colin I., Jr. 1991. "New Theories on Old Issues: Perspectives on the Prospects for Restoring Economic Growth in Latin America in the Nineties." In Emmerij and Iglesias (eds.) 1991.

Bresser Pereira, Luiz Carlos. 1978. *O colapso de uma aliança de classes.* São Paulo: Brasiliense.

1981a. *A sociedade estatal e a technoburocracia.* São Paulo: Brasiliense.

1981b. "Inflation in oligopolistic and technobureaucratic capitalism." In Bresser Pereira and Nakano 1987. Originally published 1981.

1984. "The Dialectic of Redemocratization and *Abertura*," *Development and Crisis in Brazil, 1930–1983* (Chapter 9). Boulder, Colo.: Westview.

1987. "Changing Patterns of Financing Investment in Brazil." *Bulletin of Latin American Research* (Glasgow) 7, 2.

1988a. "The Cyclical Pattern of State Intervention." Paper presented at seminar sponsored by the University of São Paulo and the Wilson Center, "Democratizing Economics," São Paulo, July. Published in Portuguese in *Revista de Economia Política* 9, 3 (July 1989).

1988b. "Da crise fiscal à redução da dívida." Paper presented at Fórum Nacional, Rio de Janeiro, November. Published in Bresser Pereira (ed.), *Dívida externa: Crise e soluções.* São Paulo: Brasiliense, 1989.

1988c. "Economic Ideologies and the Consolidation of Democracy in Brazil." Paper presented at symposium "L'internationalisation de la démocratie politique," University of Montreal, October. Published in Ethier (ed.) 1990.

1989. "The Perverse Macroeconomics of Debt, Deficit and Inflation in Brazil." Paper presented at symposium "The Present and the Future of the Pacific Basin

Economy," Institute of Developing Economies, Tokyo, July. Published in Fukushi and Kagami (eds.) 1990.

1990. "A Pragmatic Approach to State Intervention." *Revista de la CEPAL* 41 (August).

1991. *Os tempos heróicos de Collor e Zélia*. São Paulo: Nobel.

Bresser Pereira, Luiz Carlos (ed.). 1991. *Populismo econômico*. São Paulo: Nobel.

Bresser Pereira, Luiz Carlos, and Dall'Acqua, F. 1989. "Economic Populism x Keynes: Reinterpreting Budget Deficit in Latin America." Paper presented at Fundação Getúlio Vargas, São Paulo. Published in *Journal of Post-Keynesian Economics* 14, 1 (Autumn 1991).

Bresser Pereira, Luiz Carlos, and Ferrer, A. 1991. "Dolarização crônica: Argentina e Brasil." *Revista de Economia Política* 11, 1 (January).

Bresser Pereira, Luiz Carlos, and Nakano, Y. 1987. *The Theory of Inertial Inflation*. Boulder, Colo.: Lynne Riener.

1990. "Hyperinflation and Stabilization in Brazil: The First Collor Plan." Paper presented at seminar "Economic Problems of the 1990s," Knoxville, Tenn., June. Published in Davidson and Kregel (eds.) 1991.

Brodersohn, Mario. 1989. "La deuda externa de Argentina." Working paper. Fundación Centro de Estudios para el Cambio Estructural, Buenos Aires.

Bruno, Michael. 1991. "Introduction and Overview." In Bruno, Fischer, Helpman, Liviatan, and Meridor (eds.) 1991.

Bruno, Michal, Fischer, S., Helpman, E., Liviatan, N., and Meridor, L. (eds.). 1991. *Lessons of Economic Stabilization and Its Aftermath*. Cambridge, Mass.: MIT Press.

Canitrot, Adolfo. 1975. "La experiencia populista de redistribución de ingresso." *Desarrollo Económico* 15 (October).

Cardoso, E., and Helwege, A. 1990. "Populism, Profligacy and Redistribution." Tufts University, Medford, Mass. Published in Bresser Pereira (ed.) 1991.

Central Bank of Brazil. 1985. *Brazilian Economic Program*, vol. 7, May. Brasília: The Bank.

Cheibub, José Antônio. 1991. "Taxation in Latin America: A Preliminary Report." Department of Political Science, University of Chicago, July.

Cline, W., and Weintraub, S. (eds.). 1981. *Economic Stabilization in Developing Countries*. Washington, D.C.: Brookings Institution.

Corbo, V., Goldstein, M., and Khan, M. (eds.). 1987. *Growth Oriented Programs*. Washington, D.C.: IMF–World Bank.

Corbo, V., Krueger, A., and Ossa, F. (eds.). 1985. *Export Oriented Development Strategies*. Boulder, Colo.: Westview.

Cui, Zhiyuan. 1991. "Comments on Maravall–Pereira–Przeworski volume on reform." Unpublished, University of Chicago.

Davidson, Paul, and Kregel, Jan (eds.). 1991. *Economic Problems of the 1990s*. London: Edward Elgar. Papers presented at seminar of the same title in Knoxville, Tenn., June 1990.

Diáz-Alejandro, Carlos. 1981. "Southern Cone Stabilization Plans." In Cline and Weintraub (eds.) 1981.

Dornbusch, Rüdiger. 1989. "Policies to Move from Stabilization to Growth." Paper presented at conference "Economic Reconstruction of Latin America," Getúlio Vargas Foundation, Rio de Janeiro, August. Published in *Proceedings of the World Bank Annual Conference on Development Economics–1990* (supplement to *World Bank Economic Review*).

Dornbusch, Rüdiger, and Edwards, S. 1989. "The Macroeconomics of Populism." Paper presented at second meeting of IASE, Bogotá, March 30–April 1. Published in *Journal of Development Economics* 32, 2 (April 1990).

Edwards, S., and Edwards, A. C. 1987. *Monetarism and Liberalization: The Chilean Experiment*. Cambridge, Mass.: Ballinger.

Edwards, S., and Tabellini, G. 1990. "Explaining Fiscal Policies and Inflation in Developing Countries." National Bureau of Economic Research Working Paper no. 3493, October. Cambridge, Mass.: The Bureau.

Emmerij, L., and Iglesias, H. (eds.). 1991. *Restoring Financial Flows to Latin America*. Paris and Washington: OECD and Interamerican Development Bank.

Ethier, Dianne (ed.). 1990. *Democratic Transition and Consolidation in Southern Europe, Latin America and Southeast Asia*. London: Macmillan.

Fajnzylber, Fernando (ed.). 1990. *Changing Production Patterns with Social Equity*. Santiago: Economic Commission for Latin America.

Fanelli, J., and Frenkel, R. 1989. "Desequilibrios, políticas de estabilización e hyperinflación en Argentina." CEDES Working Paper, November. Published in Fanelli and Frenkel (eds.), *Políticas de estabilisación y governo en Argentina*. Buenos Aires: Editorial Thesis, 1990.

Fanelli, J., Frenkel, R., and Rozenwurcel, G. 1990. "Growth and Structural Reform in Latin America: Where We Stand." Report prepared for UNCTAD, October. Buenos Aires: CEDES.

Faucher, Philippe. 1991. "The Improbable Stabilization and Inconceivable Popular Market Capitalism: Argentina, Brazil, Mexico and Peru." Paper presented at workshop "States, Markets and Democracy," University of São Paulo, July. To be published as part of a book with Graciela Ducatenzeiler.

Feinberg, Richard E. 1990. "Comment." In Williamson (ed.) 1990.

Fernández, Raquel, and Rodrik, Dani. 1991. "Resistance to Reform: Status Quo Bias in the Presence of Individual Specific Uncertainty." *American Economic Review* 81.

Finance Ministry of Brazil. 1987. *Macroeconomic Control Plan*. Brasilia: Ministério da Fazenda, Secretaria Especial de Assuntos Econômicos, July.

Flam, H., and Staiger, R. 1989. "Adverse Selection in Credit Markets and Infant Industry Protection." National Bureau of Economic Research Working Paper no. 2864. Cambridge, Mass.: The Bureau.

Foxley, Alejandro. 1983. *Latin American Experiments in Neo-Conservative Economics*. Berkeley and Los Angeles: University of California Press.

Frenkel, Roberto. 1979. "Decisiones de precios en alta inflación." Estudios CEDES. Buenos Aires.

Fukushi, T., and Kagami, M. (eds.). 1990. *Perspectives on the Pacific Basin Economy: A Comparison of Asia and Latin America*. Tokyo: Institute of Developing Economies.

George, Susan. 1988. "Global Economic Security and the Political Implications of the Debt.'' Paper presented at symposium ''International Economic Security'' organized by Third World Foundation and South Magazine, Moscow, August. Mimeograph.

Grossman, Gene M. 1990. ''Promoting New Industrial Activities: A Survey of Recent Arguments and Evidence.'' *OECD Economic Studies* 14 (Spring).

Grossman, Gene M., and Helpman, H. 1986. ''Strategic Export Promotion: A Critique.'' In Krugman (ed.) 1986.

Haggard, S., and Kaufman, R. 1991. ''Economic Adjustment and the Prospects for Democracy.'' Paper presented at workshop ''States, Markets and Democracy,'' University of São Paulo, July. Published in Haggard and Kaufman (eds.), *The Politics of Adjustment: International Constraints, Distributive Conflicts, and the State*. Princeton, N.J.: Princeton University Press, 1992.

Haggard, S., Kaufman, R., and Webb, S. 1990. ''Politics, Inflation and Stabilization in Middle Income Countries.'' Working Paper, World Bank, September.

Heilbroner, Robert. 1990. ''Reflections After Communism.'' *New Yorker*, 10 September.

Helpman, H., and Krugman, P. 1989. *Trade Policy and Market Structure*. Cambridge, Mass.: MIT Press.

Hicks, John. 1974. *The Crisis of Keynesian Economics*. Oxford: Blackwell Publisher.

Hirschman, Albert. 1979. ''The Rise and Decline of Development Economics.'' *Essays in Trespassing*. Cambridge: Cambridge University Press, 1981.

Inter-American Dialogue. 1990. *The Americas in a New World: The 1990 Report on the Inter-American Dialogue*. Queenstown, Md.: Aspen Institute.

Islam, S. 1990. ''Whither the Brady Plan?'' *International Economy*, October. (Quoted in Bacha 1991.)

Kagami, Mitsuhiro. 1989. ''A Fiscal Comparison of Asia and Latin America'' (1989). Published in Fukushi and Kagami (eds.) 1990.

Keynes, John M. 1923. *A Tract on Monetary Reform* (1923). In *Collected Writings*, vol. 4. London: Macmillan, 1971.

Kiguel, M., and Liviatan, N. 1988. ''Inflationary Rigidities and Orthodox Stabilization Policies: Lessons from Latin America.'' *World Bank Economic Review* 2, 3 (September).

Krasner, Stephen D. 1985. *Structural Conflict: The Third World against Global Liberalism*. Berkeley and Los Angeles: University of California Press.

Krueger, Anne O. 1985. ''The Experience and Lessons of Asia's Super Exporters.'' In Corbo, Krueger, and Ossa (eds.) 1985.

Krugman, Paul R. 1987. ''The Narrow Moving Band, the Dutch Disease and the Competitive Consequences of Mrs. Thatcher.'' *Journal of Development Economics* 27, 1.

Krugman, Paul R. (ed.). 1986. *Strategic Trade Policy in New International Economics*. Cambridge, Mass.: MIT Press.

Lopes, Francisco L. 1989. *O desafio da hiperinflaçõ*. Rio de Janeiro: Campus.

Lustig, Nora. 1990. ''Agreement Signed by Mexico and Its Commercial Banks.'' Testimony before U.S. House of Representatives Banking Committee, Washington, 7 February.

1992. *North American Free Trade: Assessing the Impact.* Washington, D.C.: Brookings Institution.

Malan, Pedro. 1990. "Uma crítica ao consenso de Washington." Remarks at closing session of a conference in honor of Professor Albert Hirschman, Buenos Aires, 11 November. Published in *Revista de Economia Política* 11, 3 (July 1991).

Malloy, James M. (ed.). 1977. *Authoritarianism and Corporatism in Latin America.* Pittsburgh: University of Pittsburgh Press.

Michaely, M., Papageorgiou, D., and Choksi, A. 1991. *Liberalizing Foreign Trade.* Vol. 7, *Lessons of Experience in the Developing World.* Cambridge, Mass.: Blackwell Publisher.

Nelson, Joan (ed.). 1989. *Fragile Coalitions: The Politics of Economic Adjustment.* New Brunswick, N.J.: Transaction.

1990. *Economic Crisis and Policy Choice.* Princeton, N.J.: Princeton University Press.

O'Connor, James. 1973. *The Fiscal Crisis of the State.* New York: St. Martin's Press.

O'Donnell, Guillermo. 1973. *Modernization and Bureaucratic Authoritarianism: Studies in South American Politics.* Institute of International Studies of the University of California, Berkeley, Modernization Series no. 9. Berkeley and Los Angeles: University of California Press.

1977. "State and Alliances in Argentina, 1956–1976." In Bates (ed.) 1988. Originally published in *Desarollo Económico,* January 1977.

Oliveira, Gesner. 1991. "Sucesso de modelo do Chile tem alto custo social." *Folha de S. Paulo,* 16 June.

Pack, H., and Westphal, L. 1986. "Industrial Strategy and Technological Change: Theory versus Reality." *Journal of Development Economics* 22, 1.

Passos, Felipe. 1972. *Chronic Inflation in Latin America.* New York: Praeger.

Pérez, Carlos Andrés. 1990. Interview by Clovis Rossi. *Folha de S. Paulo,* 24 November.

Przeworski, Adam. 1989. "Why Are Children Starving When We Could Feed the World? The Irrationality of Capitalism and the Infeasibility of Socialism." University of Chicago, October. Mimeograph.

1990a. "East–South System Transformation." University of Chicago, February. Mimeograph.

1990b. "Political Dynamics of Economic Reforms." University of Chicago, November. A chapter of a book in preparation.

Ramos, Joseph. 1986. *Neoconservative Economics in the Southern Cone of Latin America, 1973–1983.* Baltimore: Johns Hopkins University Press.

Reisen, H., and Trotsenburg, A. 1988. *Developing Country Debt: The Budgetary and Transfer Problem.* Paris: OECD Development Center.

Remmer, Karen L. 1986. "The Politics of Economic Stabilization: IMF Standby Programs in Latin America, 1954–1984." *Comparative Politics* 19, 1 (October).

1990. "Democracy and Economic Crisis: The Latin American Experience." *World Politics* 42, 3 (April).

1991. "The Political Impact of Economic Crisis: Latin America, 1982–1990." Paper presented at Annual Meeting of American Political Science Association, Washington, D.C., August.

Sachs, Jeffrey. 1987. "Trade and Exchange Rate Policies in Growth-Oriented Adjustment Programs." National Bureau of Economic Research Working Paper no. 2226, April. Published in Corbo, Krueger, and Ossa (eds.) 1987.

1988. "Social Conflict and Populist Policies in Latin America." Paper presented at conference "Markets, Institutions and Cooperation," Venice, October. To be published in a book of this title edited by Renato Brunetta for the International Economic Association.

Skidmore, Thomas E. 1977. "The Politics of Economic Stabilization in Postwar Latin America." In Malloy (ed.) 1977.

Stallings, Barbara. 1991. "International Influence on Economic Policy, Debt, Stabilization and Structural Reform." In S. Haggard and R. Kaufman (eds.), *The Politics of Economic Adjustment: International Constraints, Distributive Policies, and the State*. Princeton, N.J.: Princeton University Press.

Tanzi, Vito. 1989. "Fiscal Policy, Stabilization and Growth." In Blejer and Chu (eds.) 1989.

Werneck, Rogério Furquim. 1987. *Empresas estatais e política macroeconômica*. Rio de Janeiro: Campus.

Wijnbergen, Sweder van. 1991. "The Mexican Debt Deal." *Economic Policy* 6, 2 (April): 14–56.

Williamson, John. 1990a. "What Washington Means by Policy Reform." In Williamson (ed.) 1990.

1990b. "The Progress of Policy Reform in Latin America." In Williamson (ed.) 1990.

Williamson, John (ed.). 1985. *Inflation and Indexation: Argentina, Brazil and Israel*. Washington, D.C.: Institute for International Economics.

1990. *Latin American Adjustment: How Much Has Happened?* Washington, D.C.: Institute of International Economics.

2. Politics and policy: economic reforms in Southern Europe

JOSÉ MARÍA MARAVALL

This chapter deals with socioeconomic reforms after the transition to democracy, taking Southern Europe as a case study. It will consider reforms to be policy innovations that, through legislation or executive action, are meant to change the existing pattern of economic performance and the social distribution of resources. It will examine the dilemmas faced by the new democratic governments, the types of reforms that were introduced, the factors that help to explain the path these reforms followed, the outcomes of the reforms, and their effects on democracy itself. Once democracies are reestablished after a period of dictatorial rule, new problems emerge: The efficiency of the new political system, and not just its legitimacy, becomes the main issue – that is, the capacity of democracy to solve problems and fulfill expectations. It may be argued that the margins for purposeful change (i.e., what can be done once democracy is restored) depend mostly on the nature of economic requirements and on the type of transition to democracy; that these are indeed the confining conditions of political choices and strategies. Yet economic policies may vary in their design, implementation, and impact as a result of factors other than the type of transition to democracy and economic conditions. The range of reforms that are introduced (concerning, for example, nationalization, public expenditure, the balance between state and market) is very much the result of particular combinations of constraints and choices.

Socioeconomic reforms contribute to the particular type of democracy constructed. They depend upon the political conditions of new democracies, but their success or failure also has consequences for the new political system. In the complex relationship that exists between the economy and the polity, some of the main questions have to do with the contribution of economic reforms to the consolidation of democratic institutions and to their efficiency, with variations in the pattern of reforms, and with their association with

This study is part of a larger research project carried out within the Juan March Institute. It is also related to project AME91–0257 of the PLANICYT.

political variables. I will argue that besides the need to tackle the economic crisis, to bring the state to financial solvency and to increase the competitiveness of the economy, new democracies face extended demands in the area of social rights. Stabilization and structural reforms require changes in exchange rates, limits on public expenditure, higher tax revenues, suppression of subsidies, deregulated prices, efficient capital and labor markets, and changes in the structure of property. But democracies have to respond to exigencies of social fairness as well; the citizens of new democracies often consider that their new political status has to do also with social rights. This is of course an empirical issue. It is also a normative one: Democracy can be considered incompatible with restrictions on the exercise of political and social rights or with discriminations based on social conditions. Both democracy and economic reforms may be undermined by high social costs and inequalities of distribution that erode political support. Eventually the quality of a new democracy will depend on the combination of economic efficiency and social cohesion.

New democracies usually inherit states that are too interventionist in the economy and too weak in social policies. Thus, paraphrasing a well-known political maxim, the state has to be transformed until it becomes as small as possible and as large as necessary. The World Bank has emphasized this dual requirement for the economic development of democracies:[1] Governments must intervene less in certain spheres and more in others, and the economies must be more market oriented, but the role of the state in the provision of public goods, investment in human capital, the building of infrastructure, and the protection of the environment is indispensable and must be reinforced. State intervention is also necessary for social equality. The market by itself does not guarantee that the population, especially its poorest groups, will benefit from adequate education, health protection, or pensions. Social policies, as the World Bank argues, are related to democracy, strengthen the legitimacy of the regime, and contribute to political stability; they are also associated with less economic protectionism and more growth.

Economic reforms generally seek to maximize the competitiveness of the economy, the solvency of the state, the satisfaction of demands, and the welfare of citizens, but they differ in the particular mix of these goals and in the instruments they use. Inflation, budgetary and current-account deficits, unemployment, and loss of competitiveness are serious challenges for new democratic governments, but their gravity is not always the same, nor are the political pressures for reforms that governments face equivalent.

The Southern European economies in the mid 1970s did not find themselves in the same dramatic circumstances as the Eastern European and Latin American economies over the last decade, nor were the governments confronted with economic exigencies of a similar urgency. Yet Southern European societies shared a situation of relative economic backwardness vis-à-vis the more advanced societies of Western Europe. They belonged to particular niches in the international division of labor, if we look at the composition and balance of their trade, the nature of the foreign investment they attracted, the importance of tourism in their economies, and the extent of their migration of labor to other countries. They had had long experience of state economic protectionism and autarky; their economies have correctly been described as "assisted" rather than "competitive" capitalism:[2] Since the nineteenth century, the state and public enterprises had played a central role as promoters of economic development. The state was highly centralized, and public bureaucracies were large and inefficient. Their welfare systems were very limited and did not satisfy social needs, which were great. Military intervention in government and political life had been a recurrent event in their contemporary histories. Religious pluralism had hardly existed, and the dominant religion was identified with the state. Successive failed democratic experiments were characterized by unstable party systems with fragile roots in society and by dramatic confrontations between left and right on basic questions concerning the legitimacy, nature, and structure of the state.[3] To "normalize" their societies by Western European standards, to catch up in both economic and political terms, had been the major goal of Greek, Portuguese, and Spanish reformers in this century. "Modernization," a key word in Southern European democratic politics, was thus understood to a very large extent as "Europeanization" – this was surely a major characteristic not only of the democratic transition in the three countries but also of reforms after the transition.

In this respect, similarities with the intellectual visions of many Eastern and Central European reformers are remarkable. In Poland, Hungary, and Czechoslovakia, the goal of reforms from 1989 onward was to construct a "normal" economic system – that is, to follow the model of the advanced Western European economies. Experiments with different solutions were rejected in Eastern and Central Europe from the very beginning; this was also the case in Spain, while in Portugal and Greece experiments were gradually abandoned after the two years of provisional governments, unstable politics, and economic deterioration that followed the "Revolution of the Carnations" in the former and the poor economic results achieved by Papandreou in his attempt to take Greece on a "Third Road" to a different kind of economic system.

Economic development, crisis, and conflict: the background to political transitions

Although differences existed in their respective levels of economic development prior to the reestablishment of democracy, Portugal, Greece, and Spain had experienced considerable economic change since the 1950s. The Greek economy in this period became largely integrated in international markets and went through a phase of quick growth that from 1960 to the collapse of the dictatorship in July 1974 reached an average annual rate of 7.7 percent.[4] Economic development benefited from low wages and from remittances from large numbers of workers abroad. In Portugal, Salazarism had been deeply anticapitalist and had tried to freeze the economy and the social structure in a preindustrial mold: In 1974 the country had the lowest per capita income in Western Europe, agriculture was seriously underdeveloped, and overall productivity was very low; however, from the late 1950s onward a shift in economic policies had taken place, with the country moving away from autarky and toward greater integration in the world economy. From 1960 until the putsch of the Armed Forces Movement (MFA) against the dictatorship in April 1974, the Portuguese economy had been growing at an average annual rate of 6.9 percent. While trade had for decades benefited from a colonial empire that provided protected markets and cheap raw materials, economic change in Portugal was reflected in the fact that in 1973 nearly half of commercial exchanges were with the European Community and only one-sixth with the colonies. Foreign capital was entering Portugal,[5] and new industries were established in the areas of electronics, cars, shipbuilding, and textiles. Agricultural production fell as a proportion of GDP from 20 percent at the beginning of the 1960s to 14 percent at the end of the decade; the share of industrial production went up from 27 to 33 percent.

The Spanish economy under Franco stagnated for twenty years; only in 1963 did real wages reach the (pre–Civil War) level of 1936. International political isolation went hand in hand with economic autarky. Beginning in the second half of the 1950s, however, international isolation gradually ended, in parallel with some liberalization of the economy. After a three-year stabilization plan in 1959–62, the Spanish economy benefited from general economic development in Western Europe and went through a period of rapid growth that from 1955 to 1975 reached an average annual rate close to 8 percent.[6] Labor was cheap and abundant, taxation was low, state protection was high. The resulting changes in the Spanish economic and occupational structure were dramatic: The contribution of agriculture to GDP fell from 23

Table 2.1. *Evolution of the three Southern European economies 1961–73* (*averages*)

	Greece	Portugal	Spain	EC
GDP: annual variation (%), constant prices	7.7	6.9	7.2	4.8
Inflation: annual variation (%)	4.5	3.9	7.1	5.2
Employment { Annual variation (%)	−0.5	0.2	0.7	0.3
{ Unemployed as % of active population	4.2	2.5	2.8	2.4
Real wages per wage earner: annual variation (%)	6.4	6.7	7.5	5.0
Unit labor cost in real terms[a] (100 = 1980)	106.0	86.3	95.7	97.1

[a] 1961–70.
Source: EC Commission, *Economie Européenne*, Supp. A, No. 5 (May 1991).

percent in 1960 to 5 percent twenty years later, and the agricultural population declined from five million in 1960 to two million. Financial capital played a dominant role: In 1956 five banks controlled 51 percent of the country's capital and were largely responsible for the creation of new national industry. The state was an important instrument of capitalist activity, basically through the National Institute of Industry (INI), a public holding company created in 1941 that participated directly in sixty-three companies employing over 200,000 workers and representing 10 percent of GDP. The subordination of the state to private interests was ideologically defended in terms of the *principio de subsidiariedad:* In the 1950s, reactionary Catholic socioeconomic doctrine replaced Fascist ideas of state-led mobilization and development. No modern tax system existed, but, thanks to very limited public expenditure, there was no budget deficit.

Table 2.1 shows the evolution of the three Southern European economies in the 1960s and early 1970s compared with the average for the six European Community countries. Before their transitions to democracy started, the three Southern European countries had, in different degrees, been going through a phase of economic growth and liberalization that had brought changes to their economies and their social structures.[7] However, serious economic and social contradictions existed in the three processes that characterize limited economic modernization: Protectionism remained much higher than in the other Western European economies, and industrialization was based on barely competitive industries (steel, shipbuilding); there was a permanent gap between aggregate demand and the supply of manufactured goods, which caused important deficits in the balance of trade; inflation was always high.

Table 2.2. *The economy at the time of the transition to democracy*

		Greece	Portugal	Spain
Rate of GDP growth	1970	8.0	7.6	4.1
	Initial year of transition[a]	−3.6	1.1	0.5
Rate of unemployment	1970	4.2	2.6	2.6
	Initial year of transition[a]	2.1	1.7	4.5
Rate of inflation	1970	3.9	3.4	6.8
	Initial year of transition[a]	20.9	18.9	16.8

[a]Portugal and Greece: 1974; Spain: 1975.
Sources: Economie Européenne, no. 46 (December 1990); *IMF, Government Finance Statistics Yearbook*, vol. 13 (1989); World Bank, *World Tables*, 1989–90.

The economic crisis of the 1970s overlapped with the collapse of authoritarian regimes. In 1973–4 the price of oil quadrupled; as a consequence, in 1975 Western Europe experienced negative economic growth, and average inflation went up to 8 percent. After a short-lived expansion in 1977–8, the second oil shock in 1979, in which the price of a barrel of oil increased from $12 to $31 in five months, led to stagnation in GDPs, higher inflation, and more unemployment. Economic growth did not resume again until 1986. The economic crisis was deeper in Southern Europe, which was much more dependent on imported oil; for example, Spain could cover only a little more than a quarter of its demand for primary energy from its own resources, while Greece's oil bill was equivalent to two-thirds of its revenues from exports. The international crisis thus worsened the position of Southern Europe in the world economy. Table 2.2 provides evidence about the deterioration of the three economies, particularly in their rates of growth and inflation, as the transition to democracy was about to start. The situation of the economies was, however, less dramatic than in the Latin American and Eastern European countries at the time of their transitions. Although inflation had gone up in Greece, Portugal, and Spain, it was much lower than the 66 percent for Poland in 1989, the 235 percent for Brazil in 1985, or the 349 percent for Argentina in 1983. No hyperinflation existed: The currencies were convertible, exchange rates were not artificial, and no black markets existed; to a very large extent, prices reflected supply and demand for goods and services. The debt per capita had reached $134 in Portugal and $331 in Greece in 1974, a far smaller figure than in Brazil ($769), Argentina ($1,556), Chile ($1,539), Poland ($1,113), and Hungary ($1,656). However, although politics had some margin for maneuver, the economies of the three Southern European countries had worsened considerably from their performance in the decade before.

To sum up, Portugal, Greece, and Spain had experienced a period of economic development followed by a serious economic crisis just as they embarked on their transition to democracy. In fact, the transitions were related to growing social unrest stemming from the new strains and inequalities of development. This unrest, affecting in particular the industrial labor force and the lower middle class, acted as pressures from below on the Greek dictatorship;[8] in Portugal, the expansion of urban industrial concentrations in Lisbon, Setubal, and Oporto and a growing industrial working class were the basis of the waves of strikes that started in 1968 and reached their highest level in 1973 and 1974, led by workers' commissions in the workplace defending claims that were increasingly political.[9] The pressures from below were particularly important in the Spanish case: The number of working hours lost through strikes rose from 1.5 million in 1966 to 8.7 million in 1970 and to 14.5 million in 1975, the year Franco died, and the objectives of the workers' movement took on an increasingly political dimension. Confronted by this considerable social conflict in the last two years of Francoism, the Spanish government of Arias Navarro, very much like the Greek government of Papadopoulos and the Portuguese government of Caetano, was unable to make the tough economic decisions required to tackle the economic crisis. It thought that the crisis would not last and maintained the price of oil at artificially low levels. Basic areas of production were deeply damaged by excess capacity and high production costs. Unions remained illegal, but the government was unable to control wage rises. From 1970 to 1979 wages grew forty percentage points ahead of productivity.[10] Exports lost competitiveness, and the balance of trade deteriorated sharply. At the beginning of the transition, the Spanish economy was experiencing high inflation, an important trade deficit, growing unemployment, a collapse in profits, and an increasing public deficit as the government tried to compensate for the drop in external demand by expanding public expenditure.

As dictatorships weakened, growing social demands, stemming from the very limited satisfaction of social rights, were expressed not only over wages but also in the areas of health, education, and urban problems by a diversity of organizations, neighborhood associations, movements for educational reform, and so on. This was particularly the case in Spain: Besides the strong wage demands of the 1970s, the absence of a developed welfare system was fueling social demands. Welfare legislation, which had followed a rhythm similar to that of Western European countries until 1936, had been halted by

Francoism. Thus, in 1975 public social expenditure amounted to only 9.9 percent of GDP, whereas the European Community average stood at 24 percent; only 4 percent of the social-security budget was financed by public revenues from taxes, in contrast to 26 percent in France and Italy; public expenditure in education was 1.8 percent of GDP, four percentage points below the European average; one in every four Spaniards was not covered by any public health program.

Demands for the satisfaction of social rights were much less explicit in the other two countries. However, in Greece, where no welfare system had existed, popular pressure (which had remained latent under the dictatorship of the colonels) for an expansion of the "social wage" and for income redistribution gradually emerged.[11] In Portugal as well, although workers' strikes had increased before the transition, the explosion of demands followed, rather than preceded, the end of the dictatorship. It was democracy that liberated demands. There were seventeen strikes in the first week of democracy, thirty-one in the second, eighty-seven in the third, and ninety-seven in the fourth. For several months an endless stream of strikes defended better working conditions, a shorter working day, more paid holidays, higher wages; they took place not only in the redoubts of working-class organization, but also in transportation and the mail service and among fishermen, bakers, and newspaper sellers. Warnings were increasingly made against general strikes by Intersindical, the Communist Party,[12] and the president of the republic. Decreto-lei 392 of 27 August 1974 legalized strikes but also introduced restrictions. Yet strikes continued. From the summer of 1975, they included demands for self-management, not just on ideological grounds but also in order to avoid the closing of firms and to ensure jobs and wages; houses were also occupied (two thousand in the first two weeks of democracy) by *comissãos de moradores,* and land was taken over by the peasants.

The first stage of democracy: the primacy of politics

As democracies were restored in the three countries, for some time politics took precedence over the economy. Although all the Southern European transitions were initiated from within, significant differences existed among them. In Spain, the leading role was taken by civilian politicians. Political change consisted of a mixture of pressure from below and reforms from above; it also took the form of a gradual process based on transactions and pacts. The transitions in Greece and Portugal were much more a sharp break with the past, and both started with a military problem (the confrontation with

Turkey over Cyprus, the war in Angola and Mozambique). In Greece political change was directed by a civilian leadership once the army took power away from the junta of colonels. The Portuguese transition, in contrast, was initiated by a military uprising against the Caetano dictatorship; until the constitutional change of 1982, the army occupied a central position in the new regime, first with the Movimento das Forças Armadas (MFA) assembly and later with the Council of the Revolution. The break with the past was followed by two years of political turmoil: The new rules of the game were not clearly defined, and the confusion of parliamentary and extraparliamentary politics was considerable; six provisional governments succeeded one another at short intervals. In Greece and Spain the rules were much more clearly defined from the beginning. In these two countries also, the new democratic right (the Nea Demokratia of Karamanlis and the Unión del Centro Democrático of Suárez) won the first two elections, and the left could gain experience about the possibilities and limits of pluralist democracy. But whereas Karamanlis, benefiting from an absolute majority in parliament, led the Greek transition very much on his own with little involvement on the part of the opposition (Panellinio Sosialistico Kinima – PASOK – in particular), Suárez followed a strategy of negotiations and pacts with the opposition that extended to the passing of the 1978 constitution, to the process of political decentralization that tried to accommodate nationalist demands in Catalonia and the Basque country, and to economic policies.

The major problem at that stage for the new democratic governments of Greece and Spain was to establish a viable political democracy. In Portugal the construction of a different kind of economic system was also part of the task. The ideology of the initial governments in Greece and Spain helps to explain to a considerable degree the absence of radical economic reforms and the priority of politics; an additional factor was the threat of military intervention against democracy (higher in Spain, manifested in Operación Galaxia of November 1978 and the attempted coup of 23 February 1981). Moreover, memories of past democratic failures contributed to political pragmatism. In Portugal, on the contrary, because of the sharp break with the politics of the past, the dominant presence of the radical MFA, and the vast popular mobilization that followed the collapse of the dictatorship, everything seemed possible for some time. The tasks of establishing political democracy and reforming the economy beyond capitalism were attempted at the same time. This was to produce considerable political instability and to aggravate the economic situation.

Let us examine the early economic decisions in Portugal. The provisional government that took power after 25 April 1974 immediately closed the stock exchange and froze more than $2 billion (American billion) of private capital. Shortly afterward, Decreto-lei 203/74 of 15 May presented the government's program. Its main goals were to increase public investment, to change the credit system, to reform the banks, and to implement massive nationalization. An anticapitalist ideology also guided the drafting of the new constitution once the elections of April 1975 had been held. The constitution, which was eventually passed in 1976, thus stated that "the development of the revolutionary process imposes, on the economic level, the collective appropriation of the main means of production"; Articles 89 and 105 declared that the private sector of the economy would play only a residual role and that "a progressive and effective socialization of the economy" would take place; the objective, according to Article 91, was "the creation of a socialist society." The first nationalization, that of the Lisbon water company, took place in June 1974; the big wave of *estatização* came a few months later in the radical period of Gonzalvism and included the railroads, sea transportation, the airlines, oil refineries, the steel industry, the tobacco companies, production of fertilizers and cement, the breweries, and a myriad of dependent small firms. It has been estimated that 27 percent of Portuguese companies were affected – mostly large, technologically complex units.[13] As a result, the share of total investment held by the state increased from 18 percent in 1973 to 45 percent in 1980. At the end of the period of nationalization, public enterprises contributed 15 percent of GDP and 24 percent of gross capital formation. This proportion was not very different from that of other Western European countries – the Portuguese productive public sector was smaller than the Italian. The major difference existed in the financial system, as the twenty-two national banks were in public hands.

In this first stage of the Portuguese transition, important wage increases were granted, starting with a large rise in the guaranteed minimum wage, decided on one month after the fall of the dictatorship; real wages grew 25 percent on average between 1975 and 1976. Public expenditure also went up very quickly, much faster than the GDP. A large part of the budget was spent on noncompetitive industries with shrinking markets (chemicals, shipbuilding, steel) in an attempt to preserve jobs. The satisfaction of huge social demands and an ideological program of socioeconomic transformation took precedence over strict economic management. The consequences of these big increases in public spending, of wages growing faster than inflation and productivity, and of the country living off the large foreign-currency reserves that still existed at the beginning of the transition were critical for the solvency of the state, the international position of the economy, and macroeconomic indicators. The budget deficit, which had not existed under the dictatorship, was now very large; the trade and payments balances were in heavy deficit; the external debt was growing fast. Inflation was increasing, as also was unemployment, which suffered from the additional impact of 600,000 migrants returning from Angola and Mozambique (a ratio to population roughly six times the Algerian migration to France in 1958). Decolonization represented the sudden loss of safe colonial markets. Investment declined (gross capital formation fell by 6.1 percent in 1974 and by 10.6 percent in 1975); an important capital flight took place, and capitalists left Portugal.[14] The effect on economic development was considerable: The rate of GDP growth, which had reached 7.6 percent on average between 1970 and 1974, was only 2.3 percent between 1974 and 1977.

The evolution of the economy contributed to the political turmoil and to an increasing confrontation between radicals and moderates. This confrontation had to do with both economic policies and parliamentary democracy. Economic policies divided the radical faction of the military and Melo Antunes (the officer who had been in charge of the MFA's program of reforms), particularly over the degree of state control of the economy and over the role of foreign investment. The various parties were also divided over the extension of public ownership and control. And divisions over the relative importance of parliamentary and direct democracy were deep. In the first year of the transition, political mobilization expanded greatly: A myriad of channels of political representation and organs of "popular power" were set up through commissions, assemblies, and committees of various kinds. The elections to the Constituent Assembly in April 1975 had a deeply moderating effect on economic policies: The sixth provisional government, of Pinheiro de Azevedo, formed in the midst of a serious economic crisis, stopped further nationalization and obtained important loans from the USA and the European Community. This change of course away from collectivization was to be reinforced by a new victory of the moderates in the first constitutional elections one year later. Thus, over two years, serious political uncertainties existed over the role of state and market and over the importance of direct versus parliamentary democracy.[15] Succeeding elections gradually took the country away from economic collectivism and direct democracy.

In Greece, one of Karamanlis's major concerns was to consolidate democratic institutions and insert the country into Western Europe. His reforms were political. Until the first democratic elections in November 1974 (which gave him 54 percent of the vote) he pursued a cautious strategy: The 1952 constitution was reestablished as an interim norm, Ghizikis was maintained as head of state, political parties (including the KKE) were legalized, political amnesty was granted, and civilian control over every important institution was ensured. Following the elections and a foiled coup by the military in February 1975, Karamanlis quickly set the new rules of the game: The monarchy was abolished after a referendum in December 1974, and those responsible for the 1967 military coup were brought to trial.[16] The government also applied for membership in the European Community in 1974; negotiations started two years later, the treaties were signed in May 1979, and Greece became a full member of the EC on 1 January 1981. The economy, however, had been in increasing difficulty; inflation stood at 15.4 percent in 1976 and grew to 19.8 percent in 1980; the annual rate of growth, which had been at 7.7 percent from 1961 to 1973, declined to less than half that rate (3.5 percent) between 1974 and 1980; investment fell (whereas from 1970 to 1973 gross capital formation had grown at an average annual rate of 12.4 percent, from 1974 to 1981 the rate fell to an annual average of − 1.25 percent); some three hundred enterprises were on the verge of bankruptcy. Public expenditure, however, increased at a fast rate; it was largely financed by budget deficits and foreign loans, so that the external debt went up, reaching 4.4 percent of GDP in 1978 and 7.9 percent in 1981. Karamanlis, under strong Gaullist influence, carried out a considerable program of nationalization; eventually the public sector covered most of the banks, telecommunications, the oil industry, transportation, and seaports.

If massive public deficits were to be avoided, inflation reduced, and investment promoted, serious reforms were needed in public expenditure, in the tax system, in subsidies to firms, in the financing of public debt, in the evolution of the costs of production, in labor-relations legislation, and in public administration. However, these were not the only problems: Expansion of public expenditure was fueled by attempts to satisfy social demands and by the need to dedicate much larger resources to pay for more and better education, health, and pensions. This was a common predicament in the new Southern European democracies. Governments faced the dilemma of either taking their country on a long and painful road toward economic efficiency and long-term growth, with dubious prospects of economic or political success and postponing the rewards that many people expected from democracy, or attempting to respond to more immediate political and social needs, delaying the implementation of economic reforms and hoping the economy could muddle through. In Greece no deep economic reforms were introduced by Karamanlis, and politics dominated the first seven years of the new democracy.

This was also the case in Spain. Suárez believed that his new and fragile democracy was not ready to undertake serious economic reforms. The transition to democracy was a delicate enough task, and powerful antidemocratic groups remained undisturbed; over a long period they represented a serious threat to democracy. Suárez's careful knitting of the fabric of democracy could be undone at any time. Besides, the Unión del Centro Democrático (UCD) government, which had won the first two general elections – of 1977 and 1979 – with 35 percent of the vote, was minoritarian. Thus, economic policies over most of the period from 1977 to 1981 were based on consultations and pacts. Examples are the Pactos de la Moncloa in 1977, the Acuerdo Marco Interconfederal in 1979, and the Acuerdo Nacional sobre el Empleo in 1981.

The Spanish economy was in stagflation. The annual rate of growth was no longer close to 8 percent; it fell to 1.3 percent on average between 1975 and 1982. Inflation had reached 23.2 percent in 1977; although the government was able to bring it down to 17.1 percent by 1979, it remained much higher than the Western European average. The Pactos de la Moncloa were a classical stabilization plan where wage claims were adapted to the forecast of inflation and where some structural reforms were included but were never fully carried out. The second oil crisis, of 1979, had a great impact on a productive structure that had not adjusted to the new economic conditions. Industrial production fell (by 1.1 percent in 1982); investment declined sharply; the crisis in the financial system was the deepest of any OECD country and threatened institutions that represented 30 percent of the nonowned resources of the Spanish banks; the trade deficit grew rapidly; the budget deficit rose to 5.6 percent of GDP in 1982 and was mostly financed by the Bank of Spain's printing money, which aggravated inflation. Yet, as in Greece, public expenditure increased from 24.9 percent of GDP in 1975 to 38.0 percent in 1982, largely owing to expansion of the budgets for social security, health, and education, areas where large social demand existed. Wages also grew in real terms: 3.0 percent annually on average between 1975 and 1982. The income of adult male workers improved during the transition and over the economic crisis. Unit labor costs, which had almost doubled in the eleven years from 1962 to 1973, doubled again in the following four years.[17] As a result of the crisis, unemployment started to rise dramatically; it was 4.5 percent in 1975 and 16.2 percent in 1982.[18] Indeed, unemployment became the greatest social problem in the new Spanish democracy. Francoism had kept it latent, as nearly two and a half million Spanish workers had migrated to other European countries in search of work, and only a very small proportion of women were in the

Table 2.3. *Economic performance in the first stage of the new democracies (averages for the period 1974–82)*

	Greece	Portugal	Spain	EC
GDP: Annual variation (%), constant prices	2.7	2.8	1.7	1.9
Inflation: annual variation (%)	17.2	19.8	16.7	12.0
Employment { Annual variation (%)	1.0	−0.4	−1.4	−0.1
Unemployed as % of active population (average for period)	2.7	6.4	8.4	5.6
Real wages per wage earner: annual variation (%)	3.9	3.0	2.8	2.0
Unit labor cost in real terms in 1981 (100 = 1980)	106.5	102.3	100.5	100.6
Total expenditure on public administration (% of GDP)	—	—	29.6	43.9
Total revenues for public administration (% of GDP)	29.3	—	27.9	40.0

Source: Economie Européenne, no. 46 (December 1990).

labor market. The economic crisis in Europe brought many migrants back to Spain.

Thus, the new Southern European democracies experienced serious problems of economic efficiency over the period that corresponded to what Rustow called the phase of "habituation" in democratic transitions.[19] Table 2.3 shows the economic performance of the three countries and of the European Community from 1974 to 1982. The economies deteriorated in terms of GDP growth, inflation, unemployment, budget deficits, and labor costs. Paradoxically, the crisis seemed to have an egalitarian impact on Spanish society: If we examine the share of total consumption of the top decile of population, it declined from 31.0 percent in 1973 to 19.3 percent in 1981.[20] This was very much a result of the crisis itself rather than of redistributive policies. Becoming poorer, Spanish society had also become more equal, for losses in income and consumption were greater in the better-off groups. Social demands, in any case, multiplied with democracy: Przeworski is right when he states that "the advent of democracy is accompanied by an explosion of expectations: for most people democratization promises not only political rights but also social transformations."[21]

The predicament of the democratic governments was not only about the economy but about demands for social welfare and equality. These claims were particularly important in Spain; in the 1981 "European Values" study of thirteen countries, Spain ranked highest in "reformism" and support for social policies;[22] on a scale of 1 to 5 in popular support for social equality and welfare, Spain again came out on top compared with eight other Western European countries.[23] Three in every four Spaniards believed the economic system to be very or fairly unjust, 87 percent held the view that "there would be fewer problems in the country if people were treated more equally," and 70 percent considered that the government was responsible for the welfare of each and every citizen.[24] Thus, egalitarian views were deep and broad-based and were expressed as demands against the state.

In the three countries, expectations were foiled by the economic crisis; they were also frustrated by social policies that drew ever larger resources from public funds but were always lagging behind demand. Tocqueville's discussion of spiraling expectations in new democracies was wholly appropriate: "Democratic institutions awaken and flatter the passion for equality without ever being able to satisfy it entirely. . . . [The people] are excited by the chance and irritated by the uncertainty of success; the excitement is followed by weariness and then by bitterness."[25]

The result was growing *desencanto* and disillusionment. It has sometimes been argued that transitions based on transactions and pacts tend to produce this effect,[26] yet it is the case that Portugal experienced mobilization *and* disenchantment. The Portuguese political culture only a few years after the collapse of the dictatorship was described in terms of extensive political cynicism and withdrawal.[27] Although the right was in crisis from 1974 to 1977, conservative values were influential; they were also reinforced by the economic crisis. As retrospective criticism of the dictatorship was very limited, the passage of time improved memories of that regime as a period of stability. At the end of the decade, 28 percent of Portuguese thought Caetano was a better choice to govern the country than the democratic prime ministers (he was followed by Mario Soares, chosen by 9 percent). A majority of the people believed that democracy had worsened the economy, education, housing, and morality and had improved only wages and freedom; 63 percent thought that Portuguese society was in the midst of a serious crisis, due basically to economic conditions, the cost of living, and the lack of work, and only 5 percent believed that no crisis existed.[28] Ten years after democracy was reestablished, two-thirds of respondents believed that large numbers of citizens were discontented with the existing parties, 50 percent expressed the view that the National Assembly "solves nothing," and over one-third still selected authoritarian rulers when asked which government had ruled Portugal best.[29]

The contradiction between expectations and performance, caused mainly by economic difficulties, also became a growing problem in Spanish politics.

Whereas in 1975 50 percent of Spaniards thought that the economy was in good condition, only 2 percent believed it in 1980. This pessimism was not only about economic performance: At the turn of the decade, only one in every three individuals trusted democracy to solve the problems of the country, although three in four declared themselves "unconditional democrats."[30] The relationship between political efficiency and legitimacy has often been discussed in comparative politics;[31] it has been argued that the legitimacy of democracy enjoys considerable autonomy vis-à-vis efficiency, on the grounds that general support for the political system is different from satisfaction with specific outcomes, that responsibilities are always fragmentary in democracies, and that it is always possible to change the government without destabilizing the regime. That autonomy is more limited, however, in the early phases of a new democracy, and problems of efficiency may have a greater impact on the regime. In Spain there was thus a correlation between positive orientation to democracy and satisfaction with specific outcomes; this correlation decreased over time as legitimacy became divorced from performance: It was .81 in 1978, .68 in 1980, and .57 in 1984.[32] For several years the consolidation of democracy was seen as threatened not just by *involución* but also by an economy in crisis.

Frustration and disenchantment increased over the first years of the new democracies. These feelings were related to a cynical view of politics that had for a long time been a central trait of Southern European political culture – probably a rational judgment based on long experience of politics as abuse. The view that all politicians were the same, that they all looked after their own interests, and that people had very little say in politics was much more widely held in Southern Europe than in the old established democracies. Fifty-five percent of Spaniards and 51 percent of Portuguese expressed feelings of indifference, mistrust, or boredom toward politics; 10 and 16 percent, respectively, manifested hostility. Seven in every ten Spaniards thought that politicians looked after only themselves and that voting was the only way people could influence political decisions – a proportion similar to that which existed in Hungary as democracy was established.[33] These problems of the political culture were to add to the difficulties of economic and social reform.

The second stage of democracy: the launching of economic and social reforms

Several years after democracy was refounded, ample economic reforms were needed to redress economies that were lagging in international competitiveness and facing serious problems of state solvency. Yet besides tax reform, control of public expenditure, changes in exchange rates, liberalization of trade, deregulation of prices, suppression of subsidies, and reorganization of the labor and capital markets, the satisfaction of social rights in countries where provision for welfare was very limited required extension and reorganization of social policies, particularly in the areas of public pensions, unemployment benefits, education, and health. Thus, reform of the tax system was needed not just to reduce the public deficit but also to finance welfare and redistribute income. Public administration had to be reorganized, not only with the goal of improving the solvency of the state but also to deliver more social services. Decentralization and citizen participation were needed for more satisfactory social policies. These reforms were often contradictory. For example, control of wage increases could result in slower technological development; greater social expenditure could reduce the solvency of the state. Economic together with social reforms in the particular context of the new Southern European democracies required a new balance between market and state: Whereas economic efficiency (in terms of state solvency and international competitiveness) would lead to a larger role for the market, the satisfaction of social rights would demand an extension of the state.

The European Community was, to a very large extent, the reference for many of the reforms. Catching up with Western Europe meant joining the European Community, competing effectively with the other economies, and reaching their levels of satisfaction of social rights. In Spain, the consensus about these goals was overwhelming. Adolfo Suárez presented the Spanish request for EC membership in 1977, and all parliamentary parties supported him. It was widely believed that international isolation and dictatorship had been closely connected in recent Spanish history. The European Community was seen as a symbol of democracy and development; this symbol had been very important in the struggle against Francoism. Joining the EC was believed to be a decisive step for the consolidation of democracy as well as for future economic competitiveness. In Portugal, the consensus over EC membership was also high, although differences existed – for example, in the position of the Communist Party. The socialist government of Mario Soares presented the request for admission in 1977; besides the PS, he was backed by the Partido Popular Democrático (PPD) (later Partido Social Democrático [PSD]) and by the Centro Democrático Social (CDS). As in Spain, membership was largely seen in political and symbolic terms, as a reward for the recovery of democracy and as a decisive contribution to its consolidation, rather than in a strictly economic perspective. The European Community was perceived as a global alternative to isolation and third worldism; the request for membership was thus part of the change of course from the economic and political experimentation of 1974 and 1975.

The views that existed in Greece over the European Community were much more divided. The left was opposed; the right favored membership: PASOK and KKE on the one side, the Center Union and Nea Demokratia on the other. Whereas Karamanlis and ND believed that entry into the Community would be a decisive step for Greek democracy and for future economic growth, Papandreou and PASOK thought that the EC, and NATO too, would increase Greece's dependence and limit its sovereignty. Memories of external interference in Greek turmoils (particularly in the civil war of 1946 to 1949), which led to the political exclusion of the left as well as a strategy of appropriating the right's patriotic claims, helped to shape this position of PASOK's. Both democracy and development were thought to be more viable without external influences. Thus, in the 1977 elections PASOK opposed membership and demanded a "special agreement" (similar to the one that Norway enjoyed) and a referendum. Karamanlis, however, took Greece into the EC before the 1981 elections; in the campaign for these elections, and with the prospect of forming a government, Papandreou was much more nuanced about the Community. Eventually, the PASOK government presented a memorandum for special assistance in March 1982, which was considered to be a renegotiation of the terms of entry rather similar to the one achieved by Great Britain under the Labour government of Harold Wilson in 1974, and it led to a considerable increase in the resources that Greece obtained from the Community.

Catching up with Western Europe – that is, the "normalization" of Spain – was the main thrust of the reforms that the government of Felipe González launched at the end of 1982. Political and economic considerations were intertwined; it was thought that the political transition had to be followed by an "economic transition." Whereas Suárez was concerned about the capacity of democracy to face the costs of serious economic reform, González believed that, as in past episodes of Spanish history and in many other cases of democratic experiments, a prolonged economic crisis posed a serious threat to political stability. Economic strategies for "expansion in a single country" were rejected; the objective was, on the contrary, to increase the international competitiveness of the economy. González also mistrusted nationalization; he was influenced in this by the Spanish experience of the public sector and by the skepticism of traditional Partido Socialista Obrero Español (PSOE) leaders such as Prieto and Besteiro; he also sympathized with the ideological revision of the German SPD in 1959, with Swedish social democracy (and

Palme in particular), and with the British Labour Party moderates (particularly Gaitskell and Crosland). The change of course in the economic policies of the French government in 1982 was also a useful negative example, although it only reinforced existing views.

In spite of the economic crisis, in the summer of 1982 and before the general elections in October González still believed that the future government would have a considerable margin of maneuver for expansion, for increases in public expenditure, and for substantial job creation. By September the future minister of the economy, Miguel Boyer, gradually came to know the real depth of the crisis. Large outflows of foreign capital in October and November aggravated the situation. Describing this context of decision making some years later, González stated:

We had the anguish of an economic situation that was very bad from the macroeconomic point of view, not only because there was a process of necrosis in the whole industrial structure, but because we had a balance of payments with a terrible deficit and we had less than $3,000 million in foreign currency reserves. . . . We had an extraordinarily bad set of economic data; for example, the destruction of employment was proceeding in the rhythm of a thousand jobs lost per day. In Europe, the process of economic adjustment had been going on for seven years, and we were seven years late. . . . In the electoral campaign of 1982 I had the courage to say that rather than have the IMF dictate to us what had to be done with the Spanish economy, we would do it by ourselves.[34]

González's economic policies were tough from the beginning. Devaluation of the currency and higher prices for oil were decided on the first day of the new government's tenure. Over nearly three years the Spanish economy went through a deep adjustment whose aim was to create the conditions for future sustained growth, reducing the basic macroeconomic problems of the inflation rate, the public deficit, and the external deficit; carrying out substantial reconversion of the industrial sector after 1983 (with the Ley sobre Reconversión y Reindustrialización); reforming the capital markets; introducing changes in the labor market (in 1984 establishing more flexible types of labor contracts); and reorganizing social security with the Ley de Pensiones of 1985. Reduction of the deficit from 5.6 percent of GPD in 1982 to 2.4 percent in 1990 was achieved by slowing down the rate of growth in public expenditure, so that whereas it had increased by 10.5 percentage points in the seven years from 1977 to 1982, it did so by only 4.5 points in the next seven years; on the other hand, larger tax revenues financed this expenditure and the accumulated debt. The drop in the inflation rate was due to the sharp reduction in the public deficit, very high interest rates, an increase in aggregate fiscal pressure, and wage moderation.[35] The government thus used both demand and supply-side reforms: It tried to maintain demand and avoid underconsumption, to promote profits, and to stimulate investment. Although huge resources were spent on mitigating the effects of the crisis in the productive and financial systems in order to defend the international creditworthiness of the country and employment,[36] competitiveness, not prolonged protectionism, was the goal. The state played an active part in the promotion of competitiveness: Expenditure on research and development as a proportion of GDP doubled from 1983 to 1990 (increasing from 0.48 to 0.90 percent) as a result of the 1986 Ley de Fomento de la Investigación Científica y Técnica; more than $9 billion was spent on industrial reconversion over five years; public expenditure on labor policies increased by 43 percent in real terms between 1982 and 1989, amounting to 9.1 percent of the total expenditures of the central and regional governments over this period. Labor policies cost 3.2 percent of GDP in Spain in 1988, against 1.0 percent in Portugal and 0.8 percent in Greece. The average for the European Community as a whole was 2.9 percent. These policies included income maintenance as well as active programs, which basically consisted of jobs promotion and vocational training schemes. It was the active programs that grew the most: They represented 7.9 percent of total expenditures on labor policies in 1983 and 24.6 percent in 1989.[37]

In Portugal and Greece for some time reforms were either postponed or erratic. In Portugal the combination of the international crisis, uncontrolled public expenditure, and the poor management of nationalized companies had had serious consequences for inflation, unemployment, investment, and the current account. A few months after the first elections of 1975, the sixth provisional government presented a Plan of National Reconstruction that started to turn economic policies toward austerity, labor discipline, and fiscal rigor and tried to attract foreign investment. The economic crisis became the most important issue in the campaign for the second general election shortly afterward. It was increasingly thought that political priorities had postponed painfully needed reforms. In this campaign, Soares committed the PS to an end to nationalization: "The first thing to be said to the Portuguese people, and we the socialists say it, is that there will be no more nationalizations. It is necessary to stimulate the private sector and to enable private entrepreneurs to work safely."[38] Once in government, the PS passed Decreto-lei 422/76, which established mechanisms for privatization, brought the collectivization of land to an end, and tried to protect the "competitive coexistence" between the public and private sectors.[39] There were few ideological notes in the economic program of the Soares government; social and economic "modernization" was the keyword. The government introduced more economic austerity, devalued the escudo, reduced subsidies to public firms, imposed a ceiling of 15 percent on annual wage increases, and established monetary restrictions. The government also formally requested admission to the European Community and sought a loan from the IMF, which created serious political difficulties that ended with the replacement of the minority PS government by a PS–CDS coalition again led by Soares. This coalition concluded the IMF agreement and reinforced the economic adjustments.

This government lasted only from January 1978 to July. It was replaced by three consecutive governments of "presidential inspiration" (i.e., appointed and backed by Ramalho Eanes, who had won the 1976 presidential election with 62 percent of the vote, and made possible by the bipolar executive format of the republic), which for a few months maintained policies of economic austerity. But access to power of the conservative Alianza Democrática (AD) coalition (between the PSD and the CDS) with the 1979 elections – this government lasted until 1983 – meant relaxation of these policies. The result was faster growth but also more inflation and an increase in the balance-of-payments deficit. It was this coalition that, with PS support, in 1982 removed the references in the constitution to socialization of the means of production. These interrupted and partial economic reforms were very much a product of the instability of Portuguese politics in those years.

The launching of a comprehensive program of reforms started only in 1983, nearly ten years after the transition to democracy. It was begun by the new Bloco Central (PS and PSD) coalition. Soares, on taking over as prime minister, stated that "this government will be austere, uncompromising, and unpopular if that is what is required to achieve economic recovery." Reforms were intended to promote state solvency and economic competitiveness; a deflationary program was introduced in order to tackle the balance-of-payments deficit, inflation, and the burden of debt. Subsidies to firms were cut from 15.5 percent of GDP in 1980 to 5.5 percent, credit was restricted, and the prices of public goods were raised. The deficit was reduced, to a large extent through an increase in taxation. The private sector enjoyed more favorable conditions: Competition was fostered in several economic areas, including the financial sector. In June 1985 Portugal signed the treaties of the European Community and became a full member on 1 January 1986. In between, the Bloco Central coalition broke down with the 1985 elections, won by the PSD with 30 percent of the vote; PS support fell from 36 to 21 percent. The new minority PSD government, led by Aníbal Cavaco Silva (which became a majority government after winning the 1987 elections with

50 percent of the vote), continued the course of economic reform. It reinforced the role of the market, particularly in the financial sector and in public companies, and was able to benefit later from the international economic recovery in the second half of the decade. The initial erratic economic path and the considerable political instability of the new democracy changed dramatically in the 1980s: Portugal adapted fully to the Western European pattern.

Greek economic policies also experienced several shifts in the 1980s. Karamanlis, while carrying out his impressive task of reestablishing democracy, had postponed many urgent economic reforms. At the beginning of the decade, economic stagnation, increasing unemployment, and an inflation rate of 24.8 percent made Papandreou declare after the PASOK electoral victory in 1981 that he had inherited a "scorched-earth" economy. On taking over government, PASOK opted for Keynesian policies of expansion-cum-redistribution that presented similarities to the economic policies of the first Mitterrand government in France. Papandreou tried to stimulate production by increasing low and middle incomes and by offering incentives to productive investment. The number of beneficiaries of public pensions increased sharply, the "social wage" was extended, and lower incomes were indexed to past inflation. As a result, income differentials decreased substantially; the ratio between the gross earnings of top civil servants and the minimum wage fell from 5.5 : 1 in 1980 to 2.6 : 1 in 1988. The state also intervened in the affairs of forty-four companies in order to save them from bankruptcy and prevent more unemployment. Monetary policies were expansionist. The consequence was an increase in demand but not in economic growth; the rate of GDP growth was only 0.1 percent in 1982 and 0.3 percent in 1983, and industrial production, which had increased at a rate of 4.4 percent between 1973 and 1979, declined to − 1.4 percent between 1980 and 1985. Investment also fell during these years. Inflation remained high (21.0 percent in 1982; 20.2 percent in 1983), and unemployment doubled, going up from 4.3 percent in 1982 to 9.0 percent in 1985 (particularly among youth, where the rate was four times higher than the overall rate). The public deficit grew from 9.8 percent of GDP in 1981 to 14.3 percent in 1985, as the government was unable to raise sufficient revenues from taxation. The accumulated public debt, which represented 47.2 percent of GDP in 1981, reached 84.1 percent in 1985. External debt grew from 7.9 percent of GDP in 1981 to 10.6 percent in 1983.[40]

The PASOK government reacted late to this set of poor economic results. It devalued the drachma by 21 percent, but it did not introduce tough economic measures until after PASOK had won the 1985 general election. Following these, Papandreou passed a stabilization plan that lasted for two years. The plan tried to reduce inflation and the current-account deficit by restrictive demand management: Wages were controlled by law (suppressing the indexation mechanism), public expenditure was brought under strict control, and monetary policies were much tighter. The plan also attempted to improve the competitiveness of the Greek economy by cutting the costs of production and again devaluing the currency, this time by 15 percent. These measures improved the economic climate: Inflation came down but remained at 17 percent in 1986; the public-sector borrowing requirement fell from 18 percent in 1985 to 13 percent in 1987; the rate of growth in unit labor costs decreased from 22 percent in 1986 to 11 percent in 1987. The Greek government managed to get a substantial loan from the European Community to sweeten the pill. Yet investment remained low (it declined, in fact, by 6.2 percent in 1986 and by 7.8 percent in 1987), industrial production was stagnant, and the external dollar debt doubled between 1981 and 1987, reaching 44.8 per cent of GDP. Papandreou thought that these reforms were sufficient. When the minister of the economy, Kostas Similis, argued that they should be carried on in 1988, the government refused, afraid that the political costs would be too high, and the minister resigned in November 1987. But reforms were far from complete: Competitiveness and productivity were low, structural microeconomic problems had been left untouched, and the balance between investment and consumption was too uneven. Inflation, unit labor costs, the balance-of-payments deficit, and the PSBR went up again very quickly. The trade deficit reached 20 percent of GDP in 1989; the current-account deficit, in that same year, was triple that of 1988. Thus, at the end of the 1980s, after fifteen years of democracy, important economic reforms were still due in Greece.

The ideologies of these Southern European governments were not clearly associated with the launching of economic reforms. If we examine the record of the conservative governments, state solvency and economic competitiveness were not the top priorities in the political agendas of Constantin Karamanlis and Adolfo Suárez, and the Alianza Democrática in Portugal did not continue the reforms the previous governments had introduced. However, the PSD government of Anibal Cavaco Silva from 1985 onward was reformist. If we turn to left-wing governments, the policies of Mario Soares and particularly of Felipe González were clearly dominated by the economy: They tried to improve the solvency of their states and the competitiveness of their economies. On the other hand, Andreas Papandreou made only a limited attempt in this direction between 1986 and 1987, and the performance of the Greek economy under PASOK was poor.

The reforms clearly abandoned experimentation, and there was some convergence in the three countries in this respect. From 1976 onward, Portugal moved away from collectivist policies; the neo-Keynesian attempt in Greece failed and was eventually dropped; economic pragmatism dominated Spanish policies. A relationship between political democracy and a market economy seems to have existed in Portugal, where discussions of the political and economic models were simultaneous, and the turn toward parliamentary democracy after the first two elections coincides with the abandonment of collectivism. In Spain the Pactos de la Moncloa of 1977 were not only a stabilization plan but also an implicit agreement about a market economy that was later incorporated in the 1978 constitution. The left was overwhelmingly concerned with democratic consolidation and the political feasibility of its programs. This was particularly the case in Spain, where memories of the failed democratic experience of the Second Republic in the 1930s and its long-lasting and dramatic consequences were very strong. Other episodes of leftist government (Allende in Chile, the provisional governments in Portugal) were also influential. González thus argued that his nondoctrinaire, pragmatic policies had a "utopian" component: the consolidation of democracy and eradication of the authoritarian threat. This was also clearly the major concern of Soares in Portugal. Over the 1980s as democracies were consolidated, European integration and the competitiveness of the national economies became the dominant priority. Control of inflation, the budget, and the current-account deficit was seen as a necessary condition for competitiveness, for long-term growth, and for the creation of employment. Experiments were rejected as too risky in both economic and political terms.

The major ideological difference among reformist governments was expressed not so much in the economic content of their policies as in their combination of political and social reforms. Measures to promote state solvency and economic competitiveness must therefore be examined not just on their own but as part of typical *packages* of reforms that included changes in the protection of social rights. These packages are relevant when we analyze ideological variations among governments and interpret strategic choices: Social reforms may change the impact that economic reforms have in society, and the burden of costs may change. The packages may also be related to the choice between the *decretismo* and *pactismo* options.

Democracy considerably expanded social policies in the three countries. The greater concern in all about social rights confirmed Tocqueville's argument that "when the people begin to reflect on their position, they notice a mass of hitherto unfelt wants, which cannot be satisfied without recourse to the resources of the state. For that reason public expenditure increases with civilization, and as enlightenment spreads, taxes rise.''[41]

Both public expenditure as a whole and social expenditure in particular increased very sharply from the mid 1970s under the new democratic regimes. Welfare systems and mechanisms for income distribution were extended and reorganized. The role of the state in the provision of health, education, and pensions was reinforced. Revenues from taxation increased, and fiscal systems were made more redistributive.

Reforms took place in Greece in the system of education, in public health, and in labor relations. Legal reforms extended enrollment in further and in higher education, made access to education more democratic, and promoted participation in educational institutions. Private education, however, was not integrated in the national public system and remained a privileged sector.[42] Law 1397/83 established a national health system that provided universal health care and brought together the various organs of health provision. Law 1264/82 regulated trade-union freedoms and democratized the organization of unions. New legislation in Spain changed the criteria for welfare provision: Universal entitlement was introduced. To supplement voluntary and contributory pension schemes, basic pensions were established with payouts unrelated to personal contributions, financed by the public budget, and equivalent to the guaranteed minimum wage. A national health system was created by the 1986 Ley General de Sanidad, which, as in Greece, replaced a diversity of insurance schemes with an integrated public system that provided universal protection. Educational reform was also undertaken, based on three laws: the 1983 Ley de Reforma Universitaria, which gave financial, academic, and organizational autonomy to universities; the 1985 Ley del Derecho a la Educación, which democratized the educational system as a whole and regulated the relationship between public and private schools; and the 1990 Ley de Ordenachón General del Sistema Educativo, which made education compulsory up to age sixteen, expanded technical/vocational education, and reorganized the levels below higher education. The Suárez government introduced new democratic labor legislation with the Estatuto de los Trabajadores and the Ley Básica de Empleo; the González government completed this legislation, passed a new law protecting trade-union freedoms (the 1985 Ley de Libertad Sindical), and massively expanded labor policies. The political discontinuities of the governments in Portugal probably explain why changes in the law were not so thorough. The new legislation tried to satisfy social rights and was an essential component of the reformist package, as it had an impact on the social distribution of the costs and benefits of economic reforms. The economic consequences were also relevant, for expanded social policies required larger budgets from the state. It was increasingly in this part of the reformist package that the ideological differences among governments were most clearly expressed.

Other reforms were more qualitative. They did not rely on economic resources and did not have direct effects on material inequality. Reform of civil rights, greater decentralization, and new channels of social participation were examples of this qualitative change, which was of great importance in Greece and Spain. In Greece civil-rights reforms included the full acceptance of civil marriages (Law 1250/82), the introduction of divorce, modification of the penal code, a new family law that established equal rights for husband and wife and eliminated differences between legitimate and illegitimate children (Law 1329/83), and legal equality for women in the labor market, in pension rights, and in parental leave (Law 1414/84). Reforms of a similar kind were introduced in Spain: Divorce, abortion, and conscientious objection were legalized, and the right to habeas corpus and to legal assistance was ensured. The new channels of participation that were created in Spain affected the management of schools, universities, and the health service.[43] Political and administrative decentralization resulted in seventeen ''autonomous communities,'' each with a regional parliament and government, and in an increase in the proportion of public expenditure managed by these communities; it went up by twenty percentage points in the decade of the 1980s. In Greece, more powers and resources were transferred to local governments, and the power of the nomarchs (provincial governors) was reduced, but the Ministry of the Interior retained important controls. Participatory reforms were more limited, and it was alleged that these mechanisms, rather than devolving power to society, were manipulated by the parties.[44]

Qualitative reforms may have raised fewer problems in terms of economic resources, but sometimes they engendered serious ideological resistance. Divisions between left and right, for example, were particularly bitter in Spain over abortion, divorce, and education reform. These reforms were important in terms of the social identification of political alternatives and of electoral support.[45] The quantitative reforms as a whole made the Southern European transitions expensive. In the three countries, public expenditure grew considerably; the gradual satisfaction of social rights that had remained unattended put much pressure on budgets. Table 2.4 provides information on the evolution of public expenditure, revenues from taxes, and public-sector employment after the reestablishment of democracy in the three countries.

Table 2.4. *Evolution of public expenditures, taxes, and employment* (% of GDP)

	Greece			Portugal			Spain		
	1976	1984	1988	1976	1984	1988	1976	1984	1988
Total public expenditure	20.9	44.2	51.3	37.3	46.6	43.7	26.0	38.7	41.7
Revenues from taxes	29.2	34.2	35.9	31.0	34.6	36.6	25.0	33.2	36.7
Public-sector employment	8.5	9.4	10.1	8.8	13.3	13.8	8.5	12.8	13.8

Sources: OECD economic surveys of Greece, Portugal, and Spain, 1989 and 1990; J. Borrell, *Balance general de la política presupuestaria durante el período 1981–1988*, Santander: Universidad Internacional Menéndez Pelayo, 1988.

While public expenditure grew in the three countries, it did so dramatically in Greece (by 30.4 percentage points), more moderately in Spain (by 15.7 points), and to a much more limited extent in Portugal (by 6.4 points). After all the turmoil of the early years of democracy, Portuguese governments appear to have controlled the growth of public expenditure better than their counterparts in the other two countries (though the figures from Portugal do not include the large increases of 1974–5). Portugal is also the only case where economic adjustment in the 1980s appears to have reduced public expenditure; although Greece and Spain expanded their budgets at a reduced pace from 1984 to 1988, no cuts were introduced. Government ideology seems to have been related to trends in public expenditure if we compare Portugal with Greece and Spain, but not if we compare governments within each country over time; as a whole, the annual rate of growth of public expenditure diminished in the three countries over the decade. Public-sector employment rose in the three countries as a share of GDP, but more slowly in Greece; in Portugal and Spain the rate of growth was also lower starting in 1984. This was the same pattern as in the European Community as a whole: Whereas from 1970 to 1980 public expenditure increased in every country, from 1980 to 1990 it increased only in Spain, Greece, France, Italy, and Portugal. That is, the countries with social democratic governments were among those that did not cut public expenditures; in these countries, however, the rates of growth of budgets were considerably slower than a decade earlier, not only under conservative governments (such as the Union pour la Démocratie Française–Rassemblement pour la République in France, the UCD in Spain, and ND in Greece) but also under social democratic ones.[46]

Tax revenues increased in Portugal, Greece, and Spain over the whole period. In the case of Spain, the increase was twice as much as in the other two countries, but taxes eventually came to represent a similar proportion of GDP in the three countries. If we compare the evolution of public expenditure combined with taxation, expenditure grew much faster in the first years of democracy. In the second stage, this trend was maintained only in Greece; in Portugal, taxes continued to go up in the second half of the 1980s, but public expenditure was reduced; in Spain, higher tax revenues financed both more public expenditure and a cut in the budget deficit. By 1988 it was Spain that had the smallest gap between expenditure and taxes. If we examine this country, fiscal pressure went up by 10.3 percentage points over the decade of the 1980s – the greatest increase in any OECD country. (The figures for Greece and Italy, the only other countries with relevant increases, were 8.2 and 7.7, respectively.) Three points were used to reduce the deficit, three points to pay interest on the debt, and over four points to finance higher public expenditure.[47] Taxes on incomes and wealth represented roughly one-third of the fiscal pressure (and 10.3 percent of GDP); the other two-thirds consisted basically of taxes on production and imports (also 10.3 percent of GDP) and greater contributions to social programs (12.0 percent). The largest increase in revenues took place in the first category (with four percentage points of GDP) and was due to reductions in income-tax evasion – between 1982 and 1988, two million persons declared their income for the first time; for every three income tax returns in 1982, there was an additional one six years later. At the end of the decade, however, fiscal pressure in the three new Southern European democracies was considerably lower than the average in the European Community (42.8 percent in 1987), mostly because of persistent tax fraud.[48]

These different patterns mattered in political terms. The vague revolutionary objectives that had dominated the transition in Portugal ended fifteen years later in cuts in public expenditure. Postponed economic reforms meant a huge public deficit in Greece, which after Nea Demokratia returned to power in 1990 would lead to big cuts in public expenditure there too. The position of the state was more balanced in Spain: It had expanded the public provision of goods and services gradually and without reversals, and at the same time its solvency had greatly improved during the 1980s. Solvency of the state was crucial if economic efficiency and social fairness were to go together. Otherwise U-turns in economic policies would sooner or later be inevitable and damage social reforms.

The effects of reforms: the balance between economic efficiency and social fairness

Reforms were always defended by their proponents with the argument that their final effects would be Pareto-superior to the situation at the point of departure, that at least at the end of the day most people would be better off, and that no satisfactory alternatives existed. There are considerable difficulties, however, in assessing when effects are "final." New and unexpected events may have consequences for the economy (e.g., a new oil crisis) and distort the results of reforms already undertaken, and there is no threshold beyond which governments no longer face new challenges. Nevertheless, if a crisis of solvency and competitiveness is avoided through economic reform, and several years of stable growth follow, we may consider the effects final. Reformers also argued that the transitional costs will be lower than the final benefits; temporary sacrifices should thus be accepted. Arguments about reform also distinguished between their *aggregate* and their *distributive* effects – whether what is considered is the economy as a whole or variations in the impact of costs and benefits within the society. Economic competitiveness and growth were typical final effects; wage reductions were a case of transitional costs that might also reflect modifications in the distribution of income. Reforms in taxation had both final and distributive effects.

Improving the solvency of the state and the competitiveness of the economy means inevitable transitional costs. These costs may, however, vary, according not just to the depth of the economic crisis but to two additional factors. One is whether reforms and costs are concentrated in a short period or introduced gradually. The other is whether or not these economic reforms are compatible with social policies that distribute their impact. Further, these two factors can limit the efficacy as well as the cost of economic reforms: Gradualism and considerations of social fairness may only prolong, or "humanize," the illness when surgery is urgently needed. The situation of the Southern European economies was better than that of the Latin American and Eastern European ones once the transition to democracy was completed: There was no hyperinflation, nor did a system of collective ownership and state planning have to be transformed. Gradualism and social fairness thus created fewer problems affecting economic efficiency. Deep economic reforms were much less urgent than politics when democracy was reestablished; public expenditure could generally grow in spite of the crisis.

When the governments eventually decided to tackle a crisis that had been

Table 2.5. *Economic performance in the second stage of the new democracies (average for 1983–92)*

	Greece	Portugal	Spain	EC
GDP: annual variation (%), constant prices	1.8	2.9	3.6	2.7
Inflation: annual variation (%)	17.4	17.7	8.5	5.8
Employment — Annual variation (%)	0.8	−0.1	1.4	0.8
Employment — Unemployed as % of active population (average for period)	7.6	6.9	19.2	9.9
Real wages per wage earner: annual variation (%)	0.6	1.9	0.6	1.6
Unit labor costs in real terms in 1990 (100 = 1980)	105.3	82.1	84.3	92.9
Total public expenditure (as % of GDP)	48.0	44.2	40.9	47.9
Total public revenue (as % of GDP)	34.1	36.6	36.4	43.5

Source: Economie Européenne, no. 46 (December 1990).

growing over several years, the resulting transitional costs differed in the three countries. In Greece the 1985–7 austerity package produced a drop in real wages of 11 percent on average over the two years.[49] Although the rate of growth in public expenditure was slowed down, no cuts were made. Reforms had no dramatic consequences for unemployment, either: Although the rate doubled between 1981 and 1990, it remained below the European Community average – to a considerable extent because of overmanning in many firms, which reduced their competitiveness. The final economic effects of reforms were, however, frustrated, for these were interrupted in 1987. The austerity package was rather badly balanced despite the considerable help Greece obtained from the European Community, particularly as from 1983 – net transfers on the order of $12 billion between 1981 and 1990[50] proceeding from the Community's structural programs. The poor performance of the Greek economy in the 1980s is shown in Table 2.5, which compares Greece with Spain and Portugal and with the European Community as a whole. The economic deterioration, if we consider the 1970s or the experience of the other countries, was particularly remarkable in the rates of growth, inflation, and the deficit (expenditure minus revenues).

The transitional costs of the deflationary package that the Soares government introduced in Portugal in 1983 were manifested in a drop in economic activity over the next two years and a considerable fall in real wages (of ten percentage points over two years). The effect on unemployment was, however, very limited: It climbed only from 7.9 to 8.5 percent between 1983 and 1986.

Table 2.6. *Evolution of jobs and active population in Spain, 1964–89*

	No. of jobs created	Increase in active population
1964–9	832,200	751,500
1970–4	519,400	803,700
1975–9	− 1,031,800	42,300
1980–4	− 918,500	536,500
1985–9	1,950,900	1,445,000

Source: A. Espina, *Empleo, democracia y relaciones industriales en España*, Madrid: Ministerio de Trabajo y Seguridad Social, 1990, pp. 361–7.

The adjustment, as had been the case in Greece – and also in Japan, Austria, and Sweden – was at the cost of wage levels due to very rigid legislation concerning unemployment. The final effects of the reforms were much more visible than in Greece. The average rate of GDP growth between 1985 and 1990 stood at 4 percent; gross fixed investment, which had fallen by eighteen points in 1984, reached twice the OECD average rate toward the end of the decade; direct foreign investment doubled in two years; inflation was cut from 28.0 percent in 1984 to 8.5 percent in 1990; unemployment fell by three points in two years, to 5.5 percent in 1990. As a consequence of reforms, the economy was able to benefit considerably from membership in the European Community, which also provided Portugal with transfers that in 1989 were equivalent to 2.5 percent of its GDP.

The economic reforms introduced in Spain at the end of 1982 produced serious transitional costs. In contrast to Portugal and Greece, the rate of unemployment increased dramatically over the first decade of democracy; it went up from 3.9 percent in 1975 to 16.2 percent in 1982 and 21.9 percent in 1985 (twice the rate for the European Community), and it was much higher among young people.[51] The destruction of jobs started in the mid 1970s as a result of classical and Keynesian factors: Real wages had been growing much faster than productivity, paternalistic Francoist legislation had created important rigidities in the labor market, and low investment resulted in a serious lack of productive capital. But unemployment was also fueled by structural factors, particularly the coming of age of the baby-boom cohorts of the 1960s and early 1970s, rapid expansion of the active female population since 1982,[52] and the return from Europe of the migrant workers of the 1960s. As can be seen in Table 2.6, the vast increase in the number of unemployed people was due both to the destruction of jobs in the decade 1975–84 and to the increase in the active population.

Table 2.7. *Percentage of unemployed in households according to position in the family (1986)*

	Husband	Wife	Head of single-parent family	Son or daughter	Not member of family
Spain	26.8	8.0	1.4	60.4	3.4
Southern Europe[a]	17.4	14.7	1.6	62.4	3.9
European Community	21.1	20.6	4.0	42.0	12.3
United States	18.7	16.6	9.3	35.5	19.7

[a]Italy, Spain, Portugal, and Greece.
Source: OECD, *Perspectivas del empleo*, Paris, 1989.

Unemployment was by far the greatest social and economic problem in the new democracy. It damaged support for the governments and seriously strained their relations with unions. And it brought enormous pressure on the budgets: Whereas in 1975 unemployment benefits covered 167,900 persons, the number had multiplied by more than ten by 1989, reaching 1,946,420.[53] In spite of this, families still provided ample protection for the unemployed. These were mostly young people in search of a job, so that in 1984, 73 percent of the unemployed lived in a family with an employed male provider. To a very large extent "it all was as if the adult worker . . . had sacrificed the possible employment of his offspring and, to a lesser extent, his consort in favor of the growth of his own income."[54] Table 2.7 shows the impact of unemployment on households in Spain and in Southern Europe as a whole, compared with the European Community and the United States. Within families, parents had safer jobs in Spain and in Southern Europe, and children were much more vulnerable. If we examine the evolution of wages, they did not, in aggregate terms, suffer from the economic crisis. The average income per worker grew by 13 percentage points in real terms in the period 1977–82 and, although the rate slowed down between 1983 and 1991, it still went up by 6.2 points.[55] That is, from the beginning of the economic reforms, the buying power of wages went up by 0.7 percent per year.

The final effects of economic reforms in Spain began to emerge in the second quarter of 1985, a few months before the country became a full member of the European Community. The drop in the price of oil and the depreciation of the dollar helped economic recovery, and the reforms had put the Spanish economy on a much better footing in terms of inflation, the deficit, and industrial competitiveness. Spain also benefited from considerable net financial transfers from the European Community, which amounted to $7.1 billion between 1987 and 1992, although the positive balance between contributions and transfers declined from a peak of $1.8 billion in 1989 to $0.7 billion in 1992.[56] In the second half of the decade of the 1980s, the rate of growth was, on average, twice that of the European Community as a whole – around 5 percent per year. The inflation differential vis-à-vis the European Community was cut from five to one and a half points, and the budget deficit came down to 1.9 percent of GDP. Unemployment fell by six points, as the very large number of new jobs overcame the continuing expansion of the active population. In fact, the high rate of creation of new jobs from the mid 1980s was probably the best result of the economy in comparative terms. By the end of the decade, however, the Spanish economy was, like other Western European economies, experiencing new problems with inflation (it went up to 6.9 percent in 1989) and with a deficit in the current account. The rate of creation of new jobs slowed down, together with growth – although both remained comparatively high. Greater openness to competition had also done some damage to national industries, where foreign capital penetrated deeply. Foreigners bought shares in some 22,000 firms (about 20 percent of the total number of Spanish firms), while the economy as a whole suffered relative deindustrialization and turned into more of a service economy.[57] European integration thus posed many question marks for the future performance of the Spanish economy. However, reforms had taken it out of a difficult situation: It was now more open and competitive, and the state was solvent.[58] Its problems were increasingly similar to those of other Western European economies, although the Spanish economy still lagged behind most of them.

Reforms improved the economies of Spain and Portugal. This was hardly the case in Greece, where reforms had been much less complete. The costs of the economic crisis varied. In the case of Spain, they mostly affected unemployment rather than wages; the burden fell particularly on the shoulders of young people and the long-term unemployed among men. When reforms started, unemployment remained high; only three years later did it start to decrease as wage rises slowed down, investment picked up, and growth reached a high and fairly stable rate. In the Greek and Portuguese cases, reforms were at the cost of the wages of employed workers; employment as a whole did not suffer much. The cost of reforms in each country therefore represented a trade-off between wages and employment.

Reforms also changed the balance between the state and the market. In Portugal and Spain the role of the market in the economy was reinforced. During the economic crisis income differentials were reduced: Everybody became poorer, but the rich suffered the most. Later on, economic expansion and a freer market stimulated greater differentials in the primary distribution of income.[59] Yet at the same time taxation went up in the three countries, and public expenditure grew as a proportion of GNP (except in Portugal after 1984). In the European Community as a whole, current revenues from taxes went up on average,[60] but though the new Southern European democracies had tax levels below the rest, their rates of increase were faster. To some extent this also happened with regard to public expenditure: It remained stable in the European Community as a whole (+ 0.2 percent of GDP in the period 1981–90) and went up in five of the twelve countries – the five Southern European ones.[61] Of the three new democracies, Greece and Spain in particular experienced high rates of growth of public expenditure, although only in Greece did the budget reach the proportion of GDP of most Western European countries (financed by a large public deficit). Thus, it is possible that the new inequalities generated by more unrestrained market forces were counterbalanced by the combined effect of taxation and public expenditure. In Spain the active role of the state in the distribution of income was also expressed in the regional distribution of compensatory public expenditure. Catalonia and Madrid contributed twice as much to public revenues as they later obtained from state resources, while Andalusia and Extremadura got three and four times as much. The distribution of compensatory investments (the Fondo de Compensación Interterritorial) showed a strong negative correlation with regional per capita income ($r = .90$). Thus, in the period of economic growth from 1985 to 1990, the differences between the richest and the poorest autonomous communities shrank as a whole.[62] From a regional point of view, in becoming richer Spain did not become more unequal, largely as a result of state intervention.

Reforms also resulted in a trade-off between wages and social policies. In negotiations with trade unions, governments often argued that wage increases beyond a certain point would have negative consequences for social expenditure: They would have to be paid for by reducing the budgets for more and better health, education, and so on. Governments presented wage moderation as the counterpart of a larger social wage that would include social transfers and policies leading to the collective good. Trade unions, on the other hand, tended to defend increases in wages and transfer payments and were much less concerned with the provision of social goods. Different means of satisfying social rights therefore had different, and sometimes opposed, emphases.

Democracy clearly improved the protection of social rights; it did not consist of political rights alone. Economic reforms and social expenditure were not related as a zero-sum problem. The budget for social policies grew,

Table 2.8. *Evolution of the public provision of pensions, health, and education in Spain 1975–89*

	1975–82	1982–9
Public pensions		
Budgetary growth in real terms (%)	29.3	55.5
Increase in no. of beneficiaries (millions)	1.4	1.2
Public health		
Budgetary growth in real terms (%)	8.3	30.6
Increase in no. of beneficiaries (millions)	3.7	6.3
Education		
Budgetary growth in real terms (%)	66.4	94.0
Increase in rate of enrollment in secondary education for the age group 14–17 (%)	16.6	30.5

Sources: Ministerio de Economía y Hacienda, *Gasto público en España*, Madrid, 1989; Consumption reports from the Ministries of Health, Education, and Science and of Labor and Social Security, Madrid, 1990.

financed at least partly by larger revenues from taxes. If we examine expenditure on pensions, unemployment benefits, health, and education in Spain,[63] it went up in real terms by 39.7 percent between 1975 and 1982 and by 57.6 percent between 1982 and 1989; as a proportion of GDP, it increased from 9.9 percent in 1975 to 17.8 percent at the end of the 1980s. Table 2.8 shows the evolution of budgets and beneficiaries of public pensions, health, and education.

If we look at Greece, social expenditure also went up as a whole; it was 12.8 percent of GDP in 1970, 15.5 percent in 1980, and 22.6 percent in 1987. The expansion of public pensions was dramatic: The number of beneficiaries increased at an average annual rate of 5.4 percent in the 1980s. Greece eventually spent a higher proportion of its budget on pensions than any other OECD country except Italy, and as a result the social-security deficit jumped from 1 percent of GDP in 1970 to 7 percent in 1989. Education also expanded, particularly at the higher levels (the number of university students doubled between 1981 and 1986). And more of the budget was spent on social services.[64] Portugal went the opposite way: Economic reforms from 1983 on controlled social spending much more strictly. Here a sound economy was a much clearer priority than further improvement in social rights. Democracy thus mattered for the protection of social rights, and within democracies the political orientation of the governments made a difference. If we examine the

European Community as a whole, between 1982 and 1990 social expenditure on average declined as a proportion of GDP. But it increased in France, Greece, and Spain under social democratic governments.[65]

The capacity of the states to intervene in the economy was limited under the rules of the European Community; paradoxically, it was augmented in some redistributive areas. The goal of economic and social cohesion of the European Single Act reinforced "structural funds," that is, the resources of the EC budget dedicated to the development and structural adjustment of the less developed regions, to the economic recovery of areas deeply affected by industrial decline, to the struggle against long-term unemployment, to the promotion of employment among young people, and to reform of the Common Agricultural Policy. Out of these "structural funds," Greece got 6,667 million ECUs for the period 1989–93; Portugal, 6,958; and Spain, 11,362.[66] These funds contributed to finance infrastructural investments in backward regions and labor policies – particularly vocational training, which underwent massive expansion.

The effects of economic reforms on social inequality in the new Southern European democracies were thus complex. It has been argued that the logic of democracy results in a "conservatizing formula" – a fortiori when democracy is the outcome of transition by transaction, with no sharp break with the past; the pacts of the transition impose limits on the political agenda.[67] In the case of the three Southern European countries, economic reforms were often described as "technocratic," "monetarist," or "conservative."[68] A particularly critical analysis was formulated in Spain by the *Unión General de Trabajadores* (UGT), one of the two largest unions:

Social inequality has not been redressed in our country over the last ten years, and with a very high degree of probability it will have been augmented. . . . The situation of the workers in Spanish society has not improved. The way out of the crisis has been socially regressive: Unemployment has increased; labor-market dualism has emerged; cuts have been made in important social services, which have deteriorated; work conditions in many productive sectors have worsened; the contribution of wages to the national income has decreased.[69]

The conclusion is, however, far more complex. The trade-offs among wages, employment, and social policies, the varying balance between market and state, and the different packages of economic/social/qualitative reforms have been described. As a whole, the standard of living increased in Spain, and social policies were expanded. The initial costs of economic reform were concentrated in unemployment, but even then the rates of destruction of jobs were lower than in the earlier period of delayed reforms, for the economy did not enter recession. Later on, from 1985 onward, the annual rate of job creation stood on average at 3.3 percent. Real wages did not fall, but their growth was much more moderate than in the previous period. Public expenditure on pensions, unemployment benefits, health, and education increased substantially in real terms. Dissatisfaction with social policies was considerable, but twice as many people thought that social inequalities had decreased over the 1980s than thought the opposite.[70] Almost by definition, turning the state solvent and the economy competitive is never harmless. Nevertheless, whether reforms can be described as regressive or not depends largely on how inevitable reforms were, whether costs could have been avoided, which alternative reforms were available, and which trade-offs were achieved among economic efficiency, unemployment, wages, and social policies, affecting different social groups in diverse ways.

The final pattern of economic growth, market inequalities, unemployment, wages, and redistributive policies seems to offer relevant variations in Southern Europe. Reforms improved economic performance in Spain and Portugal but not in Greece. The unemployed bore the heaviest cost in Spain – particularly young people, but also long-term unemployed male workers and women. Employed wage earners did not suffer loss in incomes; low-income groups benefited from the expanded provision of public pension schemes, health protection, and education; and regional differences diminished. In Portugal and Greece, wage earners lost purchasing power, but unemployment did not reach dramatic levels except among young people, and in Greece some welfare policies were expanded, particularly pensions. The specific packages of reforms could thus influence the social distribution of costs: Economic policies designed to improve the solvency of the state and the competitiveness of the economy were not necessarily incompatible with social policies designed to broaden social rights. Economic reforms in Southern Europe were, in comparative terms, less of a "bitter pill" than in other new democracies. Their "expensiveness" was to a very large degree made possible by the substantial increase in the revenues of the states due to higher and better-distributed taxes.

The path of reforms: dilemmas, decisions, and implementation

Governments launch reforms when they consider that the crisis has reached a particular gravity and that decisions cannot be postponed, when they think that alternative courses of action are worse options, and when they believe that reforms are likely to succeed. The "objective" gravity of the crisis in the three new democracies of Southern Europe has already been examined. The political priorities of the transition had for some time postponed reforms that were necessary, but the economy was back on top of the political agenda a few years after democracy was reestablished. Reforms were launched in Portugal when in 1977 the country had to turn to the IMF for help; in Spain, radical economic reforms were decided upon in 1982 when foreign-currency reserves were depleted, the public deficit was much larger than expected, the destruction of jobs had reached a high rate, and large capital flights were taking place.

Selection of a particular course of action depends on calculations about the comparative costs of alternative strategies; these costs may be social (i.e., reduction in wages, higher unemployment) or political (i.e., electoral losses, social conflict, divisions within the government or the party). Governments in new and fragile democracies may face a choice that leads to dramatic consequences either way. In such contexts, reformers often find themselves in the vicious circle of economic stagnation, social demands, deepening economic crisis, political destabilization, and authoritarian involution that Flisfisch has described.[71]

These dilemmas of course affect all sorts of political decisions, not just economic policies. For example, when in the 1980s the Greek and Spanish governments faced the difficult choice of whether to call a referendum on NATO membership, as they had committed themselves to do in their electoral programs of 1981 and 1982, they had to assess the consequences carefully: the likelihood of winning the referendum, the political scenario if they lost, the subsequent electoral cost, the impact on the other member countries, the social reaction if the commitment was not fulfilled. Postponements as much as decisions may have deep negative effects on the economy and the polity. If the crisis is perceived as grave enough, decisions will be seen as inevitable and urgent. This was the case in Spain in 1982; much less so in Greece in the 1980s, where reforms were very limited and always subordinated to electoral considerations; it was also the case in Portugal from 1983.

The choice of a particular package of reforms always excludes possible alternative policies. The rejection of experiments that could have serious economic and political risks was a negative determinant of the choice. Democratic consolidation and economic recovery were the overwhelming concerns of reformers. The uncertainties of the first years of the Portuguese transition were a further deterrent to economic adventures. Thus, reformers gradually converged in rejecting nationalization, economic protectionism, isolation, and experiments beyond a market economy. The change of course in economic policies that took place in Portugal was based on the conviction that the process of collectivization in 1975 had been inefficient. In Greece and Spain a very negative view existed of the nations' economic performance and of the redistributive impact of public sectors that were already of considerable size;[72] a reference to the market economy was included in the Spanish constitution of 1978 that was accepted by the left. Whereas in Portugal economic protectionism was for some time hotly discussed inside the MFA and in the Constituent Assembly, in Spain it was generally associated with dictatorship. The commitment to the European Community was seen in opposition to the protectionist model: Insofar as Europe was considered to guarantee a better and safer future not just for the economy but for democracy, the protectionist alternative was excluded.

Reforms are launched when they are thought likely to be successful. This depends first of all on the strength of reformers. It has often been argued that majority governments will be readier to undertake reforms. They will have the *right* to carry out their policy intentions, in accordance with the doctrine of the mandate of representative government,[73] and they will have the *ability* to do so. Only if a single party has all the powers of government can necessary but unpopular decisions be taken. A comparative study of economic policies in the twenty-four OECD countries appears to support this argument: One-party majority governments are associated with lower deficits and a lower ratio of debt to GDP.[74]

Whereas the Spanish experience confirms this hypothesis, the Portuguese and Greek cases do not. Greece had majority governments from 1974 to 1989, yet neither Constantin Karamanlis (with 54 percent of the vote) nor Andreas Papandreou (with 48 percent) decided to introduce and complete reforms that were needed. The several Portuguese governments do not show a clear pattern. The 1977 minority government of Mario Soares failed precisely because the IMF questioned its political strength; in contrast, the 1985–7 minority PSD government was able to continue the reforms started in 1984. Some coalitions, such as the CDS/PSD coalition of 1979–83, performed badly, but others, such as the PS/PSD of 1983–5, did much better. The Portuguese experience thus seems to provide support for the formal model of European coalition governments developed by Austen-Smith and Banks:[75] Stable policies can exist with minority governments, which can have the "political will" to introduce reforms and the ability to implement them against competing coalitions. Spain offers perhaps the clearest contrasting case: After the first five years of the new democratic regime with its poor economic performance and the postponement of necessary reforms, the major political issue of the 1980s was to have a government able to govern ("un gobierno que gobierne"). The majority support enjoyed by González in 1982 was decisive when the reconversion of industry, the expropriation of the private holding company Rumasa, the reform of public pensions, and reform of education were decided upon.

When reforms are launched, the main objective of the governments is to carry them through if they are seen as necessary. Only the survival of the government itself can modify this commitment. The future of reforms and the future of the government are more compatible if the latter enjoys majority support and if the former are decided on early and made irreversible. At the beginning of its mandate, the government still enjoys self-confidence, internal party unity has not been strained, and popularity is high. This is particularly so if the government is untainted by a recent disappointing record. Later on, the capacity to make decisions becomes more and more restricted. The Southern European experience seems partly to confirm Keeler's argument that the combination of crises and large mandates opens a large "window" to wide-ranging policy reforms for incoming governments, which then enjoy both *authorization* by society to carry out their programs and *empowerment* by an ample parliamentary majority.[76] Nelson's comparative study of nineteen third-world governments in the 1980s shows that only six introduced programs of structural reform. Of these, five had come to power after a period of turbulence and crisis that had discredited the former governments; the three that had democratic pluralist systems had all won elections with massive support.[77] Spain in particular fits Keeler's analysis well; yet governments with a considerable policy window can also fail, as in Greece, while governments with a restricted initial mandate can attempt to introduce relevant reforms and occasionally be politically successful, as was the case in Portugal. If reforms are also seen as impossible to stop and as irreversible, resistance will be lower. The Spanish reform of the industrial sector, social security, and education would have been much more difficult, even for a majority government, had measures not been taken in the first two years of the mandate. As the initial impetus wears out, reforms increasingly require a different strategy, one consisting more of negotiations and pacts. A weak government may be unable to make decisions, and reforms may be decided on too late. But *decisionismo* is not the only key to success. In addition to the ability to make decisions, cooperation from key sectors of society is needed, particularly when reforms require time; cooperation is, for example, more necessary for the success of tax and income policies than for a devaluation of the currency or for capital levies, which require surprise and irreversibility. Consultation with parliamentary forces and key interest groups may give reformers precious information about potential adversaries and allies. This strategy is not necessarily incompatible with *decisionismo* as long as consultation does not appear to be useless,[78] but it will highlight the issue of costs and may affect the rhythm, the irreversibility, and the content of reforms. It is a strategy that becomes more necessary when governments are more vulnerable; that is, when they are minoritarian or have taken too long to launch an initiative.

Consultation and concertation thus consist of choices related to strategy, to the style of policy making, and to the content of reforms. If consultation is not to be useless and if concertation is to be possible, not only will the government have to convince its partners that reforms are necessary, that the future final benefits will be higher than the transitional costs, and that they will be carried out by the government alone if need be, but costs will also have to be limited, a package with social compensations will have to be agreed on, and specific benefits will have to be allocated to the interest groups involved in the negotiation.[79]

It has often been argued that the ideology of a government is related to the choice of consultation and *pactismo*. Social democracy is thought to be more prone to neocorporatist formulas. Yet no clear association existed in Southern Europe. The PASOK government had serious difficulties with unions. The number of hours lost to strikes doubled in its first two years, and in 1983 Law 1365 restricted strikes in the public sector. Conflict increased again in 1985, following new policies for economic adjustment, and in 1987 five times the hours were lost to strikes as in 1981.[80] In Portugal the minoritary center–right government of Aníbal Cavaco Silva was able to make a pact with the UGT in 1985–6, but not with the CGTP. In Spain relations between governments and unions were particularly complex. In 1977 the Pactos de la Moncloa involved the government and the parliamentary opposition, and only indirectly the trade unions, and lasted only one year. In December 1978 a *decreto-ley* imposed wage limits unilaterally, in a purely *decretista* fashion. In 1979 a two-year agreement was signed by the employers' confederation and the socialist UGT, but not by the Workers' Commissions or the government. In 1981, a new two-year pact was agreed to by the government, the employers' confederation, and the two trade unions. Thus, some form of concertation existed in four of the five years of conservative government. When the PSOE came to power, the 1981 agreement was still in effect; until the end of the decade, only once did a pact obtain: in 1985–6, and it took in the government, the UGT, and the employers' confederation. Although the PSOE insisted strongly on the doctrine of concertation, its relations with the unions proved particularly difficult.

In Spain unions were much readier to reach agreements during the transition than after the new democracy was consolidated. Also, conflict between the UGT and the Socialist Party had fratricidal connotations: The organizations shared a common history, and the UGT had agreed to the PSOE's electoral program of 1982. Pacts were reached more easily in the early stages about key reforms: industrial reconversion, new legislation on the working week, the new law on trade-union freedom. The UGT was, however, increasingly unhappy and skeptical about economic policies and feared an eventual loss of support if it remained associated with the government; it considered that it was better to make agreements with a right-wing government.[81] The minister of the economy, Carlos Solchaga, also came to believe that concertation was expensive and inefficient as well as less needed in a phase of economic expansion. Spanish unions had a very limited membership[82] and could perhaps be thought not to be sufficiently centralized or broad-based to ensure efficient pacts; the UGT and the Workers' Commissions had, however, substantial support in union elections and a strong *capacidad de convocatoria* – a very important potential for mobilization – and they provided symbolic legitimacy for reforms. Conflict between the unions and the government also increased when the government had lost part of its initial strength. Only after the mutual bitter experience of a successful general strike in 1988 that did not seem to lead anywhere, and after new general elections in 1989, was it possible to resume concertation, although it was limited to specific issues.

It appears that the minority nature of the government was a more important factor than ideology in explaining *concertación:* The PSD and UCD governments in Portugal and Spain were minoritarian and reached agreements with unions. Cavaco Silva headed both minority and majority PSD governments in Portugal: He was much readier to reach pacts in the first situation. These governments were more vulnerable and tried to gain strength through pacts. The majority government of González in Spain was more concerned instead with the application of the mandate theory; it believed that it had the right and the duty to carry out policies conceived in terms of the general interest, although agreements could be reached if they did not distort the main thrust of reforms. A government's stage of life, which was associated with how strong it was, seems to have influenced the choice between *decretismo* and *pactismo.* For example, the choice of the PSOE government in Spain for rapid and irreversible decisions about economic and social reforms was later replaced by a strategy of negotiation – slower but arousing less antagonism. The González government thus decided to withdraw a program of youth employment that had generated bitter resistance in the winter of 1988–9 even though it enjoyed vast support in public-opinion surveys; it reached a considerable number of limited agreements with the unions (on pensions, unemployment benefits, vocational training, and so on) in 1990, and it also achieved a pact with unions on a major reform of education (the Ley de Ordenación General del Sistema Educativo) in that same year. Relations between the government and the unions, however, remained sour: Union leaders were consistently hostile to the government, while the PSOE firmly believed that the economic and electoral failure of the British Labour Party in 1979 was a excellent example of what happens when unions dominate governments. González tried to make a permanent offer of concertation compatible with the political autonomy of the government. He stated: "Our position is clear: Yes to social dialogue and social compromise, also yes to political dialogue and political compromise. But no mortgages on the conception and implementation of our project," arguing that these "mortgages" might "condition the sovereign majoritarian will of the people."[83] As for the unions, they rejected any kind of global pact, with the argument that it would provide a blank check for the government's economic policies. Thus, they did not accept the offer of a global "Pact of Progress" made by the government in the summer of 1991, which sought to achieve a high and stable rate of growth with low inflation and expanded employment based on a vast program of investment in infrastructure and in professional training and on wage moderation – but which would guarantee improvement in the purchasing power of wages. Unions were much more willing to enter into limited pacts as long as their ability to negotiate higher wages was not compromised.

The urgency of reforms seems to have had a complex relationship with the choice of strategy: *decisionismo* or concertation. Agreements were easier in Spain at the depth of the crisis: The fragility of democracy, the weakness of unions only recently legalized, and growing mass unemployment pushed the unions toward a strategy of concertation – *un sindicalismo de negociación*. In the process, they exacted legislation that protected trade-union rights, organized collective bargaining, established institutional channels of participation, and granted substantial public funds for their activities. Later on, however, the UGT came to believe that "the unions have been the Cinderella of the transition, and this has damaged the interests of the workers."[84] The unions considered that expansion would leave more room for higher wages and public expenditure; they also cared more about real incomes and social protection than about the provision of such collective goods as health and education. As for the government, it was not ready to reach agreements that would have jeopardized growth, investment, state solvency, and economic competitiveness. It also argued that excessive wage raises had hurt jobs and that increases in the budget for social transfers had been substantial. In its initial stage, and in the depth of the economic crisis, the government found least resistance from unions to early and tough economic decisions. Conflict between the unions and the government, paradoxically, multiplied when the economy was growing rapidly; it was not so much the distribution of costs but of profits that seemed to fuel the antagonism. More than the costs of reforms, it was the resistance they generated and the power of governments to push them through that influenced the choice of strategy: The less urgent the reforms, the more necessary was a strategy of negotiation if reforms were to succeed.

Reforms are implemented through sequences of decisions that have to take into consideration the results achieved so far and the resistance that has been raised. In taking successive steps in the course of reform, governments examine the transitional costs that have emerged, the likelihood that the final effects will be attained, and the possible electoral consequences of what has been accomplished and what remains to be done. The path of reforms may thus lead to their continuation and completion, the modification of their content or rhythm, their suspension in hopes of better times, their abandonment, or their reversal. Decisions taken by reformers at strategic conjunctions of a reform process are thus influenced by variables that are very largely similar to those which condition the initial decision to launch the reform. Yet reformers now have additional experience: The reforms must have had some results, however partial and limited. Too, the balance of forces between the government and its allies and adversaries, whether parliamentarian or extra-parliamentarian, may have shifted; popular confidence in the government may have changed; the political calendar will have brought elections closer. New data and assessments of the likely economic, social, and electoral evolution will determine the course of reforms from then on.

It was in part the gravity of the crisis and poor economic results that led Portuguese governments to the abandonment, and later to the gradual reversal, of collectivist economic reforms from the end of 1975. The gradual shift was started by the sixth provisional government in 1975 a few months after the constituent elections, and after April 1976 was carried on by the first constitutional government. Politics, however, also mattered: The results of these two elections moved Portuguese politics toward the center, and from then on wide swings in electoral results took place between the center–left and the center–right. The Greek government also modified its policies as a result of bad economic results: first for a brief period in 1983 and then more consistently after winning the 1985 general election when it introduced the austerity package of 1986–7. The government changed course again at the end of 1987 out of fear that the political costs might be too high. In Greece government decisions were influenced much more by political than by economic considerations. If we look at Spain, the reforms that were introduced in 1982 were reinforced a year later for economic reasons; thereafter the public debt was financed in its entirety by the public budget in order to control inflation. Unemployment reached dramatic levels, but the government stuck to its economic policies, believing that only the competitiveness of the economy and stable growth would significantly increase the number of jobs. The distribution of available employment with maintenance of wage levels offered little hope: Working hours had already been falling since 1977 at an annual average of 1.7 percent, and an additional reduction in the age of retirement would have increased further a pensions budget that went up by 495 percent in real terms over fifteen years. Toward the end of 1985, economic growth and job creation resumed, partly in response to the European economic recovery taking place just as Spain joined the Common Market. It is of course difficult to predict what would have happened to reforms and to the government if this international economic revival had not taken place, if the Spanish economy had not started to expand, and if unemployment had kept on increasing.

Evolution of the balance of forces appears to have been a crucial factor in governments' deciding whether reforms were to be continued or not. However, differences existed between the Portuguese and Greek reforms: Papandreou, with a majority government, decided to interrupt the reforms in 1987; Soares and Cavaco Silva were prepared to continue them with minority governments. The influence of the government's strength and support was clear in Spain. Resistance to reform outside parliament was important (particularly resistance to industrial reconversion, to taxation policies, to changes in public pension schemes, to legislation on abortion, and to the reform of education). The parliamentary majority and the unity of the party, together with support from public opinion, were the decisive factors in carrying through reforms. The Centro de Investigaciones Sociológicas provided regular survey data on social attitudes to policies. As a whole, confidence in the competence of the government was always in a majority; on average, twice as many people preferred the PSOE to its closest rival, the Alianza Popular, "to ensure an efficient working of the economy," and four times as many "to reduce inequalities.'' Although there was considerable criticism of the government's fairness, no opposition party was seen as a better alternative in terms of social policies.[85]

Conclusions

The varying degrees of success of economic reforms in Southern Europe appear to have been particularly influenced by the dimensions of the crisis, the characteristics of the programs of reforms, the political strength of the governments, and the periods of time used to implement reforms. At the point when the dictatorships fell, the three Southern European economies shared some important traits of ''poor capitalism'': high inflation, obsolete industries, public deficits, noncompetitive agriculture, high unemployment, underdeveloped welfare systems, inefficient public bureaucracies, and large trade deficits. Yet their situation was much less dramatic than that of other new democracies east and south. Inflation and debt, for example, were serious problems, but of an altogether different kind than in Argentina, Brazil, or Yugoslavia. The countries were also helped by the geographical accident of being part of Europe: Economic expansion in Southern Europe in the two periods 1958–75 and 1985–90 was stimulated by Western European growth. Yet the evolution of the economies in Greece, Portugal, and Spain was not determined only by outside events. Domestic reforms were crucial for economic outcomes. If the comparative economic performances varied, it was largely because of differences in economic reforms. These were not equally competent, complete, or consistent.

The second half of the 1970s was, with few exceptions (such as the limited reforms in Portugal in 1977–8 and the Moncloa Pacts of the Suárez government), a period of economic muddling through in the new democracies and also in many of the old ones.[86] The decade of the 1980s was, in contrast, both in Western and in Southern Europe a period of increasing ''realism'' in the management of the economy. As a consequence, economic policies gradually converged. The Greek government of 1981 initially followed policies that resembled those of the first Mitterrand/Mauroy government; it had to reverse them in much the same way only a few years later, although with less rigor and much poorer results. Portugal also undid much of what the provisional governments had done in 1974–5. Governments used similar instruments in order to achieve economic competitiveness and state solvency: devaluations of the currency, cuts in subsidies to industries, strict control of the money supply, increases in the price of public goods, reduction of deficits, moderation of wages, and reform of the labor and capital markets. Taxes were also raised to come closer to Western European levels of fiscal pressure, both as part of the economic program and to finance reforms to satisfy social demands more fully. Besides manifesting differences in competence, comprehensiveness, and consistency, the governments' particular mix of economic and social reforms varied according to their political orientation.

The strength of the government seems also to have influenced the eventual success of reforms. This was most clearly so in the case of Spain; much less so in Portugal. In contrast, in Greece majority support for the governments and the strict control of parties by the leaders were unrelated to what the governments did or failed to do. In Spain voting intentions did not go through dramatic oscillations after 1982,[87] and González was in full control of his party; reformers thus enjoyed considerable time to implement their policies. The minister of the economy also benefited from the unremitting backing of González, who followed the advice of Olaf Palme that this minister had to be supported by the prime minister 98 percent of the time.

This kind of long-term perspective was essential for reforms: Governments could look beyond the transitional costs. González insisted strongly on this, arguing that it was not possible "to change in four years a society that has not been able to change for two centuries. . . . In Spain we have to measure change by decades," and "if we have the political courage to withstand the demagogic pressure of some, and to sustain our policies for a long period of time, then we shall take this country out of a long relative backwardness with respect to European countries."[88] After political democracy was reestablished, the decade of the 1980s was seen as a period of growing normalization vis-à-vis the Western European socioeconomic pattern. A lot of catching up remained to be done, but the new Southern European democracies had shed much of their singularity over the decade.

Whatever the transitional or final effects of reforms and the ups and downs in their implementation, democracy was maintained in the three countries. Portugal faced problems for a few years; both political democracy and the economy presented serious uncertainties. Gradually elections and the growing economic realism of the 1980s put the country on the path of normalization. Greece had difficulties of a different kind: Confrontational politics, a lack of consensus over some basic rules of the game, and the preeminence of electoral interests over responsible policies made governance difficult and affected economic outcomes. Spain, after a successful transition, experienced serious problems of consolidation, including military conspiracies and an attempted coup in February 1981. This political instability went along with a very difficult economic situation; efficient economic policies were widely seen at the beginning of the 1980s as crucial for the consolidation of democracy. In the decade of the 1980s, then, both elections and economic policies reinforced democracy in Portugal and Spain; the case of Greece is much more doubtful. In Spain in particular, assessments of satisfaction with democracy followed a curvilinear trend: Average scores stood at 4.45 (out of 10) in 1978, declined in 1980 to 4.19 reflecting the effects of the economic crisis, and went up again to 5.54 by 1984.[89] The number who thought that democracy had become more stable doubled in the course of the decade.[90]

The Southern European experience does not conform to the arguments that new democracies based on pacts will leave very little room for reform and that transitions will be at the cost of socioeconomic change. Fifteen years after democracy was reestablished in Portugal, Greece, and Spain, the type of transition does not seem to have decisively determined the possibilities of reform. There was something in between: namely, elections, economic constraints, and the power of the government. Considerable convergence occurred as economic policies increasingly shared objectives and instruments; the differences that remained were to a considerable extent due to electoral results and to governments. These differences were manifested in economic performance and in the packages of economic and social reforms. These packages were quite expensive. Over the fifteen years of democracy, the three countries increased public expenditure and expanded social policies. This may be one of the distinctive differences between reforms in the new Southern European democracies and in Latin America and Eastern Europe. After the transitions, reforms not only sought to improve the performance of the economies but to increase the protection afforded by social rights.

Notes

1. World Bank, *World Development Report 1991*, New York: Oxford University Press, 1991, ch. 7.
2. A. Vázquez Barquero and M. Hebbert, "Spain: Economy and State in Transition," in R. Hudson and J. Lewis (eds.), *Uneven Development in Southern Europe: Studies of Accumulation, Class, Migration and the State*, London: Methuen, 1985, pp. 284–308.
3. J. Solé Tura, "Socialist Governments in Southern Europe: Between Reformism and Adaptation to State Structures," paper presented at the European Consortium for Political Research, Barcelona, March 1985.
4. Economist Intelligence Unit, *Greece: Country Profile*, London: Economist Publications, 1990.
5. The percentage of foreign capital in total current investment went up from 1 in

1959 to 21 in 1969. In the latter year foreign capital reached 52 percent of all investment in manufacturing (Economist Intelligence Unit, *Portugal: Country Profile*, London: Economist Publications, 1990).

6. This growth was to a large extent financed directly or indirectly by the new European wealth. Thus, income from tourism rose to $2,386 million in 1973 as the number of tourists increased from six million in 1960 to thirty-six million; remittances from migrant workers reached $1,718 million in 1973, and foreign investment came to $852 million in the same year. Tourism contributed 5.2 percent of GNP in Spain in 1970 and 2.1 percent in Greece.

7. J. J. Linz analyzes the economic and social changes in Southern Europe before democracy was restored in Portugal, Greece, and Spain in "Europe's Southern Frontier: Evolving Trends Towards What?" *Daedalus*, Winter 1979, pp. 175–209.

8. See P. Nikiforos Diamandouros, "Regime Change and the Prospects for Democracy in Greece: 1974–83," in G. O'Donnell, P. C. Schmitter, and L. Whitehead (eds.), *Transitions from Authoritarian Rule: Southern Europe*, Baltimore: Johns Hopkins University Press, 1986, pp. 138–64.

9. The strikes in 1973–4 took place in the airline (TAP), textile, and electronics industries (Siemens, Phillips, Plessey, Standard Electric), in the Lisbon subway system, etc. See M. L. Lima Santos, M. Pires de Lima, and V. M. Ferreira, *O 25 de abril e as lutas sociais nas empresas*, Oporto: Afrontamento 1976, and J. Pires, *Greves e o 25 de abril*, Lisbon: Base, 1976.

10. See V. Pérez Díaz, *El retorno de la sociedad civil*, Madrid: Instituto de Estudios Económicos, 1987, p. 114.

11. C. Tsoucalas refers to this in "Radical Reformism in a 'Pre-Welfare' Society: The Antinomies of Democratic Socialism in Greece," in Z. Tzannatos (ed.), *Socialism in Greece*, Aldershot: Gower, 1986.

12. At that stage of the new Portuguese democracy, the warnings emphasized that strikes were threatening democratic gains and had a counterrevolutionary impact; Alvaro Cunhal, for example, said as much in a speech in Braga on 30 November 1974.

13. See H. M. Makler, "The Portuguese Industrial Elite and Its Corporative Relations: A Study of Compartmentalization in an Authoritarian Regime," in L. S. Graham and H. M. Makler (eds.), *Contemporary Portugal: The Revolution and Its Antecedents*, Austin: University of Texas Press, 1979, pp. 156–7, and id., "The Consequences of the Survival and Revival of the Industrial Bourgeoisie," in L. S. Graham and D. L. Wheeler (eds.), *In Search of Modern Portugal: The Revolution and Its Consequences*, Madison: University of Wisconsin Press, 1983, p. 261.

14. Among others, A. Champaulimaud, owner of a very large economic group that included Sidurgería Nacional. On winning the 1976 election, Mario Soares made a trip to Brazil at the end of the summer in order to persuade industrialists in exile to return to Portugal.

15. A good example of the uncertainties faced by representative democracy was given by Alvaro Cunhal, general secretary of the Portuguese Communist Party, in an interview by Oriana Fallaci following the elections to the Constituent Assembly

in April 1975: "If you think the Socialist Party with its 40% and the Popular Democrats with their 27% constitute the majority, you are the victim of a misunderstanding" (*L'Europeo*, 15 June 1975).

16. See P. Nikiforos Diamandouros, "Transition to, and Consolidation of, Democratic Politics in Greece, 1974–1983: A Tentative Assessment," *West European Politics* 7, 2 (1984): 50–71.

17. A. Espina, *Empleo, democracia y relaciones industriales en España: De la industrialización al Mercado Único*, Madrid: Ministerio de Trabajo y Seguridad Social, 1990, p. 53.

18. Between 1960 and 1975, 2,412,317 workers had migrated to Europe in search of jobs; from 1975 onward, the flow was negative, and in 1981 the net return reached 270,000. The active female population stood at 2,804,000 in 1964, reached 3,852,600 in 1974, and was 3,908,600 in 1982.

19. D. Rustow, "Transitions to Democracy: Towards a Dynamic Model," *Comparative Politics* 2, 3 (1970): 337–63.

20. A. Bosch, C. Escribano, and I. Sánchez, *La desigualdad y la pobreza en España: 1973–1981*, Madrid: Instituto Universitario José Ortega y Gasset, 1988, p. 9.

21. A. Przeworski, "The Games of Transitions," unpublished manuscript, University of Chicago, January 1990, p. 27.

22. See J. J. Linz, "Legitimacy of Democracy and the Socioeconomic System," in M. Doggan (ed.), *Comparing Pluralist Democracies: Strains on Legitimacy*, Boulder, Colo.: Westview, 1988, pp. 75–80.

23. P. McDonough, S. H. Barnes, and A. López Pina, "Economic Policy and Public Opinion in Spain," *American Journal of Political Science* 30, 2 (1986): 453. The other European countries are studied in S. H. Barnes, M. Kaase, et al., *Political Action*, Beverly Hills, Calif.: Sage, 1979.

24. Data from surveys by Demoscopia S. A. in October 1988 and the Centro de Investigaciones Sociológicas in November 1987 and May 1988.

25. A. de Tocqueville, *Democracy in America*, New York: Harper and Row, 1988, p. 198.

26. For example, J. Solé Tura, "The Spanish Transition to Democracy," in R. P. Clark and M. H. Haltzel (eds.), *Spain in the 1980's: The Democratic Transition and a New International Role*, Cambridge, Mass.: Ballinger, 1987, p. 29.

27. This is the analysis of, for example, T. C. Bruneau, "Continuity and Change in Portuguese Politics: Ten Years after the Revolution of 25 April 1974," *West European Politics* 7, 2 (1984): 77.

28. See T. C. Bruneau, "Popular Support for Democracy in Post-revolutionary Portugal," in Graham and Wheeler (n. 13), pp. 21–42; also T. C. Bruneau and M. Bacalhau, *Os Portugueses e a política quatro anos depois do 25 de abril*, Lisbon: Meseta, 1978.

29. Data from T. C. Bruneau and A. Macleod, *Politics in Contemporary Portugal*, Boulder, Colo.: Lynne Rienner, 1986, pp. 93–4, 155, 201.

30. Data from national surveys by the Centro de Investigaciones Sociológicas in September 1979 and in July–September 1980.

31. For example, by S. M. Lipset, "Some Social Requisites of Democracy: Economic Development and Political Legitimacy," *American Political Science Review* 53,

1 (1959): esp. pp. 86–91; also Linz, "Legitimacy of Democracy and the Socio-economic System," esp. pp. 81–5.

32. P. McDonough, S. H. Barnes, and A. López Pina, "The Growth of Democratic Legitimacy in Spain," *American Political Science Review* 80, 3 (1986): 751–2.

33. From a study by the Centro de Investigaciones Sociológicas, September 1987; also from J. R. Montero and M. Torcal, "La cultura política de los españoles," *Sistema* 99 (1990): 65, which examines the results of surveys of political culture carried out simultaneously in Spain, Portugal, Greece, and Italy in 1985. Data for Hungary are from J. Simon and L. Bruszt, *Magyar Nemzet*, 23 June 1989, and J. Simon, "La revolución silenciosa y la cultura política en la transición húngara," paper presented at the 12th World Congress of Sociology, Madrid, July 1990.

34. Interview in *Tiempo*, no. 327, 15–21 August 1988.

35. The reforms are described by G. de la Dehesa in "Los límites de la política económica española," *Leviatán* 32 (1988): 27–37.

36. $25 billion was spent for this purpose. This sum includes $11 billion on helping banks in crisis, $6 billion on the economic recovery of the Rumasa group, and $9.2 billion on industrial reconversion. The data were revealed by José Borrell, secretary of state for the Treasury, in *Diario 16*, 2 August 1988, and *La Vanguardia*, 4 August 1988.

37. Espina, *Empleo, democracia y relaciones industriales en España*, pp. 467–520.

38. *New York Times*, 3 April 1976.

39. Later on, at the 1979 Third Congress of the PS, a program was adopted ("Ten Years to Change Portugal") that accepted a mixed economy and defined socialism in terms not of state ownership but of egalitarian social and fiscal policies.

40. Data from EC Commission, *Economie Européenne* 46 (December 1990); the report of the governor of the Bank of Greece for 1985; and P. Corliras, "The Economics of Stagflation and Transformation in Greece," in Z. Tzannatos (n. 11), pp. 35–9.

41. Tocqueville, *Democracy in America*, p. 211.

42. E. Kalogeropoulou, "Election Promises and Government Performance in Greece: PASOK's Fulfilment of Its 1981 Election Pledges," *European Journal of Political Research* 17 (1989): 289–311.

43. For more details, see J. M. Maravall, "Valores democráticos y práctica política," *Leviatán* 37 (1989): 13–15.

44. See, for example, Y. Papadopoulos, "Parties, the State and Society in Greece: Continuity within Change," *West European Politics* 2, 12 (1989): 67.

45. The association between noneconomic issues, ideological identification, and party support in Spain in the 1980s is discussed by J. Díez Medrano, B. García-Mon, and J. Díez Nicolás, "El significado de ser de izquierdas en la España actual," *Revista Española de Investigaciones Sociológicas* 45 (1989): 9–41.

46. See J. M. Maravall, "What Is Left? Social Democratic Policies in Southern Europe," Working Paper 1992/36, Instituto Juan March de Estudios e Investigaciones, April 1992.

47. J. Borrell, *Balance general de la política presupuestaria durante el período 1981–1988*, Santander: Universidad Internacional Menéndez Pelayo, 1988; Ministerio

de Economía y Hacienda, *Informe sobre la reforma de la imposición personal sobre la renta y el patrimonio,* Madrid, 1990, pp. 37–42; Ministerio de Economía y Hacienda, *Memoria de la Administración Tributaria,* Madrid, 1990, pp. 443–524.

48. Ministerio de Economía y Hacienda, *Actuación económica y financiera de las administraciones públicas* (annual report), Madrid, 1990.

49. *Financial Times,* 5 February 1988.

50. S. N. Kalyvas, "Parties, State, Society: Greek Politics Today," unpublished manuscript, University of Chicago, March 1991.

51. In 1985 the unemployment rate reached 55.9 percent for the 16–19 age group and 44.6 percent for the 20–4 group.

52. The active female population was 3,852,600 in 1974 (the last year of Francoism), 3,908,600 in 1982 (when the Socialist Party won the elections), and 5,109,200 in 1989. The number of unemployed women went up from 608,000 in 1982 to 1,297,000 in 1987. As for the growing size of the cohorts, whereas the 16–25 age group was over 6.5 million, the 26–35 group was only 5.1 million. This demographic trend would last until 1993.

53. This number includes beneficiaries of either direct subsidies (1,350,250, representing 52.7 percent of all unemployed) or active labor policies, particularly vocational training (645,170; that is, 25.2 percent of the total number of jobless). From 1975 to 1989, benefits rose by 3,366 percent, or ten times the rate of inflation (Espina, *Empleo, democracia y relaciones industriales en España,* pp. 456, 457).

54. Espina, *Empleo, democracia y relaciones industriales,* p. 191. On the evolution of unemployment and economic policies in Spain, see also J. M. Dolado, J. L. Malo, and A. Zabalza, *Spanish Industrial Unemployment: Some Explanatory Factors,* Banco de España: Servicio de Estudios, EC/1985/16, 6 March; L. Fina and L. Toharia, *Las causas del paro en España: Un punto de vista estructural,* Madrid: Fundación IESA, 1987.

55. Banco Bilbao–Vizcaya, *Informe económico 1987,* Madrid, 1988, pp. 67–8; Espina, *Empleo, democracia y relaciones industriales,* p. 257; *Economie Européenne,* Supp. A, no. 5 (May 1991), p. 5, Table 9.

56. Estimates of the Ministerio de Economía y Hacienda for the 1992 budget. See *El País,* 1 October 1991, p. 64.

57. O. Fanjul, "¿Es necesaria la existencia de empresas industriales españolas?," unpublished manuscript, Madrid: INH, 1991.

58. The deficit fell to one-third of its 1982 level; foreign-currency reserves went up from $3 billion in 1982 to $45 billion in 1989.

59. Data on incomes are from the Instituto Nacional de Estadística, *Encuesta de presupuestos familiares,* Madrid, 1981; Banco de Bilbao, *Informe económico 1984,* Madrid, 1985, pp. 47, 122.

60. In the European Community, total tax revenues went up from 40.0 percent of GDP in 1974–82 to 43.5 percent in 1983–92. Between 1981 and 1990, current revenues from taxes increased by 1.6 percent of GDP. In the European OECD countries, the tax burden went up from 41.4 percent of GDP in 1979–80 to 44.6 percent in 1987–8.

61. Between 1981 and 1990, public expenditure grew in Greece (12.2 GDP points), Italy (10.8), Spain (5.9), Portugal (1.6), and France (1.5). It diminished as a proportion of GNP in the other seven countries of the EC – particularly in Ireland (− 9.0), Belgium (− 7.6), and the United Kingdom (− 5.4). See *Economie Européenne*, no. 46 (December 1990), p. 274, Table 55.

62. X. Calsamiglia, "Descentralización del gasto público y financiación autonómica: Una valoración del sistema español," Instituto de Análisis Económico, CSIC/ Universidad Autónoma de Barcelona, April 1989; J. M. Esteban Marquillas y R. Gómez García, "Análisis crítico del 'sistema definitivo' de la financiación de las comunidades autónomas," Instituto de Análisis Económico, CSIC/Universidad Autónoma de Barcelona, September 1989; Papeles de Economía Española, *La España desigual de las autonomías,* Madrid, 1991. In Andalusia, family disposable income went up from 77.4 percent of the national average in 1985 to 82.9 percent in 1989; in Extremadura, it rose from 67.2 to 76.3 percent. These regions were the poorest two.

63. Analyses of Spanish public expenditure must take into account the strong decentralization experienced in the 1980s and the formula for financing the autonomous communities that was established in 1986. The impact of decentralization was such that the share of total public expenditure managed by the autonomous communities went up from 2.9 percent in 1981 to 23.5 percent in 1991. Between 1987 and 1991, the budgets of the regional governments increased by 2.2 times (from $23.6 to $51.8 billion). Decentralization was particularly important in health and education: In 1991, 56.7 percent of the education budget and 55.7 percent of the health budget was managed by the regional administrations. Thus, when total public expenditure is examined, the budgets of the central government and of the seventeen autonomous communities must be totaled.

64. Social services consumed 9.85 percent of the budget from 1974 to 1981 and 13.0 percent from 1981 to 1989.

65. EC Commission, "Proyecciones a medio plazo de los gastos, en concepto de protección social y su financión," *Revista de Economía y Sociología del Trabajo* 3 (1989), pp. 149–50; also Maravall, "What Is Left? Social Democratic Policies in Southern Europe."

66. EC Commission, *Rapport annuel sur la mise en oeuvre de la réforme des fonds structurels,* doc. COM (90) 516 final, Brussels, October 1990.

67. For example, A. Przeworski, "Some Problems in the Study of the Transition to Democracy," in G.O'Donnell, P. C. Schmitter, and L. Whitehead (eds.), *Transitions from Authoritarian Rule: Comparative Perspectives,* Baltimore: Johns Hopkins University Press, 1986, pp. 61–3.

68. See, for example, A. M. Williams, "Socialist Economic Policies: Never Off the Drawing Board?" in T. Gallagher and A. M. Williams (eds.), *Southern European Socialism: Parties, Elections and the Challenge of Government,* Manchester: Manchester University Press, 1989, pp. 188–9; D. Share, *Dilemmas of Social Democracy: The Spanish Socialist Workers Party in the 80's,* Westport, Conn.: Greenwood, 1984, pp. 4, 74–7 passim; J. Petras, "The Rise and Decline of Southern European Socialism," *New Left Review* 146 (July–August 1984): 37–52.

69. Instituto Sindical de Estudios, *Evolución social en España: 1977–1987*, Madrid: Unión General de Trabajadores, 1988, pp. 38, 214.
70. Centro de Investigaciones Sociológicas, survey of 12–16 February 1988.
71. A. Flisfisch, *La política como compromiso democrático*, Madrid: Centro de Investigaciones Sociológicas, 1991, pp. 265–72.
72. The productive public sector in Spain consisted mainly of the Instituto Nacional de Industria, created in 1941, which was a central piece of economic autarky. It became involved in concerns that ranged from the large-scale manufacture of iron and steel to fishing industries in Africa.
73. See the discussion of the actual application of the mandate theory in British politics in R. Rose, *Do Parties Make a Difference?*, Chatham, N.J.: Chatham House, 1980, chs. 2, 4, 8.
74. N. Roubini and J. D. Sachs, *Political and Economic Determinants of Budget Deficits in Industrial Democracies*, NBER Working Paper 2682, Cambridge, Mass.: NBER, 1988. Japan, West Germany, France, and Britain did better than Belgium, Italy, Ireland, Sweden, or Denmark. See also N. Roubini and J. D. Sachs, "Government Spending and Budget Deficits in the Industrial Economies," *Economic Policy* 8 (1989): 99–127.
75. D. Austen-Smith and J. Banks, "Stable Governments and Allocation of Policy Portfolios," *American Political Science Review* 84, 3 (September 1990): 891–906.
76. J. T. S. Keeler, "Opening the Window for Reform: Mandates, Crises and Extraordinary Policy Making," paper presented at the 1990 Annual Meeting of the American Political Science Association, San Francisco, 30 August–2 September 1990, pp. 7–19.
77. J. M. Nelson (ed.), *Economic Crisis and Policy Choice: The Politics of Adjustment in the Third World*, Princeton, N.J.: Princeton University Press, 1990, pp. 328–9, 335, 341, 347.
78. As André Bergeron, then general secretary of the French union Force Ouvrière, used to say in complaining about the Mitterrand government, *"La concertation ne sert pas seulement à bavarder."*
79. Concertation led the government of Adolfo Suárez to include important provisions for the financing of trade unions in the public budget.
80. Hours lost to strikes were 3.5 million in 1981, 6.5 million in 1982, and 16.3 million in 1987. See M. Spourdalakis, "The Greek Experience," in R. Miliband, J. Saville, M. Liebman, and L. Panitch (eds.), *Socialist Register 1985–86: Social Democracy and After*, London: Merlin 1986, p. 252; Kalyvas, "Parties, State, Society," p. 26.
81. Declaration of Antón Saracíbar, secretary of organization of the UGT, in the PSOE Federal Committee meeting of 2 October 1987.
82. A European Community report of 1989 indicated that the rate of affiliation was 11 percent compared with an EC average of 42 percent. Only France had a similarly low rate; in Portugal and Greece affiliation was three times higher (EC Commission, *Estudio comparado de la normativa reguladora de las condiciones de trabajo en los estados miembros*, Brussels, 1989, pp. 3–7). An OECD report gave the figures 16 percent for Spain, 25 percent for Greece, and 30 percent for

Portugal compared with an OECD average of 28 percent (OECD, *Perspectivas del empleo*, Paris, 1991, pp. 218–25).

83. F. González, "El PSOE, un proyecto renovado en una nueva sociedad," epilogue to *Manifiesto del Programa 2000*, Madrid: Editorial Sistema, 1991, pp. 126–7, and "Reflexiones sobre el proyecto socialista," *Leviatán* 41 (1990): 9.

84. Instituto Sindical de Estudios, *Evolución social en España*, vol. 1, p. 9.

85. For example, between 1984 and 1988, 31 percent preferred the PSOE and 14 percent the AP for management of the economy; 33 percent preferred the PSOE for reducing inequalities, against 8 percent for the AP, according to surveys by the Centro de Investigaciones Sociológicas (CIS). Fifty-five percent expressed their confidence in the competence of the government, against 21 percent who did not. See, for example, CIS, studies 1416, 1712, 1740, and 1745, carried out between 1984 and 1988.

86. For example, in France the Giscard/Barre governments acted as if the economic crisis was just a cyclical problem and delayed any effective action. Real incomes and public expenditure kept growing at a fast rate.

87. Over the decade, the lowest estimate of intent to vote for the PSOE was 38.8 percent in May 1988, according to CIS data.

88. Interview in *Tiempo*, no. 327, 15–21 August 1988; see also P. Calvo Hernando, *Todos me dicen Felipe*, Barcelona: Plaza y Janés, 1987, pp. 237–8.

89. McDonough, Barnes, and López Pina, "The Growth of Democratic Legitimacy in Spain," p. 743.

90. Centro de Investigaciones Sociológicas, surveys in September 1986, September 1987, and May 1988.

3. Economic reforms, public opinion, and political institutions: Poland in the Eastern European perspective

ADAM PRZEWORSKI

> I hope there will be unemployment in Poland.
> A militant in Solidarity and deputy in the parliament.

Introduction

The purpose of this chapter is to use the experience of Poland, with some side glances at other postcommunist countries, in order to present evidence in favor of three propositions: (1) Market-oriented reforms are inevitably a protracted process – the period from stabilization, trade liberalization, and privatization to resumption of growth is long; (2) political support for market-oriented reforms erodes to the point of threatening their continuation unless these reforms are accompanied by a social policy; (3) the policy style typical of market-oriented reforms tends to debilitate nascent democratic institutions.

Poland launched its transition to a market economy on 1 January 1990, liberalizing most prices, introducing partial convertibility of the złoty, putting a ceiling on wage increases, reducing subsidies to industries and to consumers, reducing social spending, increasing interest rates, institutionalizing monetary restraint, restricting monopolies, liberalizing imports and exports, and announcing a program of privatization. Bulgaria adopted its first reforms on 22 November 1990 but postponed price increases and devaluation until 1 February 1991 under pressure from mass protests. Romania attempted to liberalize prices and introduce partial convertibility of the currency on 1 November 1990 but also postponed these measures, until 1 April 1991, because of public resistance. Czechoslovakia liberalized most prices on 1 January 1991, with

I should like to thank several Polish colleagues for sharing their analyses of the situation, and even unpublished data. In addition to my coauthors, I am most grateful to Camille Busette-Hsu, Ellen Comisso, Zhiyuan Chi, and Joanne Fox-Przeworski for comments on earlier versions of this text.

increased prices for energy and heating and rent increases to follow within six months. Finally, Hungary, where most prices and import restrictions had already been freed from state control under the communist regime, after a period of hesitation decided to begin with privatization and a social policy before freeing the remaining prices, reducing subsidies to industry, deregulating wages, and introducing convertibility. All these countries passed laws giving foreign investment a favorable status, liberalized imports and abolished export restrictions, undertook some antimonopoly measures, and launched broader or narrower programs of restitution and privatization.

As this text is being written, output and demand are falling everywhere, and unemployment is increasing steadily. Real incomes are declining. Since these are precisely the effects reforms were expected to engender, evaluations of this performance bounce between extremes. For some, these changes indicate that reforms have no effect other than to lower the standard of living and generate unemployment. For others, they show that reforms are transforming economic structures in the desired direction. For still others, these effects are not yet sufficient: Reforms are too slow. Forecasts by innumerable research institutes, multilateral agencies, banks, and consulting firms also oscillate between dire warnings and rosy assurances.[1]

Since I am no wiser, I intend to keep away from this fracas.[2] I shall argue that the Polish reforms were designed with insufficient attention to political factors and that the price of this neglect is erosion of support for reforms and fragility of the nascent democratic institutions. Hence, my argument is directed against leaving economic reforms in the hands of economists – at least those economists who believe that the success of reforms depends only on the soundness of the economic plan, claim that if reforms fail it is only because of the irresponsibility of the people, and see the choice facing Eastern Europe and Latin American societies as "us or populism." The Polish experience belies the approach epitomized by the message of the main foreign architect of the Polish reform package, Jeffrey Sachs: "Once, and from the moment when economic reforms introduced are good (and I believe they are), there is theoretically no reason why they [countries] would not succeed in their transition." And "There is real danger of populism or demagogy, which can only impede the reforms" (interview in *Le Figaro,* 5 December 1990).

Economic reforms are inevitably painful. They are unlikely to be free of mistakes. And they must take time; in spite of all the urging,[3] they can never be quick enough to prevent the emergence of divergent opinions, organized opposition, and political conflict. It is impossible to build democracy by trying to beat the democratic process to the punch, to escape its verdict.[4] Economic blueprints that treat politics as nothing but an extraneous nuisance are just bad economics. This, I believe, is the central lesson of the Polish experience.

The first part of this chapter is devoted to the choice of reform strategies. I try to explain why the Polish reforms were oriented toward stabilization, liberalization, and privatization rather than toward a sectorally oriented development strategy and why they embraced shock treatment rather than a gradual posture. The second part summarizes the economic performance in the aftermath of reforms and argues that reforms must be in place for a long time before their positive effects are felt. The third part analyzes the dynamics of popular support for reforms. The fourth part is devoted to the impact of reforms on democratic institutions. The conclusion attempts to identify those aspects of the reform process that are crucial in shaping political dynamics.

Background: The choice of strategies

What made reforms necessary?

Poland attempted to modernize its economic structure after Edward Gierek became first secretary of the Polish United Workers' (PUWP, Communist) Party in the aftermath of the bloody repression of 1970. The development strategy paralleled that of South Korea: Borrow money in the West to develop production for Western markets, and use repression to keep wages down while capitalizing the profits by building basic industries. While the inflow of borrowed money and relaxation of controls over agriculture led to a marked improvement in the standard of living until 1978, the strategy collapsed in the aftermath of the recession in the West. The outcome by 1979 was that Poland acquired a $26-billion (American billion) debt (40% of GDP), developed some industries that were dependent on foreign technologies without securing foreign markets, initiated several gigantic investment projects (investment grew at 11% per annum during the 1970s), acquired a chronic current-account deficit, and did not modernize its industrial structure.

The crisis that hit in 1979 was deep and broad. National income fell for the first time in the postwar history of the country. Investment took the brunt of the collapse; wages and consumption continued to grow until 1982. Several indicators of the accumulated state of the infrastructure and of welfare services also stagnated or declined in 1979.[5] There developed an open political crisis (too well known to be recounted), which was temporarily terminated by the military coup d'état of 13 December 1981. After 1979 the immediacy of the

Table 3.1. *Poland: Some basic economic indicators, 1970–88*

	1970	1978	1979	1982	1988
National income	100	184.1	179.9	140.6	182.4
from industry (%)	44.0	49.5	49.8	49.2	49.1
Consumption	100	179.0	184.5	159.0	200.8
Investment	100	215.3	174.0	82.8	115.9
Investment/GDP (%)	27.1	30.6	25.7	21.6	19.7
National income/capita	100	171.1	166.0	126.3	156.8
Average wage, state sector	100	148.0	151.1	120.7	144.5
Imports	100	229.1	226.4	159.3	235.5
Exports	100	198.2	211.7	178.6	262.1
Balance with non-CMEA[a]	11.5	−34.0	−26.6	27.7	13.2
Budget balance/revenue	3.3	10.2	4.0	−3.5	0.8
Consumer prices	100	130.7	140.4	377.5	1,400
Gross mortality rate	8.1	9.3	9.2	9.2	9.8
Vacationers[b]	66.5	127.9	124.4	85.1	101.3
Hospital beds[c]	51.8	56.2	56.3	56.3	57.2
Visits to doctors	6.2	7.9	7.8	7.5	7.6
Users of public libraries	203	210	211	197	208
Housing built (m²)[b]	324.4	503.6	503.1	342.6	371.4
Railroads (km²)	7.1	6.8	6.9	6.7	6.4
Roads (km²)	39.9	41.6	41.5	41.3	41.9

[a]As a proportion of exports.
[b]Per 1,000.
[c]Per 10,000. CMEA, Council of Mutual Economic Assistance.
Source: Rocznik statystyczny 1989.

economic crisis – a combination of foreign debt, a public deficit, wage pressure, and overextended investments – was too great to entertain programs of industrial modernization. Thinking in terms of stabilization came to dominate the political agenda.

The government that took power in 1982 was keenly aware that broadgauge reforms of the economic system were necessary, and it was willing to engage in such reforms as part of its political strategy. The new government thought that reforms were necessary to restore the mechanism of legitimation by consumption characteristic of the Gierek period.[6] Repression would be needed – their thinking went on – until the economy began functioning well again, at which time political contestation would subside. Hence, on 1 January 1982 the government introduced the reform program that had been elaborated by the opposition in 1981. To stabilize the economy, real wages and per capita consumption were reduced by 15 to 20 percent, while employment and output fell by 3 to 5 percent. At the same time, the central planning system was abandoned and replaced by government purchases, the autonomy of enterprises was enhanced, the scope of administrative price setting was reduced, and the tax system was revamped (and complicated) (Balcerowicz 1989). Yet while investment and growth resumed, real wages and consumption remained below their 1978 levels. By 1985 it had become apparent that these reforms were not working. Resource allocation remained highly centralized, enterprise autonomy remained fictitious, the extent of price regulation in fact increased, foreign debt continued to increase through successive capitalizations of arrears, and trade with the West grew much more slowly than world trade. Moreover, the consumer market remained in deep disequilibrium, and distribution was a combination of rationing, queues, and barter with the price mechanism.

By 1987 a "consensus of termination," to use a term of O'Donnell's, had developed among elites. Both the government and the – still illegal but increasingly public – opposition arrived at the conclusion that much more profound transformations, including those of property, were inevitable if the economy was ever to recover. But a political stalemate developed. The regime wanted to use the widespread support for reform to gain legitimacy for its continuation in power; the opposition wanted reforms but also power. The government organized a referendum on economic and political reforms in November 1987 and failed to muster the support of a majority of potential voters. It then turned around and passed an even more radical package of reforms.[7] The goals of the new package were the same as of the 1981 program: to equilibrate the market and increase efficiency.[8] To reach market balance, prices of consumer products were sharply increased by administrative fiat. A commercial banking system was established. Enterprise autonomy was enhanced again. Most important, for the first time barriers to entry were reduced: All forms of property were given equal legal status, registration of new firms was simplified, and some limited access was opened for foreign capital. Hence, the first steps toward a mixed economy were made under a communist government. Indeed, the first beneficiaries of the new law were the apparatchiks, many of whom, to use Tarkowski's (1989) wonderful phrase, turned into entrepreneurtchiks.[9]

The stabilization part of the package turned out to be a typical technocratic nightmare: Workers responded to price increases with strikes, the government did not have any legitimacy to resist workers' demands, and the result was that the money overhang doubled in the aftermath of the Sadowski reform.

None of the other measures adopted after 1982 had had an effect by 1988: Government orders effectively replaced allocation by the planner, the share of regulated prices in total sales in fact increased from 1982 to 1987, the share of cooperatives in total employment declined slightly from 1980 to 1987, subsidies remained a constant factor in the state budget, only 71.8 percent of exports to dollar markets (72.2 percent of ruble markets) were profitable by 1987, and the inflow of foreign capital was minimal.[10]

The last communist government, headed by Mieczyslaw Rakowski, did succeed in briefly raising expectations in the fall of 1988, but this hope was short-lived. It was clear to everyone that reform programs undertaken by communist governments failed. In January 1989 the regime decided to hold talks with the opposition, and after tense negotiations an agreement was signed on 5 April. Yet since the legitimacy of this agreement was quickly undermined by the defeat of communists in the elections of June 1989, the political situation remained unclear and tense. By the summer, as negotiations about the composition of the future government were proceeding by twists and turns, the endemic economic crisis, combined with increasing wage pressure, caused an eruption of hyperinflation. In July nominal wages increased by 101.8 percent, and by October the monthly inflation rate had reached 54.8 percent. The first postcommunist government inherited hyperinflation.

This was, then, the situation in Poland as the first democratic government took office. The net material product was falling, the annual inflation rate was running at triple digit levels, and the budget deficit had increased to more than 8 percent of GNP (Lipton and Sachs 1990: 117), while international reserves remained low and no new money was available. The economy was noncompetitive. The state was bankrupt; it ran a deficit and could neither raise money from local economic activities nor borrow from abroad. Social services and income protection were decaying.

While each Eastern European country has its peculiarities, their economies and social conditions were not very different from Poland's on the eve of the transition to democracy. This is not the place to describe the structure of command economies: I will cite only some indicators. During the 1980s growth slowed down everywhere in comparison to the earlier decades. The net material product fell in 1989 in Hungary, Romania, and Yugoslavia and in 1990 in all Eastern European countries, including the Soviet Union.[11] Productivity was low and declining. The proportion of the labor force in agriculture remained high, and yields remained low by Western standards. Except in Hungary and Yugoslavia, most prices were controlled. Production and prices were subsidized out of the state budget; subsidies amounted to about one-third of state expenditures, or about 15 percent of gross national product. The structure of prices was quite different from the structure in market economies: Rent, energy, heating, food staples, and personal services were relatively cheap; textiles, imported food, and consumer durables, expensive.[12] The consumer market suffered from a profound disequilibrium. The degree of monopoly was exceedingly high in both production and distribution. Several countries experienced an acute housing shortage. Health indicators remained well below Western standards and were stagnating or decaying; educational systems were probably on a par. Income distribution was at least as egalitarian as in the most egalitarian Western countries: Belgium or Japan.

Responding to the visible slowdown of their economies, all Eastern European countries attempted to reform. The directions of reforms differed. One model, initiated by East Germany and later followed in the Soviet Union, Bulgaria, Czechoslovakia, and Romania, was to introduce some financial autonomy for state enterprises and to make them financially responsible by using a "profit" criterion, to remove some prices from state control, and to reduce the role of central planning in the physical allocation of resources. These reforms failed for two reasons: (1) Without a price mechanism, the profit criterion could not rationally allocate resources, and (2) the chaos introduced by this system led to spontaneous pressure to recentralize (Asselain 1985). The other model, adopted in Hungary and Yugoslavia, was to liberalize consumer prices, impose financial discipline on state firms, and allow some private activities. This strategy was in turn vulnerable to pressures from state enterprises, which used their monopoly position to drive up prices and exact subsidies from the state. Regardless of which reform strategy was pursued, the planning system was as a result weakened in all countries, albeit to differing degrees. And when political turmoil erupted, central allocation of physical resources disintegrated. The difference in the legacy left by these reforms was that Hungary and Yugoslavia emerged from communist rule with a consumer market, and the others did not.

Other differences concerned inflation, state budgets, and foreign debt. Poland had already experienced inflationary pressure in 1988, and this pressure erupted in hyperinflation just as the first democratic government was being formed. Yugoslavia was the other country that experienced hyperinflation. In Hungary prices increased by 16.5 percent in 1988, but the rate of inflation remained stable. All other countries suffered from some hidden inflation, so the data are not very reliable, but even the Soviet Union probably remained at a single-digit rate through 1989.[13] The state budget was under pressure in

Table 3.2. *Eastern Europe: Background (1989) and recent economic data*

	BUL	CS	HUN	POL	ROM	YUG	USSR
Background data for 1989							
GNP/CAP 1980 USD			2,210	1,520		3,220	1,780
GNP/CAP (EEC = 100)	45	65	55	30	20	45	35
LABOR FORCE AGRICULTURE		11.9	20.9	27.8			18.8
INVESTMENT/GNP			25.1	32.5		21.0	11.0
CURR ACCT BALANCE/GNP			−1.4	−0.2		4.8	−1.2
DEBT/CAP (CURRENT USD)			1,656	1,113		921	190
DEBT SERVICE/EXP	74.4	18.6	54.5	90.6		29.1	24
GOV EXPENDITURES/GDP	61.9	76.6	59.0	48.1			51.4
TELEPHONES PER 1,000 POP	200	226	134	118	130		
INFANT MORTALITY			17.0	17.5		25.4	25.1
LIFE EXPECTANCY AT 0		72	70.2	71.4		71.3	70
SCNDRY SCHOOL ENRLMNT			70	80		80	
SCIENTISTS (NORTH = 100)		93	179	120		137	91
DAILY CAL/ REG 84–86		141	1315	126		127	133
MILITARY/ TEACHERS		197	112	131		123	147
FEMALES/LABOR FORCE			44.7	45.5		38.7	
LARGEST ETHNIC/ POP C. 80		81	99	99		36	52
FAMILY FARMS/AGR AREA		5	2	76		75	0
Reform data							
Rate of change of NMP							
1981–5	3.7	1.8	1.3	−0.8	4.5	0.6	3.2
1988	2.4	2.3	−0.5	4.9	−0.9	−1.8	4.4
1989	−0.4	1.0	−1.1	−0.2	−2.0	0.8	2.4
1990	−11.0	−3.1	−2/−5	−13.0	−15.0	−7/−10	−4.0
Rate of change in industrial output							
1990	−14.1	−3.7	−4.5	−23.3	−19.8	−10.3	−1.2
1991 I	−26	−13	−13	−4	−17	−19	

Table 3.2 (*cont.*)

	BUL	CS	HUN	POL	ROM	YUG	USSR
Percent prices liberalized (volume)							
1989				26			
1990	14		90	90		75	
1991	72						
Inflation							
1988			16.5	66	0.5		0.6
1989	10	3	17	640		2,500	2
1990	60		35	250	18	120	5/12
1991 II		49.2		40	164		24
Unemployment							
1990			2				
1991 II	6	3.8	3.9	8.5	134	20	
*Government budget balance/*GNP *or* NMP							
1989	−1.4		−3.6	−8			−9.5
1990	−13.0		−0.0				−8.3
Joint ventures							
1990							
No. of ventures	140	16,00	5,000	2,480	1,502		3,000
Foreign equity							
(million USD)	74	850	1,200	396	129		4,615
1991 I							
No. of ventures			7,000				
Foreign equity							
(million USD)			1,600				

Sources: The background data are derived from publications of international data-collecting organizations, except for ethnic heterogeneity and family farms, which comes from Vatanen 1990. Other data should be treated with reserve, since they are pieced together from current reports by research institutes, consulting firms, and newspapers. Whenever comparative tables were available, I used those rather than local sources. The convention adopted in the table is that decimals are used if the original data are precise; whenever the reference is to "about," or other reservations are expressed, I did not use decimals.

the Soviet Union – where the deficit reached 11 percent of GNP in 1988 and 9.5 percent in 1989 – in Hungary, and in Poland. Foreign debt in Hungary was the highest in the world on a per capita basis and was very high in Poland. It was moderate elsewhere, and Romania became a net creditor in 1989. Hence, while all the Eastern European countries, including the Soviet Union, shared structural problems, only Poland and Yugoslavia, and to a lesser degree Hungary, experienced the combination of inflation, budget deficit, and foreign-account deficit that added up to a "fiscal crisis" and called for immediate stabilization.

Goals of reforms

At the most general level, there was an almost universal consensus in Poland about the goals of reforms. In his inaugural speech to the Sejm, Tadeusz Mazowiecki, the first postcommunist prime minister, announced, "The government will undertake steps initiating the transition to a modern market economy, tested by the experience of developed countries" (Domarańczyk 1990: 148). Speaking to the annual meeting of the International Monetary Fund and the World Bank in September 1989, Leszek Balcerowicz, the minister of finance and main architect of the Polish reform program, announced the government's intention "to transform the Polish economy into a market economy, with the ownership structure changing in the direction of that found in the advanced industrial economies" (*Financial Times,* 16 July 1990). According to Marcin Święcicki, the minister of economic cooperation, "in reforming our economy, we do not seek experiments. We do not want our economists to invent new systems but to adopt solutions that work elsewhere. We simply want to construct a market economy like the West's" (*Libération,* 14 February 1990, p. 32). As Sadowski, Iwanek, and Najdek (1990: 1) observed, "it is the declared objective of the present government of Poland to build a market economy modelled after the Western developed market economies." This is a canonical formulation.[14]

This formulation was based on a deeply held belief best revealed by the oft-used phrase that Poland must build a normal economic system. As Balcerowicz put it, the long-term goal of reforms is "to turn an economy of shortages into a normal economy" (*Financial Times,* 16 July 1990). The underlying conviction was what I have elsewhere termed the "Eastern European syllogism" (Przeworski 1991). The major premise of this syllogism is "If it were not for communism, we would have been like the West," and the minor premise is "Now communism is gone." The conclusion not only asserts that Eastern Europe should and will now embrace a Western-style economy but also promises that this economy will generate the glitter and glamour of developed capitalism.

Yet this reference to normalcy hides differences of views concerning specific models and directions. For one, there is an ambivalence about whether the process of reforms constitutes restoration of the prewar system or a revolution in some new direction. The term "capitalism" did not appear in the initial statements of the economic strategy (Rychard 1991a: 34). Indeed, Balcerowicz emphasized that "privatization does not mean the entering to Poland of the savage capitalism in its 19th century version" (Rychard 1991b: 21). The reform program was couched in terms of "approaching the West," "a rational economic system," "a market economy," and sometimes "a social market economy." And since "normal" economies differ significantly both in the degree of state interventionism in the markets and of provision for social welfare, this reference hides disagreements about the specific model of capitalism that is to be adopted. For a second difference, Poland is a country with strong anticapitalist traditions, originating both in the noncommunist left and in traditional Catholicism.[15] Hence, while it was obvious to everyone that Poland had to move in the direction of the "normal" and the "rational," the consensus ended here.[16]

The long-term objectives of reforms were formulated mainly in the language of efficiency, rationality, or normalcy. Creating a framework for competition was not only to make resource allocation efficient but also to change, without any industrial policy, the patterns of sectoral allocation. Privatization would make the owners maximize profits and workers work hard, hence completing the transformation to a rational economy. Efficiency appears in these statements as the ultimate goal; there are no explicit references to resuming growth.

I could find no references to building a welfare state or extending social protection in any formulation of the reform program. Sadowski et al. (1990: 1) state the goal of reforms as establishing "the fundamentals of a working market economy while dealing simultaneously with the current economic and social problems of the country," but this is where references to social problems stop. Indeed, the program promises to base income insurance and delivery of social services on market criteria.[17] In fact, responsibility for social problems was defined as a separate task from the reform process itself and relegated to the inventiveness of the minister of labor and social security, Jacek Kuroń, and the charity of individual citizens. Hence, this was a pure trickle-down model of reforms.

In turn, the government and the media were forthright about the transitional costs of reforms. All politicians, beginning with Mazowiecki and Balcerowicz, warned that the program would generate temporary inflation, unemployment, and a decline in living standards. Mazowiecki emphasized in his inaugural speech that "there is no example in the economic history of the world of inflation being squelched without serious social difficulties, including bankruptcy of some enterprises and the unemployment associated with it."

The government offered specific predictions. It expected the inflation rate to be 45 percent in January, 15 percent in February, and 5 percent in March and then to stay around 1 percent per month. Forecasts of unemployment varied widely, from 400,000 to 5 million out of a labor force of about 16 million. Output would fall by 20 percent during 1990.

Thus, the overall goal of reform was to move as quickly as possible to a market economy patterned on developed capitalism. This goal was formulated in the language of efficiency rather than explicitly of growth, and without any program of social policy.

The reform program

The reform program of the first postcommunist government was made public in September 1989 and implemented as of 1 January 1990. Its proximate goals were formulated explicitly. Stabilization was the first task; it was to be accompanied by structural adjustment and followed by privatization. The inflationary spiral must be arrested, the consumer market must be equilibrated, and the current-account balance must be improved and the government deficit eliminated; these were the most urgent goals of reform. These measures must be undertaken simultaneously with rationalizing the economy by creating competition and liberalizing trade. Finally, privatization should complete the reform process.

In his inaugural speech of 12 September Premier Mazowiecki emphasized that the fight against inflation was the first task of the government and listed as a priority the reduction of the government deficit. He announced that the government would not tolerate tax delinquency by state enterprises ("Credits should be given by banks, not the budget"), that it would reduce subsidies and investment credits, increase interest rates, and tax excessive wage increases punitively. Antimonopoly measures would be directed in particular against food-distribution enterprises. Most specialized credit funds would be abolished, and a banking system would be developed. Price controls would be eliminated, and the currency would be made convertible. The government would undertake measures to organize labor markets, including initiating manpower programs, and would introduce protection for the unemployed. In the realm of social policy, the government would "use such methods of adjusting pensions and other income supports as would prevent the deterioration of living standards of the poorest social groups and an increase of the distance between them and those gainfully employed." (The speech is reproduced in Domarańczyk 1990: 141–53.)

Balcerowicz presented the broad outlines of his program twenty-five days later. He distinguished two directions for government activity: counteracting the deterioration of the economic situation and preparing legal and organizational conditions for transforming the economy. He also made a distinction between measures leading to squelching inflation and those oriented toward structural transformation of the economy.

According to the communiqué of the Council of Ministers published on the eve of the parliamentary debate, the reform program was to include:

1. transformation of property designed to turn efficiency into a permanent feature of the economy and to propel the necessary changes in the sectoral structure;
2. introduction of market mechanisms and institutions and demonopolization;
3. reform of the financial and banking system; introduction of currency convertibility, allowing the opening of the economy to the world; stabilization measures oriented to fight inflation; restoring economic equilibrium by reducing demand and the money supply; and
4. measures designed to assuage difficulties accompanying the process of fighting inflation, oriented particularly to defend a social minimum for the weakest economic groups.

The stabilization program – a term that appeared in the public domain only at the beginning of December – was to rest, according to Vice-Minister Dąbrowski, on five pillars: a balanced budget, a tough fiscal and monetary policy, the convertibility of the currency, and a tough policy against wage pressure (Domaranczyk 1990: 323).

In the end, the reform package passed by the Sejm at the end of December 1989, the "Balcerowicz Plan," comprised (based on *Tygodnik Solidarność*, 5 January 1990):

1. changes in the Law on the Finances of State Enterprises, designed to cause bankruptcy of plants that were energy- or investment-intensive;
2. Law on Taxation of Wage Increases, designed to punish wage pressure in excess of guidelines;
3. Bank Law, which liberated banks from any externally imposed priorities and allowed foreign banks to operate;
4. Credit Law, which gave equal status to all forms of property, eliminated subsidies, abolished all interest-rate preferences except for housing, some agricultural investments, and handicapped persons;

5. Employment and Unemployment Law, which reduced protection from layoffs, established an employment service, and regulated unemployment compensation;

6. Law on Foreign Exchange, which allowed free sale and purchase of currencies by physical persons and required legal persons to sell their foreign currencies to the state and permitted them to buy them to import;

7. Law on Economic Activity of Foreign Subjects, which extended to six years the tax haven for foreign direct investment and exempted foreign firms from the Law on Taxation of Wage Increases;

8. Customs Law, which abolished export tariffs, introduced a uniform (with some exceptions) import tariff, and abolished quantitative restrictions; and

9. Tax Law changes, which concerned eleven laws, with the purpose of increasing state revenues.[18]

In addition, the package comprised a number of other laws, decrees, and administrative decisions, passed earlier or within the next few months, which

10. reduced the indexation of wages;

11. deregulated almost all prices and increased the prices of utilities;

12. reduced subsidies from 31 to 14 percent of state expenditures (about 8 percent of GDP) during the first year;

13. increased interest, to reach a positive real rate;

14. devalued and introduced partial convertibility of the Polish currency;

15. instituted a ban on the Central Bank's financing the government deficit;

16. institutionalized monetary restraint; and

17. promised that the government would close down firms that had not fulfilled their fiscal obligations to the state by 1 July 1990.

Hence, the features of the Polish reform strategy were twofold. On the one hand, the package contained an orthodox element of stopping inflation by inducing a recession and depressing wages. On the other hand, it was introduced as a part of a broad set of measures designed to change the structure of the economy. Altogether these measures amounted to the most radical program of promarket transformations attempted anywhere.

Most of the elements in the Polish package were eventually introduced in Bulgaria, Romania, and Czechoslovakia.

On 22 November 1990 the Bulgarian government attempted to liberalize most prices, except for those of thirteen staples, energy, and transport, and to introduce partial convertibility of the currency, but under the pressure of strikes it was forced to postpone price liberalization until February 1991. The leva was devalued but remained nonconvertible. The original reform package also contained a reduction in subsidies, antimonopoly steps, tax reform, and liberalization of exports and imports. A tripartite agreement among the government, trade unions, and employers reached in January 1991 pegged the minimum wage to the cost of living. The intention to privatize was announced, but no timetable was set (*IMF Survey*, 18 March 1991).

The Romanian story is almost identical: Most prices, including rents but not staples, energy, or heating, were to be liberalized on 1 November 1990, and the currency was to be devalued, but these reforms had to be postponed until April 1991 under pressure from mass demonstrations. First steps toward convertibility of the lei were made. The original package also included antimonopoly measures, reduction of subsidies to industry, liberalization of trade, and legalization of foreign investment. Plans to privatize 50 percent of the capital stock were announced.

Yugoslavia, which faced hyperinflation in 1989, liberalized 75 percent of prices in January 1990 and adopted a series of measures that comprised a rigorous fiscal and monetary policy, partial convertibility of the already devalued dinar, liberation of 87 percent of imports from restrictions, and a low uniform tariff. Privatization was postponed until the fall but not pursued because of conflicts among the republics.

Czechoslovakia introduced a similar package on 1 January 1991. It devalued the koruna, liberalized prices in sectors believed to be competitive, including staples, fixed a schedule for freeing rents and the prices of energy and heat, reduced price subsidies and subsidies to industry, and liberalized imports while preserving restrictions on the export of goods in short supply. It passed restitution and privatization legislation soon afterward. A tripartite agreement specified that real wages were not to fall more than 15 percent.

Other than to provide for some protection of wages, no social measures were included in any of these reform packages. When asked about the danger of unemployment, government officials from several countries invariably responded, "We will pay compensation."

Hungary did not follow the same course. After a long period of hesitation and debate, the first program of reforms emerged after Mihaly Kupa became the finance minister in December 1990. According to this program, the transition to a market economy and to Europe was to proceed gradually. A strict monetary policy was to be assured by the creation of a central bank. Wage regulation was to be maintained. These two measures were necessary to control inflationary pressures. Yet some subsidies to prices and to industry were to be maintained to prevent massive bankruptcies. The program defined 1991 as the year of privatization and the definition of property rights, 1992 as the year when inflation would be lowered and the convertibility of the forint would be prepared for, 1993 as the year when growth would resume, and 1994 as the year of preparation to enter the European Community. A restructuring of social policy, including social security, education, and health, seen in a perspective of three years, was to precede the full introduction of market mechanisms.[19]

Why was the particular strategy chosen?

The alternatives that entered the public domain in Poland comprised (1) tinkering with the current system by using stronger administrative measures to enforce the earlier reforms;[20] (2) a gradual transition to a market economy that would begin with the producer goods sector, wait for the effects, and only then move to equilibrate the consumer goods market,[21] and (3) a radical "jump to the market," the strategy chosen in the end. Thinking in sectoral terms, particularly of energy and agriculture, guided some discussants, but no program of industrial reconversion, or even of limited industrial policies, appeared.[22] Antistatism was so intense that no strategies based on the Far Eastern model were proposed.[23]

The status quo – a restructuring of the socialist system – was not a viable option by 1989; the general public, politicians, and technicians agreed on this point. The opening statement of the Economic Program asserted that "the causes of the striking economic indolence of the economy rest deeply embedded in the previous economic system. Without their fundamental change we will continue to be stuck in an atmosphere of general indolence and a situation of permanent crisis. No partial measures can change this situation." A thick line had to be drawn between the past and the future. The society was prepared to draw this line. In a national sample of youth, 59.3 percent thought in 1986 that "it is worth continuing socialism in our country"; 58.0 percent still thought so in 1987, but only 43.3 percent in 1988 and 28.8 percent in 1989 (Mokrzycki 1990: 12). Acceptance of the idea limiting the highest incomes declined from 89.7 percent in 1980 to 53.0 percent in 1989; support for full-employment policies fell from 77.8 percent in 1980 to 49.3 in 1989; support for laying off inefficient workers was almost unanimous (90.5 percent) as early as 1980; support for making incomes depend on qualifications rose from 53.9 percent in 1980 to 79.0 percent in 1989 (Kolarska-Bobińska 1991).[24] Support for closing unprofitable firms, for laying off unnecessary employees, for limiting subsidies to unprofitable firms, for allowing prices to form freely, and for limiting state subsidies to some products and services increased secularly from 1987 to 1989.[25] By 1989, support for private property and a market economy and tolerance of their deleterious effects were widespread by comparative standards: Poles were less egalitarian than Brazilians in 1989, and Polish workers were about as egalitarian as Spanish workers in 1977.[26]

As Rychard (1991b) emphasizes, disgust with the status quo need not translate into enthusiasm for reforms. One reason is that the term itself has been worn out by the whole history of the People's Republic. Reforms were an endemic phenomenon in all socialist economies, for reasons spelled out by Staniszkis (1984) and others: Since the economy itself did not contain feedback mechanisms, political mechanisms had to be utilized every time disequilibria occurred. Reforms have been innumerable: of the planning system, of functional administration, of territorial administration, of incentive systems, of what not. Moreover, the failure of Poland's reform programs of 1982 and 1987 bred widespread skepticism about the success of any reforms. The "second stage" of reforms, the 1987 package, was at best treated as the butt of innumerable jokes. Yet in spite of this reform fatigue, even the communist government's last reform package did evoke a jump in confidence in the government – from 33.6 percent for the old government in August 1988 to 72.4 percent for the new government in November of that year. So Poles were already showing a combination of desperation and hope.

Reform, Rychard (1991b) argues, was always a project originating and propelled from above. And there was above a consensus that a profound structural transformation of the economy was necessary. Nevertheless, given widespread fear that the "jump to the market" would make the crisis even more profound and raise the already high social tensions, and given that a more gradual approach was chosen during the Magdalenka negotiations, the reason for choice of the radical strategy is not apparent. I do not know the inside story of the events that led to the decision to embark on the "bitter pill" strategy, but some aspects of this decision are visible from the outside:

1. Several elements of the crisis were perceived by the new elite as threatening in the immediate future. The concern that dominated most official statements was that the state was insolvent. The state deficit was the first target of reform mentioned by Mazowiecki in his inaugural speech. Balcerowicz began his first declaration of the program by announcing that "we must rapidly rescue the financial situation of the state in order to salvage the economy" (cited in Domarańczyk 1990: 173). The specter of bankruptcy was used by the government to push its program through the Sejm in December.

2. A radical reform program was urged on Poland by foreign creditors,

while foreign economists reassured Polish politicians that this program would be effective. Both factors played a role: Poland had to pass several pieces of legislation by 1 January 1990 to get stabilization funds from the IMF and debt relief and any other help from abroad. The case of Poland was obviously important, since it merited a personal lobbying visit from Michael Camdessus of the IMF, who arrived just as the legislation was being discussed by the Sejm. "What you are planning to do is the best program for your country," Camdessus assured the legislators. "If I were not certain of that, I would not be here" (cited in Domarańczyk 1990: 341). Foreign economists were important not so much because there was a shortage of local ones but to assure politicians and the population that the reform package was supported by experts.

3. One theme constantly hammered at by politicians and technicians alike was that Poland had no choice but to proceed at the greatest possible speed. The greatest danger facing the country was to procrastinate. Few people, including politicians, understood the technicalities involved, but a general consensus developed that the faster, the better; whatever could be done immediately should be. The title of Balcerowicz's interview in which he detailed the reform program was "Quickly or Not At All" (Albo szybko, albo wcale, *Polityka,* December 1989). "Swallowing the bitter pill," "horse therapy," "drawing a thick line" were portrayed as necessary to finish once and for all with the irrationality of the command system. The general principle was that unless it tasted bad, it could not be good for you; the impending hardships were presented as proof that something was finally being done. And while the Balcerowicz package was criticized in detail, no coherent alternative emerged.[27] Ultimately, I suspect, the radical strategy won because it was the only coherent plan around. A title in the Solidarity weekly during the parliamentary debate on the reform program was "Balcerowicz's Program Has Only One Virtue: No Sensible Alternatives" (*Tygodnik Solidarność,* 22 December 1989).

To summarize, the radical reform strategy was adopted in Poland because of the urgent pressure of fiscal deficit and hyperinflation. It was based on a widespread consensus among elites that a profound transformation of the economic system was inevitable. While particulars were criticized, no coherent alternatives emerged. The fact that radical reform was perceived as a high-risk venture did not temper the zeal of its architects and did not tempt the government to hide its social costs. And a radical program was credible precisely because it was sufficiently different from everything attempted thus far.

None of the three factors cited implicitly in the analysis of the Polish choice explain why all other Eastern European countries but Hungary adopted a similar strategy. The combination of inflation and fiscal crisis was not an overriding consideration in Czechoslovakia and Romania. And whereas the Polish government was politically very strong when it assumed office, the Bulgarian and Romanian governments were not competitively elected and did not enjoy the same legitimacy. Indeed, they were so weak that both were forced to postpone the introduction of reforms in the face of mass opposition. Pressure from foreign creditors also fails to explain the choice: Hungary had a debt higher than Poland's, while Czechoslovakia and Romania had almost none.

One factor that does play a role is that Hungary was the only country where a consumer market already operated: 90 percent of prices and 90 percent of imports were free from state control by June 1991 (interview with Bela Kadar, minister of foreign economic affairs, *La Tribune de l'Expansion*, 7 June 1991). But another factor that played a role was that Hungarian elites were divided about the strategy to follow. These differences did not seem to follow clear partisan lines; they cut within the parties and found repeated expression within the government itself. Proponents of the Polish strategy, who included the president of the Central Bank, Gyorgy Suranyi, and the first finance minister, Ferenc Rabar, argued, "A Radical Shock Therapy Is Inevitable" (*Financial Times*, 17 September 1990). Yet others within the government were concerned about the political, including purely electoral, consequences of this strategy. Unable to pursue a radical strategy, Rabar resigned at the end of November. The budget for 1991 proposed at the beginning of December was described as a "messy compromise," mainly with regard to subsidies, and a proponent of the radical solution complained that "the government is not ready to undertake such a project. The government is too weak" (*Financial Times*, 5 December 1990). In February 1991, Hungary succeeded in concluding an agreement with the IMF that did not include recessionary measures but concentrated on institutional issues. And by the spring of 1991 a gradual approach seems clearly to have emerged. The arguments in favor of this approach were spelled out by Kupa, the new finance minister:

There are only two solutions: Either you focus on a very rapid transition to markets expecting that the profits generated by the private sector will then be distributed to those abandoned along the way or you proceed more prudently, committing yourself not to exclude anyone from this process of transition. Since the actual state of our economy does not permit the first solution, we have adopted the second, placing priority attention on the social aspects of the reform.

When asked explicitly why Hungary would want to advance more slowly than Poland, Kupa continued: "We cannot risk social tensions that would put everything in question" (interview in *Le Figaro*, 4 June 1991).

Economic effects of reforms

To provide background for what follows, here is a brief summary of Polish economic dynamics during the eighteen months after the shock treatment was applied on 1 January 1990. Selected economic indicators are presented in Table 3.3.

The effect of price liberalization was immediate and dramatic. In a few days, most prices increased 60 to 80 percent; meat jumped 100 percent. The January inflation rate was 79.6 percent, well above the 45 percent predicted by the government. The February rate was still 23.8 percent, but, except for January 1991, the monthly inflation rate was in single digits over the next eighteen months. Hence, the deregulation operation was a double success: Prices were liberalized, and at the same time hyperinflation was arrested. True, as Blanchard et al. (1991) emphasize, the money overhang had been eaten away already by the hyperinflation of the autumn of 1989: The ratio of the population's money supply to expenditures fell from 3.8 in February 1989 to 1.4 on the eve of price liberalization, December 1989. Yet price liberalization turned out to be a one-stroke operation: Inflation jumped sharply and then fell to a reasonable and stable level. The exchange rate remained stable. Confidence in the złoty was built; people were selling dollars and putting the money in three-month złoty deposits.

The effect of price liberalization in other countries was similar. Prices flared up immediately, particularly those of meat and some other foodstuffs. The rate of inflation in the first month after prices were freed was about 250 percent in Bulgaria, 48 percent in Romania, and 25.8 percent in Czechoslovakia. Yet in all these cases inflation subsided almost immediately: In Bulgaria, the inflation rate three months later was 3 percent; in Czechoslovakia, it fell to 7.0 percent during the second month, and the total increase in prices after six months was only 49.2 percent; in Romania, the overall increase for the first six months of 1991 was 164 percent. Hence, thus far it appears that the inflation caused by freeing prices from state control is a passing phenomenon.

In Poland, inflation for 1990 as a whole fell to about 250 percent after being 640 percent in 1989. The inflation that lingered was due to increases in utility rates and rents and to monopolistic pricing by state enterprises: The

Table 3.3. *Poland: Economic indicators during reform*

	WAGE	INFL	RWAGE	FOOD	SALES	EMP	UN	COL
1989								
January	−37.1	11.0	−43.3	38.0	4.4	−1.3		
February	29.0	7.9	19.6	38.0	−2.9	−0.1		
March	33.6	8.1	23.6	37.3	−1.5	−1.0		
April	−3.0	9.8	−11.7	36.1	−4.5	−0.9		
May	−3.6	7.2	−10.1	37.1	−0.5	−1.1		
June	13.5	6.1	7.0	38.5	3.1	−1.1		
July	5.7	9.5	−3.5	41.2	−16.3	0		
August	101.8	39.5	44.7	48.5	0.2	−1.0		
September	0.8	34.4	−25.0	50.1	13.6	−0.5		
October	27.2	54.8	−17.8	55.7	−2.3	−0.1		
November	25.1	22.4	2.2	51.2	−2.7	−0.3		
December	47.5	17.7	25.3	51.0	11.7	−1.2		
1990								
January	1.8	79.6	−43.3	57.4	−31.6	−1.1	0.3	4.3
February	15.0	23.8	−7.1	51.3	−2.1	−1.1	0.8	4.5
March	36.7	4.3	31.1	48.5	0.9	−1.1	1.5	5.7
April	−5.8	7.5	−12.4	54.0	−1.5	−1.3	1.9	7.8
May	−3.0	4.6	−7.3	52.9	0.3	−1.9	2.4	9.5
June	2.3	3.4	−1.1	53.0	4.9	−1.1	3.1	10.2
July	10.8	3.6	6.9	52.4	−12.2	−1.6	3.8	11.3
August	5.0	1.8	3.1	50.8	7.6	−1.6	4.5	12.3
September	7.6	4.6	2.8	48.2	8.0	−1.4	5.0	13.6
October	13.6	5.7	7.5	47.7	0.4	−1.3	5.5	14.6
November	12.0	4.9	6.8	45.7	0	−1.4	5.9	15.2
December	3.1	5.9	−2.6	45.7	3.2	−3.0	6.1	16.3
1991								
January	−0.2	12.7	−11.4	48.0	−18.7	−0.8	6.6	18.3
February	12.5	6.7	5.4	46.1	0.8	−0.9	7.0	18.9
March	3.7	4.5	−7.7	46.8	0.1	0.1	7.1	18.9
April	−1.2	2.7	−3.8		−8.3		7.3	19.6
May	−2.1						7.7	19.9
June	2.0	4.9	−3.0		0.2		8.5	21.0

WAGE: Monthly change in nominal wages (including profits paid out to employees) in state sector.
INFL: Monthly change in consumer price index.
RWAGE: Monthly change in real wages in state sector.
FOOD: Proportion of food in the expenditures of employed households.
SALES: Monthly change in sales by state sector (in comparable work time).
EMP: Monthly change in employment in state sector.
UN: Ratio of registered unemployed to labor force.
COL: Cumulative proportion of those laid off collectively among the unemployed.
Source: GUS, *Biuletyn Statystyczny*, 1990, no. 1, to 1991, no. 3.

rate of profit of state enterprises was very high and continued to increase during the first quarter of 1990. But since it did fall sharply in the end, from 29.4 percent in December 1990 to 7.6 in April 1991, there is evidence that some structural change was occurring. The state budget was in surplus for 1990 as a whole, as was the trade balance in both dollar and ruble markets. The economy was stabilized.

Yet whether this stabilization is permanent remains to be seen; thus far it has been achieved by a profound reduction in demand. The main instrument of stabilization was a sharp reduction in wages. By the end of the first quarter of 1990, consumer demand was down 47 percent, and output was down 27 percent from the same period of the preceding year. Both output and demand picked up somewhat during the second part of the year. For the first year of reforms as a whole, industrial output fell by 23 percent and total output by 13 percent. The situation is similar elsewhere: Having declined everywhere in 1990, during the first quarter of 1991 industrial production fell by 26 percent in Bulgaria, 13 percent in Czechoslovakia, and 17 percent in Romania. It also fell by 13 percent in Hungary.

The effect of these changes on real incomes and welfare is difficult to assess, in part because information about the new, and to a large extent informal, private sector is sketchy, but also for conceptual reasons (Lipton and Sachs 1990). In Poland real wages in the state sector tumbled, and real incomes of households (including incomes from additional employment) fell drastically during the first half of 1990 and recovered somewhat during the second part of 1990. For the year as a whole, real wages fell by 28 percent. But two corrections must be introduced when evaluating the initial impact of reforms. First, in the pre–1990 shortage economy, money was not a sufficient title to access goods and services: At the beginning of 1989 households held more than three times as much money as they could spend on the available supply. Hence, the drop in real purchasing power was lower than ''real'' income figures would indicate.[28] Second, under the shortage economy, an average household spent over two hours a day standing in line. In January 1991 queues evaporated overnight. For the first time in postwar history, the majority of respondents ranked not having enough money as more of a problem than shortage of supplies.[29] Hence, in spite of the declining ''real'' wages, the result of the liberalization operation must have been a gain in welfare: The excess liquidity had been useless anyway, and the saving in transaction costs was enormous. This argument is borne out by survey studies, which report that people perceived living conditions as better while ''real'' wages were declining: The difference between the proportion of respondents who thought that living conditions were bad and those who thought they were good fell from 82 in September 1989 to 73 in January 1990 and to 57 in April (see Table 3.4 below).

Yet purchasing power continued to decline after the money overhang and the queues had vanished. While wages in the state sector and household incomes recuperated somewhat during the second half of 1990, they fell again by 17.2 percent during the first four months of 1991. The same pattern is true of almost all other indicators. Sales by the state sector (in comparable work time) fell by 18.7 percent in January 1991 and continued to decline during the second quarter of 1991. Particularly affected were light industry and construction. The state budget went into deficit during the first half of 1991. Imports from the dollar zone outpaced exports by $525 million at the end of April 1991, and hence the government was forced to devalue the złoty by 15 percent in May.

Official unemployment appeared in January 1990 and continued to increase by about 100,000 per month. But for several months, many people who registered as unemployed had never before been employed. There were few layoffs and no plant closings. By the end of the first quarter, employment was down by 6 percent. Most enterprises continued to hoard labor, and productivity tumbled. In June the minister of industry decided to close the first factories; collective layoffs accelerated, and employment fell more rapidly. By the end of September, employment was down 10 percent and productivity about 20 percent. By this time the unemployment rate had reached 5.0 percent of the economically active population. By the end of 1990 the unemployment rate was 6.1 percent, and 16.3 percent of the unemployed had lost their jobs as a result of collective layoffs. At the end of August 1991 unemployment reached 9.4 percent, and over 25 percent had lost jobs as a result of collective layoffs. In other countries as well, official unemployment was the offspring of reforms. It appeared in January 1991 and continued to creep up: By the end of the second quarter, it had reached about 6 percent in Bulgaria, 3.8 percent in Czechoslovakia, and 0.9 percent in Romania. It also increased to 3.9 percent in Hungary.

Although no systematic data are available for Poland,[30] there are several indications that the reform process did not increase the inequality of household incomes. Answers to survey questions concerning the family economic situation and spending patterns remained more or less the same during the first eighteen months of reforms. In November 1987 and also in November 1989, 42 percent of families perceived their situation as bad and 12 percent as good; in May 1990, 37 percent saw it as bad and 14 percent as good; in May 1991,

40 percent classified their situation as bad and 11 percent as good (CBOS). Questions concerning family budgets indicate that about 10 percent of households managed to save and that something between 50 and 60 percent had barely enough money to buy the cheapest food and clothing. The rest either did not consume enough, borrowed, or dissaved. Hence, a rough guess is that about 10 percent of households were doing well and about a third hovered on the brink of absolute poverty. The rest survived.

To summarize, the main achievement of the reform process thus far has been introduction of a consumer market. Lines and rationing were successfully replaced by allocation by price. Even if this operation was accompanied by a sharp decline in "real" wages, it must have increased welfare. Indeed, no numbers can convey the experience; for people who for decades "hunted" the streets carrying "just-in-case" bags (*anuzka*) for whatever might "appear," who joined lines because lines meant that "they must have thrown something," the spectacle of stores filled with products one could acquire just by paying a price was a wonder. Moreover, the initial flare-up of inflation turned out to be short-lived, and the foreign exchange rate had been stabilized. Hence, reforms simultaneously introduced a consumer market and succeeded in stabilizing the economy.

Yet thus far inflation has been controlled mainly by restricting demand. Unemployment has been increasing slowly but steadily. All other indicators show the same pattern: After a sharp decline during the first half of 1990 and relative recovery during the latter half of that year, the first half of 1991 witnessed a marked deterioration in all aspects. Most important, after eighteen months of reform the economy continues to decline: Real wages are falling along with demand and output, and unemployment is growing faster. The exchange rate finds itself under renewed pressure. Meanwhile, as the budget deficit mounts, expenditures on social services are being reduced further.

My point is not that the reform process has been a failure; in many ways it has already changed people's lives for the better. Moreover, the reason why output, employment, and living standards declined is not exclusively reform; one indication is that net material product and industrial output declined in several countries before the shock treatment was introduced; another is that the Hungarian economy followed a path similar to the economies of the countries that adopted a more radical posture. These economies declined in part because the old system of resource allocation, including trade relations with the Soviet Union, disintegrated; in part because of a coincidental increase in oil prices and international interest rates; and only in part because of reforms.

In turn, I believe that this experience demonstrates that even if a reform program is as radical as the Polish package has been, the transition to a market economy is inevitably a long process. After eighteen months, the end of the road is not in sight.

Unemployment is far from having reached bottom. There are several indications that the great majority of state firms have not changed their traditional behavior and have decided to wait things out.[31] The best evidence for the posture of state firms is that during the first eighteen months after reform their sales fell by about 50 percent while employment fell by about 20 percent. Hence, sales per worker fell by nearly 40 percent; state firms were continuing to hoard labor. The privatization law that was passed served only to perpetuate uncertainty: Few firms have been privatized thus far, but many know they will be. Most markets are still missing: There is no effective stock market, no labor market, and no credit market. The introduction of the new tax system was delayed by a year; the new system was adopted only in July 1991 for 1992.[32] Private foreign investment, as distinct from aid from governments and multilateral agencies, has been minuscule. By August 1990, eighteen months after the Law on Joint Ventures was liberalized, the Agency for Foreign Investment had issued 1,903 permits out of 2,309 applications, and 800 firms were operating. The total investment was on the order of $100 million. By February 1991, some 3,000 companies with foreign capital were registered, with foreign equity of about $400 million.

Moreover, although the evidence is limited, little indicates that the jump to the market induced the monetarist miracle of an explosion of popular entrepreneurship. In the words of Lipton and Sachs (1990: 111), "the object of competition is the rapid emergence of markets for goods, labor, and capital, thereby creating an appropriate environment for the massive resource reallocation necessary for a fundamental transformation of the economy." Nothing of the sort has occurred thus far, and there is little support for this claim at the level of individual attitudes. As Elster (1990) argued, in the presence of externalities preferences for economic systems differ drastically from individual decisions. While private property and markets enjoyed widespread support by 1988, Rychard (1991a: 422–3) shows that 78.7 percent of parents wanted their children to find a job in the state sector, and only 14.5 percent wished their children to work in the private sector. In a survey conducted at the end of June 1990, 72.2 percent of respondents supported privatization of state enterprises, but 52.3 preferred to work for state firms (Życie Warszawy, 25 June 1990). The proportion of state employees who said they would open their own businesses if they lost their present jobs remained almost constant, around 30 percent, from February to November 1990, while the proportion willing to become independent climbed slowly from 36 percent in February to 42 percent in November (CBOS). And whereas the support of public opinion for the market economy was overwhelming, by August 65 percent of respondents agreed with "The state should control prices and not allow them to increase too much," while only 23 percent thought prices should be freely determined by the market (OBOP).

Economic indicators show a more complicated picture. Optimists claim that the expected explosion of local entrepreneurship did materialize. During the first six months, 175,000 private firms were established, and, according to some Western sources, 500,000 private firms were formed by the end of the year. Yet during the six months for which we have systematic data, 147,000 private firms closed or suspended their activities. Hence, the net increase was only 28,000. The new firms were predominantly in commerce – 90,000 new firms were engaged in ambulatory trade – while the number of craft and service firms declined by 53,000. Average employment in the private sector fell from 1.98 employees per firm in 1989 to 1.75 in August 1990 (*Gazeta Bankowa*, 9 September 1990). Some light is cast on this phenomenon by the research of Buchner-Jeziorska (1990), who shows that entrepreneurs who were very successful at the margin of the socialist economy are unlikely candidates for the new entrepreneurial class. Given the uncertainty and the exorbitant profitability of their activities, they have learned to engage only in ventures that can be liquidated quickly, and they learned to consume at a very high rate.

None of these numbers should be considered as the final verdict; it would be unreasonable to expect attitudes and behavior to change overnight. Indeed, the most recent data indicate that the private sector is showing new life as the state sector continues to decline. Yet the transformation will be at best a slow one: Reaping quick rents in thin markets is a different form of entrepreneurship from investing in fixed assets to get a competitive rate of return.

Hence, after eighteen months of reforms, in the words of a Polish joke, "there is a tunnel at the end of the light." As new reform measures are being introduced, economic conditions continue to deteriorate, and the bottom is not yet in sight.[33] The period between stabilization and resumed growth is inevitably long. Mexico grew for the first time a full six years after a successful stabilization program; Bolivia has not grown yet. This is why political questions are crucial for the success of reforms. Will the reform program continue to be supported as an expression of the democratic process?

The dynamics of public opinion

The evolution of public opinion

When it was initiated, the reform program did shatter the accumulated skepticism, did generate confidence, and did mobilize widespread support. The very idea of radical reforms was supported by a margin of three to one; the Balcerowicz Plan specifically, by almost the same margin. Optimism soared. A question asked by OBOP in November of every year since 1979 – whether the next year would be better for the country and for the respondent – in 1989 showed the highest levels of optimism ever recorded.[34] The net percentage difference between people who thought the economy would improve and those who thought it would deteriorate in the next two years jumped from − 6 in July 1989 to 45 in December and was still 44 in April 1990 (CBOS). In another survey, the net difference between those who thought the economy would improve rather than deteriorate within the next three years went from − 18 in March 1989 to 48 in November 1989 and 49 in January 1990 (OBOP). Moreover, this was not uninformed optimism; the government had warned that hardships would ensue, and people expected them to ensue. Yet they were willing to bear the brunt. In February 52 percent said they "would support the government if it announced that your situation must still worsen somewhat during the forthcoming months," while 33 percent said they would not. In March 53 percent agreed with the statement "People think it is hard, but we need to suffer so that it will be better in the future." They were willing to suffer, and they were willing to support the program that generated this suffering because they believed that the suffering was inevitable, that the reform program was sound, and that it would bear fruit in the foreseeable future.[35]

Since the data presented in Table 3.4 speak for themselves, we can avoid delving into the details of the evolution of public opinion. Only let me indicate a periodization.

Most indicators of public opinion showed that the perception of current conditions and hopes for the future continued to hold steady until May 1990, which marked the first significant decline in support. The levels reached in May remained quite stable until the end of 1990. Indeed, most indicators showed slightly higher levels of satisfaction and optimism in November than in May. In 1991 the diagnosis of the current situation, optimism, willingness to bear sacrifices, and support for the Balcerowicz program all began to decline again. After a temporary respite in April, May witnessed the largest turn against reforms thus far recorded. The August data indicate that dissatisfaction with the reforms became even more pronounced. In August 1991 the Balcerowicz Plan had a net score of -32. The proportion of respondents who thought that current sacrifices would bear fruit in the future declined to 23 percent, and 71 percent thought their sacrifices would not bring improvement.

In sum, reforms enjoyed overwhelming support from the time they were announced through the first four months of their implementation. This support declined sharply after a few months but remained stable and sizable during the rest of the first year. During the subsequent six months, confidence in reforms fell sharply again, and after eighteen months a clear majority of public opinion turned against them for the first time.

Economic dynamics and public opinion

Why did support for reforms decline? To what extent are the assessment of current conditions, optimism about the future, and support for the specific reform program shaped by the dynamics of the economy? Which economic variables matter for the dynamics of public opinion, and how?

Since monthly data on economic variables and various aspects of public opinion are available from January 1989 to the present, we can engage (with all the appropriate caveats) in simple statistical analyses. The public opinion data listed in Table 3.4 include assessments of current conditions, forecasts, and an evaluation of the Balcerowicz Plan. Both the assessments and the forecasts include three questions, two so closely related that they provide a reliability check: One asks about the economy and the other about living conditions. (The third asks about tensions in the society.) Moreover, forecasts for the economy are asked for by two survey organizations. In total, we have eight questions that have been asked at least sporadically from January 1989 through May 1991.[36]

The correlations among the answers are presented in Table 3.4A.[37] Note that the forecast variables cohere (WIMP is the OBOP variable; all the others come from CBOS), and so do assessments of the current situation. It seems that, particularly once reforms were in place, people formed forecasts about the future independently of their assessment of the current situation. The indicators of social tension do not correlate with other attitudes for the entire period, but they do after January 1990. A glance at the data is sufficient to

Table 3.4 *Attitudes toward the economy and the reform program (percentages)*

	WE	WIMP	WM	WT	IE	IM	IT	BP
1989								
January	− 3	− 7		− 34	− 84		− 70	
February		3						
March	8	− 18	− 16	− 24	− 90		− 89	
April	8	− 1		− 1	− 87	− 74	− 54	
May		1					− 59	
June	17		− 2	− 1	− 81	− 65	− 44	
July	− 6		− 31	− 39	− 92	− 75	− 76	
September	23	11	− 3	3	− 92	− 82	− 59	
October		21						
November	45	48	11	12	− 81	− 70	− 32	
December		27						
1990								
January	33	49	5	− 31	− 84	− 73	− 76	33
February	42		12	− 21	− 71	− 72	− 65	26
March	37	24	15	− 22	− 43	− 62	− 63	11
April	44	27	25	− 17	− 37	− 57	− 55	15
May	30	15	10	− 43	− 46	− 63	− 70	9
June	32	5	10	− 42	− 43	− 64	− 67	15
July	28		7	− 33	− 52	− 69	− 80	2
September	28	22	8	− 37	− 39	− 63	− 64	14
October	33	5	12	− 42	− 38	− 62		15
November	36		17	− 26	− 57	− 76	− 79	7
1991								
January	32		12	− 16	− 40	− 61		1
February	21		0	− 40	− 42	− 59	− 72	− 12
March	24	10	5	− 48	− 38	− 62		4
April	32	16	12	− 30	− 28	− 56	− 60	12
May	16	− 10	− 4	− 55	− 62	− 67	− 83	− 17
June	6	− 13	− 12		− 53	− 69		− 18
July	7		− 12	− 51	− 66	− 78	− 85	− 28
August	16		− 6	− 47	− 54	− 78	− 76	− 32

WE: "Will the economy improve or deteriorate during the next two years?" Net score = "Improve" − "Deteriorate."

WIMP: "Will there be economic improvement during the next three years?" Net score = "Improvement" − "Deterioration."

WM: "Will the material conditions of people's lives improve or deteriorate in the next two years?" Net score = "Improve" − "Deteriorate."

WT: "In your view, will social tensions decrease or increase during the next weeks or months?" Net score = "Decrease" − "Increase."

IE: "How do you evaluate the economic situation of the country?" Net score = "Good" − "Bad."

IM: "How do you evaluate the current material conditions of people's lives?" Net score = "Good" − "Bad."

IT: "In your view, does our society experience calm and release or anxiety and tension?" Net score = "Calm" − "Tension."

BP: "How would you describe your attitude toward the Balcerowicz Plan?" Net score = "Support" − "Opposition."

Sources: CBOS, *Servis Informacyjny*, various issues (except for WIMP, which is from OBOP).

Table 3.4A. *Correlations among attitudes toward reforms (January 1989 to May 1991 at lower left, January 1990 to May 1991 at upper right)*

	WE	WM	WIMP	WT	IE	IM	IT	BP
WE	1.00	0.86 (13)[a]	0.64 (8)	0.73 (13)	−0.27 (13)	−0.21 (13)	0.53 (8)	0.62 (13)
WM	0.93 (17)	1.00	0.39 (8)	0.64 (13)	0.17 (13)	0.07 (13)	0.50 (8)	0.27 (13)
WIMP	0.71 (12)	0.61 (12)	1.00	0.69 (8)	−0.32 (8)	−0.21 (8)	0.29 (8)	0.89 (8)
WT	0.15 (20)	0.11 (17)	0.36 (12)	1.00	−0.23 (13)	−0.13 (13)	0.37 (8)	0.20 (13)
IE	0.54 (20)	0.60 (17)	−0.37 (12)	−0.51 (20)	1.00	0.83 (13)	0.89 (8)	−0.63 (13)
IM	0.22 (17)	0.42 (17)	−0.17 (12)	−0.34 (17)	0.82 (17)	1.00	0.78 (8)	−0.44 (13)
IT	0.30 (14)	0.18 (17)	0.54 (12)	0.81 (14)	−0.22 (14)	0.16 (14)	1.00	0.55 (8)
BP	Not relevant during this period							1.00

Note
WE: "Will economy improve?"
WM: "Will living conditions improve?"
WIMP: "Will economic situation improve?" (OBOP)
WT: "Will tensions decline?"
IE: "Is economy well?"
IM: "Are living conditions good?"
IT: "Are tensions low?"
BP: "Balcerowicz Plan."
   All variables are measured as a net difference between positive and negative answers.
[a]Parentheses indicate number of observations.

show that in 1989 tensions rose and fell as a function of political events rather than of economic moods.

How are these attitudes shaped by economic variables? Table 3.4B shows correlations between economic and attitudinal variables: the upper panel after January 1989, the lower panel for the period after reforms; that is, since January 1990.

The general patterns during the reform period are the following:

1. Nominal wages have no effect on attitudes toward reform; there is no evidence of money illusion.

2. When real wages grow, inflation declines, food expenditures decline, and demand increases – in short, when economic conditions are better – more people assess them as good. They have a realistic perception of the situation.

Table 3.4B. *Economic variables and attitudes toward reforms*

January 1989 to May 1991

	WE	WM	WIMP	WT	IE	IM	IT
NWAGE	0.35	0.08	0.23	0.18	0.06	−0.02	0.29
	(20)[a]	(17)	(17)	(20)	(20)	(17)	(14)
RWAGE	0.18	0.13	−0.13	−0.05	0.34	0.38	0.11
	(20)	(17)	(17)	(20)	(20)	(17)	(14)
INFL	0.15	−0.10	0.54	0.22	−0.45	−0.45	−0.04
	(20)	(17)	(17)	(20)	(20)	(17)	(14)
FOOD	0.79	0.53	0.76	−0.15	0.44	0.01	−0.13
	(20)	(17)	(17)	(20)	(20)	(17)	(14)
SALES	−0.00	0.18	−0.38	0.10	0.14	0.10	0.39
	(20)	(17)	(17)	(20)	(20)	(17)	(14)
EMP	−0.25	−0.55	0.09	0.21	−0.31	−0.25	0.33
	(20)	(17)	(17)	(20)	(20)	(17)	(14)

January 1990 to May 1991

	WE	WM	WIMP	WT	IE	IM	IT	BP
NWAGE	0.07	−0.04	−0.05	0.14	−0.04	−0.15	−0.14	−0.07
	(13)	(13)	(9)	(13)	(13)	(13)	(8)	(13)
RWAGE	−0.11	0.12	−0.60	−0.08	0.57	0.25	−0.18	−0.51
	(13)	(13)	(9)	(13)	(13)	(13)	(8)	(13)
INFL	0.15	−0.23	0.78	0.17	−0.83	−0.47	0.44	0.65
	(13)	(13)	(9)	(13)	(13)	(13)	(8)	(13)
FOOD	0.36	0.11	0.63	0.13	−0.52	−0.19	0.35	0.65
	(13)	(13)	(9)	(13)	(13)	(13)	(8)	(13)
SALES	−0.05	0.18	−0.80	−0.34	0.62	0.36	0.48	−0.29
	(13)	(13)	(9)	(13)	(13)	(13)	(8)	(13)
EMP	−0.29	−0.29	−0.12	−0.13	0.14	0.21	0.26	−0.18
	(13)	(13)	(9)	(13)	(13)	(13)	(8)	(13)
UN	−0.65	−0.31	−0.73	−0.35	0.58	0.29	−0.56	−0.77
	(13)	(13)	(10)	(13)	(13)	(13)	(8)	(13)
COL	−0.67	−0.34	−0.72	−0.36	0.58	0.33	−0.54	−0.78
	(13)	(13)	(10)	(13)	(13)	(13)	(8)	(13)

[a]Parentheses indicate number of observations.

In turn, their forecasts are to a large extent independent of the current situation and its perception: evidence that people do not simply extrapolate current conditions but have theories about the dynamics of reforms.[38]

3. Approval of the Balcerowicz Plan is more widespread when the current economic situation is bad and more people assess it as such; support for the reform program is lower when the situation is better and more people see it as good. This is true for real wages, inflation, food expenditures, and demand (sales by state enterprises). People seem to accept the argument that low wages and inflation are a necessary cost of transforming the economy, and they seem to have been successfully persuaded that reforms are the remedy for, not a cause of, declining incomes and increasing prices. Yet reforms are painful, and when the economic situation shows signs of improvement, more people are likely to conclude that reforms have been sufficient: Since things are already better, there is no need to continue.

Thus, people seem to be reading the current situation symptomatically; they see bad conditions as indicating that the economy needs treatment; good conditions as a sign that it has recovered. This is not a rational belief.[39] Hence, these findings may indicate individual myopia, albeit with a twist: Continuation of reforms is threatened when the economy shows the first signs of recovery.[40] But they may also indicate a warranted risk posture: If people are highly uncertain whether reforms will make them better off in the long run, it is rational for them to want to avoid short-term deprivations and at the same time to be averse to making additional sacrifices when things are better. Hence, the decision whether or not reforms should be continued depends on whether one believes that the reform program will increase welfare in the long run. This is why the postures of economists and of the population often diverge.

These aggregate patterns do not imply that it is those who are worse off who support the reform program. Quite the contrary; as Table 3.5 shows, those who earn lower incomes, those who see their economic situation as bad, and those with little education and in manual occupations persistently express less support for the Balcerowicz Plan than those who are better off by all these criteria. Hence, the class structure of attitudes toward the reform program is pronounced. These cross-sectional findings are not inconsistent with the results derived from analyzing the time series of average responses, since the differences among the categories are almost constant over time, determined by the initial positions as of January 1990. Hence, different categories start from different initial positions that are shaped by their place in the socioeconomic structure, but all categories are affected in the same way

Table 3.5. *Some cross-sectional data*

Net support for Balcerowicz Plan	Feb. 90	Apr. 91	June 91
Assessment of own material situation			
Very bad and bad	− 3		− 36
Good and very good	50		39
Income			
Second-lowest category		2	− 35
Median category		21	− 20
Second-highest category		35	18
Occupation			
Professionals and managers		32	46
Other white collar		28	3
Skilled workers		17	− 28
Unskilled workers		0	− 18
Farmers		− 12	− 47
Private entrepreneurs		23	− 10

Those supporting Balcerowicz Plan in sample of state employees					
	Feb. 90	Mar. 90	Apr. 90	June 90	Sept. 90
Assessment of own material situation					
Very bad and bad	28	26	18	16	12
Good and very good	57	56	38	57	47

by changing economic conditions. Poor people are less willing to make intertemporal trade-offs to begin with, and they continue to be less willing to make them throughout the period; but poor people react to changing conditions in the economy in the same way as those who are better off, and with the same irrationality.

4. While the pattern described above is perplexing, its importance is dwarfed by the effects of unemployment. Unemployment, which appeared officially only with the introduction of reforms, affects both current diagnoses and future forecasts. As it increases, people tend to assess the current situation as good, but they become pessimistic about the future. The reason, I think, is that the proportion of the labor force touched by unemployment has remained relatively low during most of the period under consideration, and, what with unemployment compensation, severance pay, and moonlighting, consumption has not been seriously affected by unemployment. People tend

Table 3.5. (*cont.*)

Net confidence in the government, by occupation

	Professionals and managers	Other white collar	Skilled workers	Unskilled workers	Farmers
1990					
January	82	69	62	55	60
February	81	67	58	50	52
March	52	60	53	40	16
April	65	53	41	28	28
May	70	54	38	37	17
June	65	49	34	29	31
July	74	35	16	22	− 7
August					
September	55	41	26	40	− 10
October	64	42	27	24	4
November	66	27	20	22	− 2
December					
1991					
January	21	32	30	34	13
February	44	21	38	25	0
March	39	22	26	7	− 21
April	55	44	30	20	0
May	38	7	0	− 2	− 37
June	21	− 4	− 19	4	− 55
July	61	− 20	− 6	− 45	− 37
August	18	− 2	− 10	16	− 51

to read the unemployment rate as an indication that the reforms are working, and they assess the current situation as good. On the other hand, fear of unemployment is widespread and increasing. Hence, as unemployment grows, people simultaneously believe that reforms are necessary and deleterious; they are more inclined to support reforms because the economy is in bad shape and to oppose them because they bring the peril of unemployment.[41] Fear of unemployment overwhelms the effects of all other economic variables combined, and it makes people turn against the reform program.

Moreover, cross-sectional evidence shows that those who feel threatened by unemployment are much more likely to oppose reforms. A sample of employees in the public sector (about 80 percent of the nonagricultural sectors) were interviewed on five occasions between February and November 1990.

The more threatened by unemployment they felt, the less willing were they to support the Balcerowicz Plan:

"Are you facing the danger of losing your job?"

Those supporting the Balcerowicz Plan

	Feb. 90	March 90	Apr. 90	June 90	Nov. 90
Very great danger	29	27	21	15	20
Great danger	37	32	25	24	20
Some danger	44	38	33	38	22
No danger	42	42	34	44	36

In conclusion, whereas many people are willing to accept that continued reforms are necessary to prevent a further fall in real wages and to control inflation, and whereas they are willing to believe that unemployment indicates that reforms are working, losing jobs is a price they are not willing to pay. The prospect of unemployment erodes support for the reform program.

The feedback from public opinion to reforms

From the perspective of architects of radical reform programs, any political opposition to reforms appears to be irresponsible populism. Yet two questions merit more serious reflection. First, is it reasonable to expect politicians competing under democratic conditions not to exploit dissatisfaction with reforms for partisan advantage? Second, and more important, should we not expect that unless opposition to reforms finds an expression through the democratic process, it will erupt in some other ways and threaten democratic institutions?

Wałęsa said the latter and did the former. With his incredible nose for popular sentiment, he broke off his support for the government at the end of May 1990, just when all indicators of support were beginning to show erosion. Wałęsa declared that the government was too isolated, that it stifled discussion and generated a false impression of consensus. He thought that popular discontent had to be vented politically. The people needed "war at the top" – his phrase – since otherwise they would have war at the bottom. His role up to that point had been limited to extinguishing strikes, and he had good reason to fear that his ability to maintain social peace could be quickly exhausted. By April 68 percent of the population thought strikes were unavoidable or very likely (up from 58 percent in March), and almost half said they would join in. And indeed, on May 20 a railroad strike paralyzed half the country. Wałęsa did succeed in extinguishing the strike, but afterward he declared that "the patient does not tolerate the operation" (Gazeta Wyborcza, 8 June 1990). Then Wałęsa began to criticize the reform program, and he began to campaign against the prime minister in the race for the presidency.

Around the same time, the Solidarity trade union, of which Wałęsa was chairman, declared that it could not tolerate the continual decline in living conditions. It wanted to talk to the government about unemployment, minimum income protection, a minimum wage, a struggle against recession, transformation of the economic structure, and the law on unions. Speaking at the meeting, Wałęsa complained, "We are building democracy, but simple people do not benefit from it" (Gazeta Wyborcza, 17 May 1990).

Wałęsa's message on the reform program combined a defense of living standards with a call for accelerating reforms. By the end of June, a pro-Wałęsa political party, the Union of the Centrum, broke away from the Solidarity coalition. The Union elaborated a systematic critique of the Balcerowicz Plan and an alternative. The preamble of their statement showed the ambivalence of the critics. It read as follows: "A modern market capitalist economy, that is to say, Western European capitalism . . . is the only economic order assuring civilized development and economic welfare. Only such an economic order − and not an abstract 'market economy' − can save Poland from catastrophe and dictatorship. . . . It must, however, include a system of social security appropriate to the level of our economic development." The preamble rejected any intermediate solutions and any search for a "third road." It called for shortening the transitional period. The document gave a positive evaluation of the government's antiinflation program, convertibility of the currency, and equilibration of the consumer market. It attacked the government for the drop in output, decline in real incomes, unemployment, and reduction in demand. The positive part of the program followed both Wałęsa's call for acceleration and his defense of incomes and employment. It demanded an immediate reactivation of the economy by eliminating restrictions on wages, reducing taxes, and introducing guaranteed prices in agriculture. For the first time since the departure of the communist government, it spoke in favor of state intervention.[42]

Hence, Wałęsa and his followers found themselves in the same contradictory situation as public opinion. On the one hand, they wanted to register popular dissatisfaction with the economic situation; on the other hand, they did not want to threaten the reforms. In the end, Wałęsa campaigned for the presidency not with an attack on the social costs of reform but with a slogan of "acceleration": in the political realm, getting rid of the legacy of the Magdalenka agreement and purging the remnants of the nomenclatura, and in the economic realm, privatization. Yet Wałęsa's moderation did not protect the presidential campaign from unabashedly populist appeals: In Latin American style, a completely unknown candidate appeared who attacked the social costs of reforms and promised the proverbial manna. In the end, Stanisław Tyminski won 23 percent of the vote in the first round of the presidential election in November, beating the incumbent prime minister for a place in the second round.

The economic fix offered by Wałęsa's campaign was privatization. The reason reforms limp, Wałęsa's forces argued, was that the government did not privatize.[43] Privatization – first of banks, insurance companies, and retail outlets and then of productive firms – would reduce the bureaucracy, liberate popular entrepreneurship, and create a middle class.

Privatization was the fix that was offered, in my view, because it was something not yet attempted.[44] Since the initial reform package did not resolve the uncertainty and reduce the social tension, something qualitatively new was required to rekindle hope. As promised by local and foreign ideologues, privatization was to be the final wonder.[45] Privately owned firms would enjoy the interested attention of their owners.[46] People would work harder in private firms.[47] The state would be freed from the pressures from firms.[48]

Support for privatization grew in public opinion as disenchantment with the reforms undertaken thus far was setting in. In March 1990, 56.3 percent thought that privatization was necessary, and 11.5 percent, unnecessary, but 34.8 percent knew nothing about it. Among the supporters, 45 percent cited better work as the rationale; among opponents, 25 percent thought it would increase inequality. In April the proportion who thought privatization was necessary rose to 60.1 percent. In July 64 percent saw privatization as necessary, and only 8 percent were against it; among the supporters, 25 percent were for selling to those who could afford it and 36 percent for distributing shares to all citizens. In September almost 75 percent supported privatization.

In response, a privatization law was passed on July 13, with an overwhelming majority of 328 to 2. Privatization was accelerated at the beginning of September by the decision to "commercialize" about 40 percent of the state sector without waiting for private buyers and to offer seven firms for sale.[49]

In the meantime, the government continued with its program. But the first signs of hesitation appeared, and social policy took a higher place on its agenda. As planned, milk subsidies were reduced in March 1990; energy prices were raised by 100 percent on 1 July, along with fees for postage and radios; most export restrictions were abolished; import tariffs were reduced several times to increase competition; new businesses were offered tax abatement. The government resisted pressure to increase subsidies to coal mines, prepared a new tax system (but delayed its implementation); on 16 June the minister of industry decided to close the first factories; on 11 August the government launched an antimonopoly investigation against sixty firms. Yet resolve seems to have been weakened; signs of wavering appeared. In the middle of May the Economic Council of the Council of Ministers declared itself in favor of some state intervention, particularly in agriculture, calling for preferential credits and minimum prices. On 1 June the government decided to increase its subsidies for housing and to loosen fiscal discipline. The closing down of delinquent state firms, scheduled for 1 July, was postponed.[50] And at the end of July the Sejm reduced the tax on excess wages, for the first time contradicting the government.

At the same time, concern over social policy reached the legislative agenda. In March the funds saved by reducing milk subsidies were symbolically directed to the Fund for Social Assistance, and somewhat later a one-time donation of 2,000 Zł per child was made (the cost of mailing it was 5,600 Zł). But by the end of April several social measures had been passed or announced. An old-age-insurance system for farmers and a program against unemployment among graduates were prepared. A retirement bill was passed by the Sejm 172 to 130, with 20 abstentions, after a heated discussion with many populist overtones. The issue of the minimum wage was also discussed during this period. The government wanted the rate to be 35 percent of the average wage; Solidarity, 42 to 45 percent; OPZZ (the postcommunist trade union), 50 percent. It was introduced on 1 July, at 35 percent. A minimum retirement pension was also set at 35 percent of the average wage. At the end of August the unemployment and retirement systems were overhauled: The qualifications for unemployment compensation were tightened, and a minimum income payment, at 90 percent of the minimum pension, was introduced.

Hence, the reaction to declining support was as ambivalent as Wałęsa's criticism of the reform program. To restore confidence, the government reached in its bag and pulled out new medicine: privatization. At the same time, it lost some nerve in proceeding with its initial program and became duly concerned with its social costs.

Once Wałęsa became the elected president, a new government was formed at the beginning of 1991. Most important ministers, including Balcerowicz, were retained in their positions. A new Ministry of Privatization was created with a program entailing partial distribution of free shares in mutual funds, and a list of firms to be privatized was announced. Otherwise, the new government continued to pursue the original program. Calls for reactivation and for social policies became louder.

My conjecture is that Wałęsa's call for a "war at the top" and his call for acceleration did stave off more profound divisions over the reform program. By pursuing his political ambitions and by using populist language, he helped diffuse public disenchantment with the reform process. Moreover, by criticizing the government, he forced it to maintain at least an appearance of being responsive to public opinion. Although Geremek, the Solidarity leader in the parliament, maintained (*Libération*, 27 November 1990) that "the Tyminski phenomenon was created by Wałęsa," this analysis suggests that space for populist appeals was created by the hard economic facts, specifically by the fact of unemployment growing in the context of disintegrating social services. Indeed, I think that the nascent democratic institutions have been insufficiently representative to keep public dissatisfaction within their limits. This is the topic to which we now turn.

Economic reforms and democratic institutions

Public confidence in institutions

The central institutions of the communist regime – the Communist Party (PUWP), the government, and the official unions – became totally discredited as successive attempts to reform the economy were fumbled during the late 1980s. The proportion of respondents who expressed confidence in the party fell from 66 percent in June of 1985 to 18 percent in July 1989. Confidence in the government enjoyed a short-lived jump when Rakowski's government seemed to open the way to economic and political reforms, only to fizzle two months later. Only the church and the army continued to enjoy popular confidence.

When the first postcommunist institutions were finally installed, confidence in all representative institutions soared. By November 1989 the government was enjoying net confidence (the difference between those who thought that the government was acting in the best interest of the country and those who thought it was not) of 83 points; the lower house of the parliament, the Sejm, 84 points; and the upper house, the Senate, 81 points. Hence, at that point the representative institutions of the nascent democratic regime enjoyed enormous popular confidence.

Confidence in the representative institutions fell throughout the first year of reforms (see Table 3.6). By the end of 1990 the government had a net score of 26, the Sejm of 21, and the Senate of 14. After a temporary increase in January 1991, both houses of parliament suffered a precipitous fall in confidence in the next four months of 1991. By July the score of the Sejm was −33 and of the Senate −29. The election of Wałęsa to the presidency and the instauration of the new prime minister, Jan Krzysztof Bielecki, protected the government from the same public opprobrium, but confidence in the government also tumbled to −18 in July 1991.

The only two representative organizations about which questions have systematically been asked are Solidarity ("S" in Table 3.6) and OPZZ. The evolution of confidence in Solidarity closely paralleled that of the government and the parliament: From its peak net confidence score of 78 in November 1989, Solidarity declined to 17 in November 1990 and to −11 in July 1991.[51] OPZZ never enjoyed public confidence; its score went from 4 in November 1989 to −10 in November 1990 and −36 in July 1991. Since political parties continued to be ephemeral throughout this period, survey organizations did not ask a similar question concerning confidence in the parties until June 1991. By July, they vied with OPZZ for last place, with a score of −36.

Systematic data are available for two nonrepresentative institutions, the church and the army, and recently the confidence question has also been asked about the police. The church traditionally enjoyed the highest confidence, and this trust rose with the emergence of democratic institutions, reaching a peak of 83 in November 1989. Although this confidence was gradually eroded, in November 1990 the church was the most trusted institution in the country, with a net score of 52. During subsequent months it experienced an unprecedented decline, falling to 22 by July 1991. The army always enjoyed the confidence of Poles: It had a score exceeded only by the church even under the communist regime. And it is the only institution in which people developed more confidence under democracy. From a score of 38 in November 1989, it increased to 48 in November 1990 and to 56 in July 1991. The reorganized police also saw confidence in it climb, from 16 in November 1990 to 21 in July 1991.

The net effect of these changes can best be summarized by comparing the confidence enjoyed by various institutions at the time when democratic institutions were first firmly installed, November 1989, with the end point of our data, August 1991. In November 1989 the Sejm was the institution that

Table 3.6. *Net confidence in institutions*

	GOVT	SEJM	SENATE	"S"	OPZZ	CHURCH	ARMY	POLICE	PARTIES
1989									
January	15*								
February	19*								
March	11*			25*		69*			
April	19*			45*		74*			
May	4*			50*		69*			
June									
July									
August									
September			66*	60*		71*			
October	46*	57*	54*	48*		71*			
November	83	84	81	78	4	83	38		
December	58*	65*	60*	62*		74*			
1990									
January	63	69	65	65	6	78	40		
February	60	60	55	57	11	69	44		
March	50	59	49	47	7	74	41		
April	45	57*	50	44	0	70	36		
May	43	44	44	38	0	67	43		
June	39	41	39	30	− 11	59	43		
July	28	34	37	29	− 14	62	44		
August									
September	29	32	34	24	− 6	56	45	16	
October	30	29*	22	27	− 11	54	44	18	
November	26	21	14	17	− 10	52	48	6	
December									
1991									
January	30	40	33	34	− 9	56	60	34	
February	26	− 1	1	− 2	− 20	41	49	22	
March	17	− 15	− 12	− 12	− 24	28	49	24	
April	33	− 2	− 2	− 1	− 17	28	57	24	
May	7	− 18	− 22	− 6	− 36	23	59	30	
June	− 9	− 8	− 15	1	− 26	26	53	21	− 23
July	− 18	− 33	− 29	− 11	− 36	22	56	21	− 36

Note: Net confidence is the difference between those who think that the activity of a particular institution serves the society well and is consistent with its interests and those who think it does not and is not.

Sources: All data are from CBOS, except for the numbers marked *. These are regression interpolations of CBOS scores on the basis of OBOP data.

enjoyed the most confidence, followed by almost identical scores for the government, the church, the Senate, and Solidarity. Twenty-one months after democratic institutions were in place, the army was the most trusted institution in the country, followed by the church and the police. These were the only institutions in the country that enjoyed the confidence of a majority. The two chambers of parliament, the government, the two trade unions, and the political parties – all the representative institutions and organizations – had negative net scores. Hence, two years after the transition to democracy, Poland was a country in which the three institutions in which people had the most confidence were the army, the church, and the police.

The weakness of democratic institutions is also revealed by a survey (conducted in August 1990) in which people were asked who really ruled Poland. Few gave institutional answers: 34 percent thought it was Solidarność, as contrasted with 21 percent indicating the government; 14 percent pointed to Wałęsa (not a public official at the time), as compared with 11 percent for the actual prime minister, Mazowiecki; 4.5 percent thought it was still the nomenclatura; and 4.3 percent, the church. Only 4.1 percent pointed to the highest legislative power in the land, the Sejm. By July 1991, 31 percent still identified Solidarność as the force that ruled the country, followed by 24 percent for President Wałęsa and 22 percent for the church. Six percent thought Poland was ruled by the government, and 4 percent pointed to the parliament.

Economic dynamics and confidence in institutions

To what extent is this progressive erosion of confidence in democratic institutions due to the deteriorating economic conditions, and to what degree is it caused by the policy style with which economic reforms were introduced and implemented? Let us first examine the effect of economic conditions and then concentrate on the political determinants.

As Table 3.6A demonstrates, the state of the economy and the material well-being of the population have a clear impact on the confidence enjoyed by political institutions.[52] As they do with regard to the radical reform strategy, people place more confidence in the democratic institutions and the church when the state of the economy is bad and when it is perceived as such. They also place more confidence in these institutions when they think that there is a high level of social tension and that this tension will increase. Hence, except for unemployment, people see democratic institutions not as a cause of their deprivation but as a solution to economic and political problems. And the

Table 3.6A. *Correlations between economic variables and confidence in institutions, January 1990 to May 1991 (N = 13)*

	"S"	GOVT	SEJM	SENATE	CHURCH	ARMY	BP
RWAGE	−0.40	−0.42	−0.33	−0.38	−0.27	0.07	−0.51
INFL	0.57	0.65	0.48	0.50	0.46	−0.20	0.65
FOOD	0.73	0.72	0.72	0.79	0.73	−0.61	0.65
SALES	−0.46	−0.37	−0.38	−0.39	−0.37	−0.14	−0.29
EMP	−0.47	−0.29	−0.51	−0.54	−0.61	0.40	−0.18
UN	−0.89	−0.94	−0.88	−0.88	−0.91	0.74	−0.77
BP	0.75	0.84	0.74	0.75	0.70	−0.61	1.00

Table 3.6B. *Correlations between attitudes toward the economy and confidence in institutions, January 1990 to May 1991 (N = 16; for IT, N = 13)*

	WE	WM	WT	IE	IM	IT
"S"	0.78	0.43	0.72	−0.61	−0.40	0.55
GOVT	0.79	0.37	0.76	−0.56	−0.30	0.71
SEJM	0.81	0.52	0.72	−0.49	−0.32	0.56
SENATE	0.78	0.47	0.70	−0.50	−0.32	0.57
CHURCH	0.75	0.49	0.65	−0.48	−0.35	0.46
ARMY	−0.61	−0.44	−0.36	0.30	0.21	−0.47

confidence in democratic institutions is associated with support for the specific reform strategy these institutions generated, the Balcerowicz Plan.

Yet once again, all this is true except for unemployment. As unemployment increases, confidence in all the democratic institutions and in the church declines; confidence is placed instead in the army (and in the police). And the impact of unemployment overwhelms all other economic variables: Unemployment alone explains 87 percent of the variance in confidence in the government, 82 percent of the variance in confidence in the Sejm, and 59 percent of the variance in confidence in the army. Real wages or inflation explain only an additional 3 to 4 percent of the variance in confidence in these institutions.[53] Hence, among economic factors, the decline of public confidence in democratic institutions (and in the church) and the increase of confidence in the army (and recently in the police) are due almost exclusively to mounting unemployment.

Policy style and democratic institutions

Although confidence in democratic institutions in Poland seems to have been undermined largely by the growing unemployment, there is abundant evidence that purely political factors also played a role. In my view, the weakness of the democratic institutions is a systematic result of the particular policy style that accompanied the reform strategy.

Let us first examine the effect of this policy style on the representative institutions, specifically the Sejm.[54] It is noteworthy that the reform strategy was adopted in Poland the same way as in most other recent cases: by surprise and independently of public opinion and of representative organizations and institutions. The agreements between the communist regime and the opposition concluded on 5 April 1989 included several stabilization measures. They also called for equalizing the legal status of all forms of property and for abolishing barriers to entry. But the strategy was to be gradual; these measures were to be introduced over two or three years. Moreover, several agreements concerned government activity with regard to sectoral priorities (energy, agriculture, military spending); a long section was devoted to workers' self-government; and the longest and most specific text concerned wage indexation and social policy (*Porozumienia Okrągłego Stołu* 1989). No other programs were offered during the first semicompetitive parliamentary elections in June 1989. Hence, nothing intimated the choice of the eventual strategy.

Neither the eventual deputy prime minister and minister of finance, Leszek Balcerowicz, nor his vice-minister, Marek Dąbrowski, participated in these negotiations. The head of the opposition group in the economic round table was Witold Trzeciakowski, who was widely expected to become minister of the economy in any noncommunist government. The nomination of Balcerowicz, a person not known outside a group of specialists, caused widespread surprise, the more so since Balcerowicz himself had declared two weeks before Solidarity decided to take the reins of government, "We do not have an economic program" (*Gazeta Wyborcza*, 5 August 1990). The first details of the reform strategy were presented by Balcerowicz during a press conference on 16 September. As a result, several Solidarity parliamentarians complained about not having been consulted. Geremek noted, "The situation in which members of the parliament learn about the economic program of the government from newspapers is unacceptable" (cited in Domarańczyk 1990: 193). As Balcerowicz himself emphasized, "We needed to take radical measures. We did not have any more time to wonder about the method, not even to try to convince the leaders of Solidarity" (*Libération,* 14 February 1990, p. 32).[55]

Elaboration of the individual measures lasted until the beginning of December. Only then was the Sejm given sixteen pieces of legislation and told that it must approve the nine most important before the end of the month to meet the IMF conditions. As the parliament was continuing to debate, Wałęsa became impatient and suggested that the Sejm should simply give the government decree powers and be done with it. Under all this pressure, the parliament managed not only to pass the economic legislation but also to change the name of the country, to put a crown on the emblematic eagle, and, after a long and stormy discussion, not to place a cross on the crown.

The televised spectacle of the government ramming through the parliament a package of complicated legislation, with the argument that the government knew what it was doing and speedy adoption was required by foreign creditors, took its toll. After the peak in confidence reached in November 1989, by February net confidence in the government was down 23 points; in the Sejm, 24 points; and in the Senate, 26 points – the sharpest drop any institution experienced until a full year later. The fall in confidence in the government was due entirely to economic conditions, whereas only half the drop experienced by the Sejm can be attributed to the economy. Examining the residuals from the regression of confidence scores on economic variables (unemployment and inflation) shows that in November the government enjoyed 3.3 points' more confidence than was warranted by the economic situation, whereas the Sejm had 9.4 points' more confidence than would be predicted by economic variables. By January the government outscored its economically determined confidence level by 3.8 points, while the Sejm found itself with 3.6 points' less than the economy warranted. By February, confidence in the government was exactly at the level predicted by economic conditions, and the Sejm had 6.8 points' less confidence than economic conditions would predict. Hence, the first blow against the parliament was dealt by those who thought that getting the reform program through rapidly was more important than having it discussed by the people's representatives.

This policy style continued as the process went on. The message harped on by Balcerowicz and his colleagues had been that the greatest danger would be to yield to political pressure for a deceleration of reforms. Interviewed by the *Financial Times* (16 July 1990), Balcerowicz argued: "It is absolutely crucial to be credible. This is why we are going to persist, despite all the political pressures upon us."[56] In January 1991, after Wałęsa and the new government assumed office, all institutions experienced a sudden jump of confidence, the Sejm and the Senate above all. Yet, impatient to accelerate reforms, Wałęsa immediately initiated a systematic campaign against the Sejm, portraying it as inert and dominated by remnants of the old system. This campaign had an obvious toll: Confidence in the Sejm lost 41 points in one month, the largest fall recorded by any institution at any time. And this fall continued until May. Examining residuals from regression on economic variables shows that whereas confidence in the government stayed slightly above the level predicted by the state of the economy, confidence in the Sejm was well below the level warranted by economic variables. And in June 1991 Wałęsa returned to the idea, which he had proposed at various moments in the past, of giving the government vast decree powers over all economic issues. The minister of justice, a lawyer, invented a wonderful legal instrument – "constitutional laws" that could be passed by a simple majority to modify the constitution – to be used to shift legislative power from the Sejm to the government. An elaborate project of one such law was made public by the president's advisers, but it was shelved by the government, which concluded that it did not need this law to continue its legislative agenda. Yet the sword of decree power still hangs over the head of the parliament, which duly passes whatever the government proposes while the confidence it enjoys among the population continues to fall.

Confidence in the government as an institution is throughout the entire period well predicted by economic variables alone.[57] Only two political events mark popular attitudes toward the government. The first is the tension accumulated by the end of May 1990, when surveys showed that 40 percent of respondents felt that the government did not know how people lived and 69 percent thought that price increases had been higher than official data admitted. As strikes erupted and Wałęsa broke off support for the Mazowiecki government, the confidence it enjoyed fell in June to 3.6 points below the level predicted by economic variables, and in July to 7.5 points below. The second marking point, but one with a surprisingly small effect, was the formation of the second democratic government, headed by Bielecki, in January 1991. Confidence in the government in January increased to 3.4 percent above the economically predicted level, and this is where it has more or less remained.

Since its nature remains undefined and has continued to be the subject of intense political conflict, the presidency as an institution has not been an object of survey questions. But it is worth noting that while the Mazowiecki government was responsible to the parliament (the president was still General Jaruzelski), the Bielecki government was a creation of the president. Hence, the relatively good performance of the government during the most recent period is probably a reflection of the public's preference for a strong executive, a preference demonstrated by several surveys.

So much for the legislative and executive institutions. What about the representative organizations? When the reform program was made public, all the existing representative organizations, with one exception, supported its general direction. The Solidarity coalition stood solidly behind the government and the Balcerowicz Plan. Most important, Wałęsa stated, "As chairman of the Solidarity trade union, I declare that I will undertake all possible actions to facilitate the difficult task of the government. I know that the union I direct approaches this matter in a fully responsible way, thinking about the future but also with a concern about living conditions today and tomorrow" (cited in Domarańczyk 1990: 165). The Communist Party greeted the choice of the variant of immediate and general "marketization" with the slogan "Your government, our program," while its heir, Social Democracy, was satisfied with opting in its program for "whatever forms of property are most efficient" and making vague noises about social policy. Other parties remaining from the communist regime concentrated on defending the corporate interests of their particular constituencies, most importantly the peasants. Only the post-communist trade union, OPZZ, took an open position against the reform package and garnered increased confidence.

Hence, the reform program did not divide representative organizations. No alternatives were discussed. Neither organized support nor organized opposition emerged from such representative systems as existed. As we have seen, the choice of reform strategy was simply removed from the realm of representative politics when it was first elaborated. The idea of a political pact that would keep economic issues away from partisan conflicts was floated each time tensions mounted. As the parliamentary elections of October 1991 approached, the government suggested that all political forces should commit themselves not to campaign on issues related to the reform strategy.

Because any transition to a market economy entails intertemporal trade-offs, no responsible political force can take a clear stand in favor of or against reforms. All are equally torn between supporting the general direction of reforms and having to defend the immediate interests of their particular constituencies. As Kuroń remarked in the aftermath of the Mazowiecki government's electoral defeat, "Having been thrown out of office, we now find ourselves in opposition. But we cannot be in opposition, because the government is weak and we support the reforms" (*Libération,* 9 April 1991).

This predicament is shown best by the dilemma confronted by Solidarity as a trade union.[58] Once the government was formed and the economic program announced, Solidarity found itself in the situation of having to support a program that would drastically hurt the immediate interests of its members. On the one hand, its leadership saw reforms as inevitable, and, as we saw above, Wałęsa swore that he would support the Mazowiecki government through the difficult moments. On the other hand, the union faced the threat of losing control over workers. The strikes of the summer of 1988 had already been initiated by a new generation of workers, against the strategy of the Solidarity leadership. During the Magdalenka talks and again during the parliamentary debate over the reform program, Solidarity union representatives found themselves in the position of supporting deindexation of wages against the more militant OPZZ. And although OPZZ's rating in public opinion was always low, in 1989 it had more members than Solidarity. Moreover, nothing comparable to the explosion of Solidarity membership of 1980 occurred in 1989; in fact, Solidarity found it difficult to recruit workers.

As reforms unfolded and their effects made themselves felt, the dilemma facing the Solidarity union sharpened. Committed by Wałęsa to support reforms, the union found it increasingly difficult to control the rank and file and was forced to make several public gestures in defense of living conditions, in favor of economic stimulation, and against further austerity. The ability of the leadership to control strikes dwindled.[59] In the end, the first political defeat suffered by Wałęsa was that after his election as president of Poland he was unable to name his successor to the chair of the Solidarity trade union. The new leadership decided to distance itself from the government.

The dilemma encountered by Solidarity is obviously inherent in situations when trade unions support austerity programs. But the facts that the Balcerowicz Plan was adopted without any consultation with unions and that neither of the two governments was prepared to compromise its plans to satisfy union demands undermined the union movement as a representative institution. As a result, public confidence in Solidarity continued to fall, together with confidence in the parliament and in the government. When Wałęsa left the leadership of Solidarity and an independent candidate became its new president, the union assumed a more militant stance with regard to the government and for the first time extracted a significant compromise: a lowering of the highly unpopular tax on excessive wages. Yet by the spring of 1991 confidence in the union among the general public had fallen well below the level predicted by economic variables alone.

Finally, to complete the picture, we need to examine the role and effect of elections. First, the turnout in elections started low by comparative standards and continued to fall, from 68 percent in the first round of the parliamentary elections in June 1989, to 50.2 percent in the local elections of May 1990, 62 percent in the first round and 53 percent in the second round of the presidential competition in November–December 1990, and 40 percent in the parliamentary elections of October 1991. Second, neither parliamentary nor presidential elections had any effect on economic policy. Economic issues were almost completely absent from the electoral campaign of June 1989, since both sides – communists and the opposition – were committed to the agreements concluded at the beginning of April. Reform *was* an issue in the presidential election; Wałęsa moderately and Tyminski strongly attacked the government over the Balcerowicz strategy. Most observers read the results of the presidential election as a defeat of the Balcerowicz Plan, and survey studies show that people opposed to the plan were more likely to vote for Wałęsa and against Mazowiecki.[60] Yet Balcerowicz kept his position in the new government, and his reform program was pursued without major modification.

Hence, radical reform was a project initiated from above and launched by surprise, independently of public opinion and without the participation of organized political forces, such as there were. It was rammed through the legislature without modifications that would have reflected divergences of interests and opinion. The parliament's repeated response to any doubts about the reform process has been to propose decree powers for the government. And even when support for the particular reform package declined and opposition became organized, the reaction was largely to embrace calls for a new fix, in the same political style. As a result, citizens were taught that they could vote but not choose, the legislature was trained to think that it had no role to play in the elaboration of policy, and the nascent political parties and trade unions were taught that their voices did not count. In the end, public confidence in representative institutions and organizations fell well below the level warranted by the economic effects of reforms alone. The policy style with which reforms were introduced and continued had the effect of weakening democratic institutions.

Conclusions

Why is unemployment so important politically?

While Poles support promarket reforms and the institutions that forge them when incomes decline and prices mount, they are not willing to continue reforms and withdraw confidence from democratic institutions in the face of mounting unemployment. And, in the end, fear of unemployment overwhelms all other considerations.

Unemployment increases uncertainty.[61] As the actual rate of unemployment continued to climb, from none to almost 10 percent of the labor force, so did fear: In February 1990, 42 percent of respondents feared they would lose their jobs; by July 1991, 55 percent. Moreover, among those who felt threatened, increasingly many saw the prospect of finding another job as dim: By November 1990, the latest period for which data are available, the proportion of respondents who thought they were likely to lose their present job and not find another one reached 30 percent.

Fear of unemployment is enormous. Even during the first few months of reform, though people seemed to be quite sanguine about the decline in their incomes, which were in fact declining, they were terrified of unemployment, although in fact almost no one had lost a job. In March 1990, 19 percent of respondents said that someone had been laid off at their place of employment. One month later, the proportion of those who said that someone had been laid off jumped to 57 percent. Twenty percent said it had happened to a member of their family; 33 percent, to a neighbor; and 50 percent, to a friend – all this when in fact collective layoffs touched only one-third of 1 percent of the labor force (43,000 persons) and total unemployment, including those who had never held a job, was 1.5 percent. At the same time, the expectation that unemployment would be widespread jumped from 63 percent in February to 87 percent in April. In a survey of secondary school graduates conducted during the late summer of 1991, 82 percent of women and 67 percent of men said they felt greatly threatened by unemployment. The same was true of 55 percent of the children of professionals and managers, 75 percent of the offspring of skilled workers, and 80 percent of the children of employees in commerce and services as well as of unskilled workers.

A political reaction followed. The proportion of those who found the very phenomenon of unemployment ''despicable'' jumped from 73 percent in March to 85 percent in April. In turn, the proportion who thought unemployment necessary declined from 50 percent in April 1990 to 26 percent in July 1991. And those threatened with unemployment were willing to resist it: 65 percent of them said, in both April and November 1990, that they were willing to strike in defense of their jobs.

Why is unemployment so frightening, and why is it so important politically?

On the one hand, while incomes were quite secure and welfare services relatively developed under the communist system, this system was not a welfare state. In a welfare state, income-maintenance schemes are an insurance against unemployment. Under communism, incomes were protected by the guarantee of full employment. They may not have been high, but they were certain. Moreover, many social services, including housing, child care, vacations, and health services, were in part financed and administered by places of employment. Finally, other social services were allocated by the central planner in the same way as other resources – the planner distributed steel, shoes, doctors' visits, and vacation places – and when central planning disintegrated, so did government-administered social services. Indicators presented in Table 3.1 showed that the gross mortality rate was higher in 1988 than in 1978, the number of people going on vacation was lower, the number of doctors' consultations was lower, and so was the number of users of public libraries, while housing construction simply tumbled.

In contrast to Hungary, Poland embarked on the transition to a market economy without having even a plan to protect individuals from the vicissitudes of the market economy. In fact, social expenditures were the main victim of fiscal austerity. The budget for 1990 reduced health expenditures by 50 percent and education by 54 percent. Culture was hit even harder. Prices of medicines jumped by 75 percent in March 1990 alone. Further cuts were introduced in the 1991 budget, and even these appropriations had to be reduced as state revenues plummeted in the spring of 1991. The health budget for 1991 was spent by June, and doctors in some Warsaw hospitals hung black flags on the buildings, announcing that they had no means of keeping their patients alive. Several traditional functions of the state were spontaneously privatized, with visible distributional effects. Many health clinics were effectively privatized, and imported medicines became available at exorbitant prices. Private schools appeared; in March 1990 their fees were about 20 percent of the average monthly income. Hence, wealthy households gained access to higher-quality social services while public services were disintegrating.

Under these conditions, the mere possibility of losing a job is frightening. While those laid off draw compensation, the amount is well below subsistence level. And no other income protection is available, and social services are few. Losing a job means losing an income, and in the present Polish market economy, having an income is the only way to survive.

Policy style and policy outcomes

Facing hyperinflation and a fiscal crisis of the state, urged by international institutions, and advised by foreign economists, the first Polish democratic government launched a program of transition to a market economy with the hope that by moving ahead as resolutely as possible it could avoid submitting reforms to public discussion, to political conflicts, and to the uncertain interplay of representative institutions. The architects of reform were persuaded that their blueprint was sound – no, more: the only one possible. They viewed all doubts as a lack of understanding, even a lack of responsibility. They were determined to proceed at all costs despite all the political pressures upon them.

Yet the experience shows, I believe, that the political conception that underlay the entire strategy was pernicious to the continuation of reforms under democratic conditions and that the technical blueprint was faulty in one crucial respect.

The Polish reforms are generally recognized as the most radical strategy of moving toward a market undertaken anywhere. The central reason why this strategy was adopted was to make the transition fast and the material deprivation it would generate brief. Yet eighteen months into the reform process it was apparent that the moment when the economy would begin to grow and when living conditions would improve was not yet near. The period between the initiation of a reform program – even the most radical one – and the launching of an economy on the path of sustained growth just is long. And this period is filled not only with material deprivation but also with uncertainty about the future of the country and with fear about one's own fate.

The technocratic style of reform is counterproductive. If reforms are to proceed under democracy, they must enjoy the continued support of a majority, expressed repeatedly through representative institutions. No reforms, regardless how well planned and how rapid they may be, can short-circuit this requirement. In the words of Bela Kadar, the Hungarian minister of foreign economic relations, "We must take into account not only economic but also political rationality. It is better to wait one year more than to charge ahead and risk losing all by inciting violent political resistance" (interview in *La Tribune de l'Expansion,* 7 June 1991).

The technocratic policy style inevitably leads to a moment when the political choice becomes one of beating a retreat or risking a political explosion. In Poland this moment occurred eighteen months after the reforms were launched. In June of 1991 the government was forced for the first time to devalue the złoty. Most tariffs, which had been reduced several times during 1990, were adjusted sharply upward in July of 1991. Reactivation of the economy was placed at the top of the political agenda, even at the cost of rekindling inflation. Calls for supporting agricultural prices and maintaining subsidies to industry became irresistible. Privatization was put on the back burner. Interviewed on 11 September 1991 (*Le Monde*), Wałęsa summarized as follows the lessons of the Polish reforms:

The West told us: Close the factories, put people on unemployment. Take a shipyard, say: Building ships is no longer profitable, so it should be closed. . . . In Poland, in our reforms, we made a mistake: We decided to go fast. . . . The result is that today we have terrible problems, lots of unemployment, machines that are stopped. If we had gone slower, we would have had half the unemployed. . . . We were naive, we believed in these slogans, and we have been had.

The proponents of the "jump to the market" did succeed in persuading the population, already prepared for this message by reform cycles under the communist regime, that radical reforms were inevitable and that the specific program adopted was a remedy for most of the economic ills. Analysis of postures toward the Balcerowicz Plan and toward democratic institutions shows that people saw the radical reform strategy as a solution to, rather than a cause of, falling incomes, increasing prices, and declining output. Yet we also discovered, quite serendipitously, that this message did not work with regard to unemployment. Growing unemployment breeds fear, causes people to turn against reforms, and erodes confidence in democratic institutions.

An overriding fear of unemployment and its political consequences are not unavoidable. After all, the Spanish program of industrial reconstruction caused unemployment rates to stay above 15 percent for a decade while the Socialist government that adopted this program continued to win elections. And Hungary, which decided to build the necessary institutional framework before taking the decisive step toward a market economy, may very well repeat this feat. The reason unemployment turned out to be so damaging politically in Poland is due to a "technical" error in the reform blueprint: Measures that would cause widespread unemployment, necessary to cause "a massive reallocation of resources across sectors," were undertaken without putting in place a social net or even labor institutions. No steps were taken to prepare for unemployment: No manpower programs were introduced to retrain the laid-off workers, no information system was organized to reduce search costs, no housing arrangements were made to facilitate mobility. As the minister of labor in the Mazowiecki government, Jacek Kuroń, observed, unemployment offices registered the unemployed, paid compensation, and stopped there. In May 1990 the ratio of employees of the Unemployment Service to the unemployed was four times lower than in Portugal (*Gazeta Wyborcza*, 1 June

1990). As firms began to lay off workers, the ratio of the unemployed to job ads increased from 2 in January 1990 to 15 by September and to 31 by May 1991. And those who were laid off and did not get that one job for thirty workers received temporary compensation and faced a de facto private health system, a public education system reserved for those who could not afford private education, and a housing market with prohibitive prices. No wonder fear of unemployment turns people against reforms and lowers their confidence in the institutions that generate them.

These errors were "technical." If the purpose of their architects was to make reforms politically palatable, the blueprint was not well designed. But the reason technocrats commit "technical" errors is that they do not consult and concert with those who are affected by their blueprints. There is something paradoxical when believers in the informational efficiency of decentralized decisions fear them most. Fearful that the democratic process will force them to moderate – perhaps even to compromise – the "soundness" of their plans, proponents of radical reforms see the greatest danger to the reform process in populism. The main obstacle to reforms is the people. Even if a reform strategy formulated in public discussion, concerted among political forces, and duly deliberated by the representative institutions had entailed more inconsistencies and compromises than the technocratic blueprint, it would have strengthened democracy and hence reduced the political space for populism.

Notes

1. Here are some headlines: "L'hiver de tous les dangers" (*Le Figaro*, 29 November 1990); "Bank Predicts Deep Downturn in E. Europe" (*Financial Times*, 19 December 1990); "Nouvelles difficultés en vue pour l'URSS et l'Europe de l'Est" (Agence France Presse, 20 December 1990); "Worst Shocks Still to Come for Eastern Europe" (*Times*, 5 April 1991); "Crunch Time for Eastern Europe" (*International Herald Tribune*, 8 July 1991). In turn, *International Business Weekly* (15 April 1991) was almost lyrical: "Reawakening: A Market Economy Takes Root in Eastern Europe," while the *Wall Street Journal* (4 July 1991) maintained that "Economic Shift Appears to Work in Eastern Europe."
2. The economic aspects of the Polish stabilization package have already been analyzed several times, and "lessons" have even been drawn. (See Blanchard, Dornbusch, Krugman, Layard, and Summers 1991; Chilosi 1991; Kołodko 1991.) These analyses converge to the judgment that the stabilization package was well designed but not free of mistakes. In particular, the recession it engendered was deeper than necessary because of reliance on the exchange rate as the anchor and because of the emphasis on privatization at the expense of reforming the state sector.
3. One might think that given the conjectural nature of the model that underlies market-oriented reforms, their proponents would be inclined to proceed cautiously, by

trial and error. Yet the voices of caution are rare. According to the *Guardian* (30 April 1991), "A steering group of the larger industrial economies [G10] yesterday called on the new democracies of eastern Europe to abandon 'gradualism' and adopt the Polish model of rapid economic reforms." According to Reuter (6 June 1991), finance, trade, and foreign ministers of the OECD countries hoped "that the USSR and the Republics would move quickly to introduce the broad range of ... reforms necessary to move to a market economy." In contrast, the general secretary of the OECD, Jean-Claude Paye, emphasized that the transition to a market economy is not just the business of economists; it is necessary, he stated, to "evaluate with caution that which is politically and socially feasible" (Agence France Presse, 29 November 1990). A report of the UN Economic Commission for Europe suggested that "the creation of a political consensus and the establishment of firm institutional foundations for private enterprise may be more crucial than the choice between shock treatment and more gradual reform." (The quotation is from an article by Anatole Kaletsky in the *Times*, 5 April 1991.)

Moreover, pressure to rush is not just a matter of advice. As Michael H. Wilson, Canada's minister for international trade, commented after an OECD meeting, "It has been made pretty clear by a number of countries that until there has been a substantial demonstration of the will to take those decisions on reform and their actual implementation, there simply is not the money available" (*International Herald Tribune*, 6 June 1991). And indeed the Polish government interpreted the 50 percent debt reduction granted Poland by the Paris Club as "a compensation for courage" demonstrated by the country in its pursuit of a market economy (Janusz Lewandowski, Minister of Privatization, *Libération*, 16 March 1991).

4. In the words of an OECD statement in "Transition from the Command to Market Economy" (OECD 1990: 9), "While a gradualist approach may cause lesser social tensions, a long period of moderate reforms entails the danger that both reformers and the population will 'become tired of reforms,' as they do not seem to bring visible changes. Also during a long period of reforms various anti-reform and other lobbies may mobilize their forces and may gradually strangle the reform process." Or, as Nelson (1984: 108) observed, "Advocates of 'shock treatment' are convinced that public tolerance for sacrifice is brief and that the courage of politicians is likewise limited. If the adjustment process is too gradual, opposition will gather and the process will be derailed." Thus, a standard argument for radical reforms is that they prevent "political fatigue" from setting in.

5. The timing is important. Many Western observers tended to blame Solidarity and the strike wave that ensued in 1980–1 for the downturn of the economy. Indubitably, wage pressure contributed to the crisis under the conditions of balance-of-payments deficits and an overextended investment program. But the collapse of the Polish economy predates the rise of Solidarity and the strikes.

6. On legitimation in Poland, see the collection edited by Rychard and Sulek (1988), in particular the article by Tarkowski.

7. The government went to the referendum with the announcement that it would take only a majority of possible votes as a mandate for reform. In fact, a small majority of those who voted said yes, but they were fewer than half of the total electorate. There are two interpretations of the regime's strategy: Either they

miscalculated their strength, or they were in fact not willing to go ahead at that point without overwhelming support.

8. The goals of the plan for 1986–90 included a number of social targets. The housing shortage was to be reduced through increased construction, health care was to be improved by building new hospitals (a major disaster in Poland) to increase the number of hospital beds to 58.3 per ten thousand by 1990, and 18,000 new classrooms were to be constructed. These social goals were not, however, part of any reform package; they were included among innumerable other targets on the regime's wish list.

9. During the first half of 1989, the last hours of the Rakowski government, 1,302 joint ventures (*spółki*) were registered. Subsequent investigation showed that 60 percent in fact did something other than what was declared in the registration statement, mainly "commercial intermediation," a euphemism for influence peddling.

10. Based on Balcerowicz 1989, Beksiak 1989, and Mujzel 1989. Total foreign investment in joint ventures was on the order of $25 million.

11. The NMP, net material product, is a narrower measure of output than the Western GDP, since it does not include services to households and government, but it is more reliable (Blades 1991).

12. This observation is based on a comparison of the West and East German price structures in 1985 (Lipschitz and McDonald 1990: 63).

13. Soviet data are based on "The Economy of the USSR," a report prepared by four international organizations for the G7 meeting in Houston in 1990.

14. The document "Economic Program: Main Assumptions and Directions" adopted by the Council of Ministers in October 1989 began with the following declaration: "The Polish economy requires basic systemic changes. The goal is to construct a market system similar to the one existing in developed countries. This must happen quickly, with the help of radical actions, to maximally shorten the transitional period burdening the society" (published by *Rzeczpospolita* in October 1989; I refer to it below as the "Economic Program").

15. Perhaps most telling is the programmatic book Mazowiecki wrote in 1970: "To defend from totalitarianism, man need not return to individualism. . . . Only responsibility for the society, for forming its organizations and institutions, so that the social community will strengthen the development and the respect for human personality . . . can restore equilibrium and sanity to the society and proper conditions for the individual development of a human being" (cited in Domarańczyk 1990: 92).

16. In a 1989 survey conducted simultaneously in several European countries, 3 percent of Poles said that the word "communism" had a positive connotation for them (compared with 15 percent of Hungarians, 38 percent of Soviets, and 2 percent of West Germans), the phrase "democratic socialism" had a positive connotation for 30 percent of Poles (54 percent of Hungarians, 57 percent of Soviets, 41 percent of West Germans), the phrase "social democracy" had a positive affect among 52 percent of Poles (68 percent of Hungarians, 34 percent of Soviets, 67 percent of West Germans), and the word "capitalism" was viewed as positive by 42 percent of Poles (37 percent of Hungarians, 24 percent of

Soviets, 41 percent of the British, 31 percent of West Germans and the French, 25 percent of Italians, 24 percent of Spaniards). A direct question about the system preferred for the future showed a clear advantage for social democracy (44 percent in Poland, 53 percent in Hungary, and 35 percent in the Soviet Union) over liberal capitalism (27 percent in Poland, 24 percent in Hungary, 4 percent in the Soviet Union) and over communism (1 percent in Poland, 4 percent in Hungary, 31 percent in the Soviet Union). Most Poles (30 percent) thought that France was the most social democratic country in Europe, followed by West Germany (26 percent) and Sweden (23 percent). They perceived social democracy as prosperous (57 percent), involving workers' participation in the management of enterprises (43 percent), and reducing inequalities (39 percent) but not as involving state intervention in the economy (15 percent) or egalitarianism (11 percent) (*Libération*, 19 February 1990).

17. Section V of the Economic Program is devoted to social policy. It is the shortest section in the statement. Its Paragraph 1 announces that social policy must be changed both because of the need to protect incomes during the transition and because of reliance on the market in the posttransition economy. Paragraph 2 specifies four types of measures designed to protect the lowest-income groups during the transition: distribution of food, support for rents and heating, partial indexation of pensions, and development of charities. Paragraph 3 speaks of organizing a system of unemployment insurance, to be financed by enterprises, and of manpower programs. Paragraph 4 proclaims that future social policy will be based on efficiency criteria and will be guided by "the principle of the dominant role of income from employment in the family budgets of employed persons." Paragraph 5 states that in the realm of social services (e.g., health and education) the principle of efficiency will signify assuring a minimum standard of living for all citizens and creating a market for levels above the minimum. In the future, tax mechanisms will be used to provide incentives for the private provision of welfare services. Paragraph 6 announces that in 1991 the social insurance system will be revamped to bring about a closer relation between contributions and the value of services.

18. Except for Domarańczyk (1990: 322), everyone makes reference to eleven pieces of legislation on economic matters. I could find only nine.

19. This summary is based on an interview with Kupa in *Le Figaro*, 4 June 1991.

20. See the article by Paweł Bożyk, "Cudu nie będzie" (There will be no miracle), *Polityka*, 16 December 1990. Perhaps the only intellectual in Poland to pronounce such views at the time, Bożyk concluded as follows: "The most important matter is not leaving everything to spontaneity. The state must assume the duty of introducing a market economy. No one can have or has the right to abdicate from this duty. This is confirmed by the experience of developed capitalist countries. Let us use it."

21. This was the Baka plan of 1985. Władysław Baka, who eventually became president of the Central Bank, resigned from the Political Bureau in 1989 because he opposed Rakowski's one-step marketization program. An alternative gradual plan was proposed by Maurice Ernst in the *Christian Science Monitor* (8 November 1989) and publicized in Poland by Rafał Krawczyk ("Czy istnieje inna droga?"

(Is there another road?), *Tygodnik Solidarność*, 22 December 1989). According to this proposal, in the first phase the supply of consumer goods should be increased, using foreign aid and reducing investment; the second phase should be deregulation of the consumer goods industry; the third, the privatization of heavy industry; and only the last should be stabilization.

22. The programmatic statement of the Economic Program (point II.5) claimed that sectoral issues did not belong in this package: "This program concentrates on the problem of the economy as a whole. This is why it does not comprise tasks of economic policy in its traditional substantive approach (sectors of national economy, branches)."

23. When asked about industrial policy in general and Japan in particular, the minister of industry, Tadeusz Syryjczyk, thought the proper role of the state was to (1) promote exports, (2) promote entrepreneurship, (3) undertake antimonopoly measures, and (4) support backward regions, the last being a goal of social policy. He also noted that wealthy countries finance research and technology. But this is where the state sectoral policy should stop; the market should do the rest. The state has no criteria on which to choose firms to support; MITI, for example, was against the development of the automobile industry, which grew only because firms did not obey state policy (interview in *Polityka*, 15 September 1990).

24. It is interesting to note for future reference that all these trends turned around in 1990: 1.9 percent more supported limitations on the highest incomes, 17.9 percent more supported a full-employment policy, 1.1 percent fewer were in favor of laying off inefficient workers, and 0.8 percent fewer thought that incomes should depend on qualifications.

25. According to a different survey, by 1989 86 percent of respondents in a national survey supported closing unprofitable firms, 81 percent supported laying off unnecessary employees, 77 percent supported limiting subsidies to firms, 67 percent supported allowing prices to form freely, and 66 percent supported limiting state price subsidies – in all cases 10 to 15 percent more than in 1987 (Ośrodek Badań Opinii Publicznej [henceforth OBOP], Komunikat no. 0921, 1990).

26. In Brazil 78 percent agreed with the statement "Everything the society produces should be divided among everyone in the most equal way possible," and 60 percent disagreed with "If the country were rich, it would not matter that there would be many social inequalities" (*Folha de S. Paulo*, 24 September 1989, p. B–8). In Spain 62 percent of workers thought there should be an upper limit on incomes (Maravall 1981: 33), while in Poland by 1988 63 percent of skilled and 70 percent of unskilled workers accepted this principle ("without or with reservations").

27. Perhaps the only coherent alternative, centered on the economic role of the Solidarity union, was sketched by an American, Anthony Levitas ("Inna Solidarność," *Tygodnik Solidarność*, 28 July 1989).

28. If we take real wages as 100 in January 1989, this index reached 136 in December, on the eve of price liberalization. It fell to 77 in January 1991 and to 66 in February and climbed to 69 in March. But if we correct for the money overhang (ignoring voluntary savings and dividing real wages by the ratio of household money supply to household expenditures), then the corrected index climbed from

100 in January to 336 in December and fell to 205 in January 1991 and to 133 in March. Hence, real purchasing power was higher in March 1991 than in January 1989.

29. In February 1989, 60 percent of respondents complained that they were hurt by inadequate supplies; 31 percent, by insufficient income. By March 1990 only 14 percent thought supplies were insufficient, and 76 percent complained about not having enough money (OBOP). Five months into reforms, only 3.7 percent saw shortages as a problem; 68.5 percent saw not having enough money as most important (Centrum Badań Opinii Społecznej [henceforth CBOS]).

30. Polish statistical sources do not provide any systematic distributional data. They only distinguish the households of state employees from those of retired people.

31. The assertion by Lipton and Sachs (1990: 120) that "in response, most managers have begun a two-pronged strategy that includes reevaluating their production processes and, in the face of undesired inventory accumulation, looking for new markets at home and abroad" is wishful thinking. Lipton and Sachs are so eager to justify the reform strategy that they fail to observe that at the time they were writing there was no reason for state enterprises to change their behavior, since they were extremely profitable. During the first four months of reform their profit rate increased 15 percent. A study of fifteen state firms by Dąbrowski, Federowicz, and Levitas (1990: 26) concludes that reactions of firms vary widely and refrains from quantitative assessments. Nevertheless, the authors conclude: "The observed changes were thus often far from the dynamism that is required for market expansion. What is particularly striking is the lack of patterns of appropriate behavior, particularly the habit of looking at the future of the firm for its prospects for economic survival. Instead of posing the question what can we sell, too often respondents ask themselves only what can we produce." The authors cite several cases in which firms responded to a fall in demand for their products by raising prices and in which managers adopted a wait-and-see attitude, hoping to use their personal contacts to obtain state contracts. My own conversations in September 1990 with several sociologists who study state enterprises indicate that most managers adopted a conservative stance, taking care of their own interests and waiting to be forced to do something. This temporizing posture was exacerbated by delay of the privatization law; managers of state firms did not know what would happen to them. The privatization law finally adopted did not clarify property rights. It introduced a temporary solution according to which state firms would be turned into public enterprises owned by the state until private buyers appeared.

32. The reason was purely technical: lack of computers and offices (*Gazeta Wyborcza*, 13 September 1990).

33. According to a study by the World Bank (*Poland: Economic Management for a New Era*, 1990) conducted in 1989, the results of a true one-shot approach in Poland would be that one-third of industrial output would disappear and the GDP would fall by 15 percent. This prediction seems overly optimistic. The experience of East Germany is illuminating here. The East German economy did transit to the market in one stroke. Unemployment in the former GDR reached 32.5 percent in April 1991 (counting the official unemployed, who constituted 9.5 percent of

the labor force, and those on "partial work time," who added another 23 percent) and declined for the first time, to 31.8 percent, in May. According to simulations conducted by McDonald and Thumann (1990: 82, 88), if by the year 2001 the East German economy reached output per worker equal to 80 percent of the West German level (it was 31 percent as of 1991), unemployment would peak at 26.5 percent in 1991 and fall to 6 percent by 2001. If labor productivity reached only 60 percent of the West German level, then unemployment would peak at 36 percent in 1991 and fall to 9 percent by 2001. Industrial production fell by one-half in East Germany in the six months following 1 July 1990, and GNP fell 15 percent. General predictions are that industrial production will fall by a further 40 to 50 percent and GNP by another 15 to 20 percent in 1991. Hence, the bottom for East Germany is somewhere around 30 percent unemployment and a 30 percent decline in industrial output. And note that, along with Czechoslovakia's, the East German economy was supposed to be the most efficient among command economies. If we use these numbers as a yardstick, Poland has a long way to go before it sees an upturn.

34. The proportion saying next year would be better for the country increased from 28 percent in 1979 to 32 percent in 1980, fell to 22 percent in 1981, and increased to 41 percent in 1982 when the military government announced the first program of reforms. It declined in 1983 and 1984 and increased again in 1985 as the government tried to invigorate economic reforms. It fell again in 1986 and 1987, to climb up to 32 percent in 1988 when the Rakowski government tried reforms again. It jumped up to 54 percent in November 1989 and landed at its 1984 level of 30 percent in November 1990. Hence, it seems that each of the reforms announced, either under a military regime or under democracy, gave a new injection of hope.

35. I have no idea on what grounds the OECD/World Bank Conference on the Transition to a Market Economy in Central and Eastern Europe decided that "in countries with newly elected democratic governments, the authorities have to contend with the unrealistic expectations of their population that throwing off the yoke of a command society would yield immediate economic improvements; in all transition economies there is lack of public understanding of the unavoidable costs of systemic changes" (Marer 1991).

36. The variables that assess the current situation begin with an "I", for "Is . . . ," while the variables that concern forecasts begin with a "w," for "Will . . ." CBOS does not conduct its monthly surveys in August and December. In turn, the data from OBOP at my disposal have several holes. Hence, the number of observations for the particular analyses ranges from eight to twenty. The CBOS data are available by subscription to *Serwis Informacyjny*, a monthly publication. The OBOP data are unpublished; I appreciate the generosity of Director Jacek Szymanderski, who dug out these results for me.

37. These are correlations between time series of average responses. I cite some cross-sectional data when they are available.

38. The WIMP variable, originating from OBOP, shows persistently higher correlations with economic variables than do the forecasts generated by CBOS.

39. This belief would have been rational if the dynamics of consumption during

reforms had been "single-bottomed"; that is, if it were true that once the economy showed improvement, a continued amelioration was guaranteed. This may be the theory many people have; hence, given their beliefs, the decision to support or oppose reforms may be instrumentally rational. But I suspect that such beliefs are not cognitively rational: They are not based on the best available evidence but on wishful thinking induced by foreboding about the costs of further deprivation.

40. A useful analogy may be to patients who, told that they must continue treatment for a specified time, interrupt it as soon as they get better and resume it again when symptoms recur.

41. With all the appropriate caveats, let me report a regression experiment that shows the role of unemployment in shaping attitudes toward the Balcerowicz Plan. Presented in graphic form are results of a seemingly unrelated regression in which the impact of unemployment is traced separately via its effect on optimism and on the current assessment of the economy. Numbers above each line are coefficients, in parentheses are t-statistics and significance levels. (I do not report constants for lack of space.) Remember that these results are flimsy: There are fourteen observations to estimate eight coefficients.

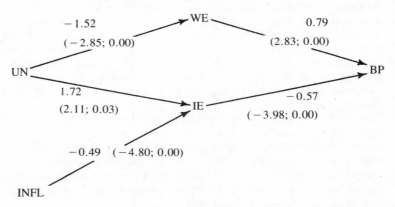

42. "The government, and not 'the invisible hand of the market,' should be responsible for structural policy. Given that the economy that constituted the point of departure for reforms was highly centralized, state intervention in the processes it undergoes is inevitable." (Text published in *Gazeta Wyborcza*, 29 June 1990.)

43. Privatization was initially delayed because there was no agreement about the method. The bill went through seventeen drafts. Every conceivable proposal was entertained at one stage or another, ranging from selling all state assets to whoever would buy them, through their free distribution to employees or to citizens as tradable shares in mutual funds.

The issues involved in privatization must be generic, for the debate over methods raised the same issues and similar proposals in Czechoslovakia, Hungary, and Poland. According to Stark (1990), the discussions in Hungary concerned the role of foreign versus domestic ownership, tolerance of spontaneous privatization, ownership by institutions versus natural persons, and the desirable degree of concentration of ownership. Reasonable arguments were offered on all sides of each issue. A proposal offered for Poland by Frydman and Rapaczynski (1990) considered the same issues. The authors opted for free distribution to all citizens of vouchers that would be used to purchase shares in mutual funds that, in turn, would own firms. The rationale for free distribution was the difficulty of attaching a value to firms in the absence of a market; the rationale for institutional ownership, in the spirit of Bardhan (1990), was the need to create incentives for monitoring performance.

44. My view of privatization as a fix is supported by the fact that those most immediately concerned are much more sober about it than the elites and the public at large. Privatization in the narrow sense – that is, sale to private owners – is supported only by directors of enterprises. Here are views on privatization derived from a survey conducted in June 1990:

	State firms should		
	Remain in state hands	Be privatized	Become property of employees
Workers	36.3	13.2	35.3
Managers	20.6	20.6	46.6
Executives	13.3	37.3	37.3

Moreover, a predominant percentage of respondents thought privatization was in only the government's interest (based on unpublished material by Jarosz and Jawlowski, who kindly shared these results). According to a journalist who followed the visit of Balcerowicz and a parliamentary delegation to the first firm to be privatized (a glass factory that was attractive to buyers because of its traditional technology!), the main incentive for employees to accept privatization was that the government excluded private companies from the tax on excessive wage increases (Jerzy Baczynski, "Niewiele pytan, skape odpowiedzi" [Few questions, miserable answers], *Polityka*, 15 September 1990).

45. I am struck that whereas the manner of privatization has been a subject of serious discussions, the idea itself is justified on purely ideological grounds. Here are Frydman and Rapaczynski (1990: 6): "Insofar as privatization consists in a transfer of control into the hands of private shareholders who, in a mutually competitive environment, are trying to maximize the returns on their investment, it is an indispensable condition of an efficient control of management performance. . . . Unless this process is completed, the reform efforts in Poland and the other East European countries will probably fail and the economic situation is likely to deteriorate even further."

46. In his speech to the Sejm on 12 July 1990, Balcerowicz motivated privatization as follows: "A market economy based on broad participation of different forms of private ownership permits the achievement of the highest – among all economic systems known in practice – degree of effectiveness in using the material and

spiritual resources of a society. It generates as a result the quickest improvement in the level of life of citizens. This is so because economizing costs, good organization of work, high quality of production, and an effective search for new markets as well as technical progress and development are in the interest of *the proprietors who direct the work of enterprises*" (speech reproduced in *Gazeta Wyborcza*, 13 July 1990; italics added). This nineteenth-century conception of the firm is characteristic of most arguments in favor of privatization.

47. In my view, the hopes attached to privatization are based on three mistaken assumptions: (1) that private property will solve principal–agent problems, forcing managers to maximize profits; (2) that the market is a source of incentives for employees rather than of information for managers; and (3) that enough capital will be forthcoming to infuse investment into newly privatized firms. The first two assumptions are based on the nineteenth-century model of capitalism. The last requires only elementary accounting.

48. Lipton and Sachs (1990: 127) are more sober in their rationale for privatization, claiming financial discipline as the main motive: "Experience around the world, plus the logic of the soft budget constraint, strongly suggest that it will be difficult to maintain the financial discipline of the state enterprises beyond the short run . . . " Yet they neglect to observe that experience around the world also suggests that it is difficult to maintain financial discipline of private firms.

49. The law distinguishes between "commercialization" – a temporary solution in which state firms would be transformed into public corporations owned by the Treasury – and privatization proper – sale to private persons (excluding public bodies). The initiative for privatization can originate from the enterprise itself, from its founding organ, or from the minister of ownership transformation. Privatization can take place at auction, through a public offering, or through negotiations following an invitation to the public. Foreigners can buy up to 10 percent of shares without special permission. Employees are offered preferential terms (a 50 percent discount up to one year's wage) to purchase 20 percent of the stock (within one year of the offering). Article 25 announced that the Sejm would enact a resolution governing the issuance of privatization vouchers, which could be used to purchase shares, rights in mutual funds, or the physical assets of a firm. Paragraph 2 of this article says that these vouchers are to be provided free of charge to all Polish citizens living in Poland, with the details to be determined, but Article 26 says that the Council of Ministers may decree that some vouchers will be available on credit. The "commercialized" public corporations are owned by the Treasury until they are sold, and they should be sold within two years unless there are no buyers. These corporations were to have one-third of the board of directors chosen by the employees and the rest by the state (Słupiński 1990).

Obviously this law was passed in response to political pressures and bears all the marks of an interim compromise among conflicting views. Most decisions were relegated to the future; indeed, passage of this law did not resolve the controversies about the manner of privatization.

50. This decision caused the first split in the Balcerowicz team. His first vice-minister, Marek Dąbrowski, resigned in defense of the hard line.

51. The question that is asked in surveys concerns the Solidarity trade union. But people probably tended to interpret this label more broadly during the first phase, before Solidarity's representation in the parliament broke into competing political parties in June 1990.

52. The data on confidence are based on CBOS but, except for the army, are supplemented by data from OBOP. The correlations between CBOS and OBOP results are in the range of 0.95 for all institutions except the army. Hence, I regressed CBOS on OBOP results and used regression to fill in some missing CBOS data. The army results are exclusively from CBOS.

53. The regression results with INFL ($N = 16$) are

$$\text{GOVT} = 78.4 - 3.54 \text{ UN} + 0.095 \text{ INFL}; \quad R^2 = 0.91, \text{ DW} = 1.48$$
$$(0.00) \quad (0.00) \quad (0.02)$$

$$\text{SEJM} = 73.8 - 9.58 \text{ UN} + 0.018 \text{ INFL}; \quad R^2 = 0.85, \text{ DW} = 1.67$$
$$(0.00) \quad (0.00) \quad (0.18)$$

$$\text{ARMY} = 35.9 + 2.24 \text{ UN} + 0.06 \text{ INFL}; \quad R^2 = 0.62, \text{ DW} = 2.30$$
$$(0.00) \quad (0.00) \quad (0.31)$$

Results with RWAGE are almost identical, and the sign of RWAGE is negative. AR1 does not change the significance levels of coefficients on UN, and it lowers the significance of other variables somewhat.

54. Confidence in the Senate and in the Sejm are almost perfectly correlated. Hence, I speak only about the Sejm, which alone has legislative powers. At the same time, the finding that confidence in these two chambers is so highly correlated and has the same determinants implies that the reason confidence in the Sejm declined is not that, unlike the Senate, it was only in part competitively elected and housed remnants of the communist nomenclatura.

55. When questioned in the Sejm about the divergence of his program from the Magdalenka agreements, Balcerowicz observed that both the political and economic situations had changed, the latter through the appearance of hyperinflation. Given hyperinflation, wage indexation could not be continued, he argued (*Życie Warszawy,* 18 December 1990).

56. This message has not always been popular with Mazowiecki, who argued in another interview (*Libération,* 28 May 1990), "We need to accelerate all the reforms but also to avoid those that could destabilize the situation and jeopardize the future of economic reforms. I think that the greatest danger for a country that just came out from the spiral of inflation would be to fall into a spiral of chaos. . . . I have enormous respect for the patience of society, but rulers should never forget that patience has limits." As the presidential campaign developed, Mazowiecki and his supporters did belatedly emphasize the importance of institutions.

57. Economic variables explain more variance of confidence in the government than in the Sejm. The largest positive residual for the Sejm was 29.4; the largest negative residual, 20.6. The largest positive residual for the government was 3.8; the largest negative residual, 7.5.

58. Solidarity emerged as a broad movement in September of 1980 to a large extent because it was the only mass organization the communist government tolerated. It became a general umbrella for the opposition to the communist regime during the 1980s. After April 1989 the Solidarity trade union gradually separated itself from the general Solidarity movement.
59. I could not find systematic strike data on a monthly basis. The average number seems to have been about one new strike per day; on one day there were 150 strikes going on (*Gazeta Wyborcza,* various issues).
60. For example, Andrzej Wróblewski, the editor of *Gazeta Bankowa,* observed in a Reuter (27 November 1990) interview, "Balcerowicz's policy has been rejected, that's a fact."

    Surveys showed that people supporting the Balcerowicz Plan tended to opt for Mazowiecki. Among the opponents of the plan, preferences were more divided: 23 percent said in July that they would vote for Wałęsa; 16 percent, for Mazowiecki; and 25 percent, not at all.
61. The idea of distinguishing intertemporal risk aversion from pure time preferences is due to Kreps and Porteus (1978). Alternative interpretations of the dynamics of public opinion toward reforms are discussed by Przeworski (1991: ch. 4).

References

Asselain, Jean-Charles. 1985. *Planning and Profits in a Socialist Economy.* Oxford: Blackwell Publisher.

Balcerowicz, Leszek. 1989. "Polish Economic Reforms, 1981–1988." In *Economic Reforms in the European Centrally Planned Economies.* Economic Commission for Europe, Economic Studies no. 1. New York: United Nations.

Bardhan, Pranab. 1990. "Risk-taking, Capital Markets, and Market Socialism." East–South System Transformations Working Paper no. 5. University of Chicago.

Beksiak, Janusz. 1989. "Role and Functioning of the Enterprise in Poland." In *Economic Reforms in the European Centrally Planned Economies.* Economic Commission for Europe, Economic Studies no. 1. New York: United Nations.

Blades, Derek. 1991. "The Statistical Revolution in Central and Eastern Europe." *OECD Observer,* no. 170 (June–July).

Blanchard, Oliver, Dornbusch, Rüdiger, Krugman, Paul, Layard, Richard, and Summers, Lawrence. 1991. *Economic Reform in the East.* Cambridge, Mass.: MIT Press.

Buchner-Jeziorska, Anna. 1990. "Psycho-social Barriers to Transformation of the Polish Economy." Manuscript, Institute of Sociology, University of Łodź.

Chilosi, Alberto. 1991. "L'economia polacca tra stabilizzazione e trasformazione istituzionale." Manuscript, Istituto di Economia e Finanza, Pisa.

Dąbrowski, Janusz M., Federowicz, Michał, and Levitas, Anthony. 1990. "Stabilization and State Enterprise Adjustment: The Political Economy of State Firms after Five Months of Fiscal Discipline, Poland 1990." Program on Central and Eastern Europe Working Paper no. 6, Minda de Gunzbrug Center for European Studies, Harvard University.

Domarańczyk, Zbigniew. 1990. *100 dni Mazowieckiego*. Warsaw: Wydawnictwo Andrzej Bonarski.

Elster, Jon. 1990. "Introduction." In Jon Elster and Karl Ove Moene (eds.) *Alternatives to Capitalism*, pp. 1–38. Cambridge: Cambridge University Press.

Frydman, Roman, and Rapaczynski, Andrzej. 1990. "Markets and Institutions in Large Scale Privatizations." Manuscript, Columbia University.

Kolarska-Bobińska, Lena. 1989. "Poczucie niesprawiedliwosci, konfliktu i preferowany lad w gospodarce." In *Polacy 88*, pp. 81–159. Warsaw: CPBP.

1991. "Preferowany lad gospodarczy i opoje polityczno-ekonomiczne: poczatek okresu transformacji." In *Polacy 90*, in press.

Kołodko, Grzegorz W. 1991. "Polish Hyperinflation and Stabilization 1989–1990." Working paper, IRSES. Paris.

Kreps, David M., and Porteus, Evan L. 1978. "Temporal Resolution of Uncertainty and Dynamic Choice Theory." *Econometrica* 46: 185–200.

Lipschitz, Leslie, and McDonald, Donogh (eds.). 1990. *German Unification: Economic Issues*. Occasional Papers, no. 75. Washington, D.C.: IMF.

Lipton, David, and Sachs, Jeffrey. 1990. "Creating a Market Economy in Eastern Europe: The Case of Poland." *Brookings Papers on Economic Activity*, pp. 75–145.

Maravall, José María. 1981. *La política de la transición, 1975–1980*. Madrid: Taurus.

Marer, Paul. 1991. "The Transition to a Market Economy in Central and Eastern Europe." *OECD Observer*, no. 169 (April–May).

McDonald, Donogh, and Thumann, Gunther. 1990. "East Germany: The New *Wirtschaftswunder?*" In Lipschitz and McDonald (eds.) 1990.

Mokrzycki, Edmund. 1990. "Dziedzictwo realnego socjalizmu, interesy grupowe i poszukiwanie nowej utopii." Manuscript, Instytut Filozofii i Socjologii PAN, Warsaw.

Mujzel, Jan. 1989. "Aims of Economic Policy and Their Implementation in Poland." In *Economic Reforms in the European Centrally Planned Economies*. Economic Commission for Europe, Economic Studies no. 1. New York: United Nations.

Nelson, Joan M. 1984. "The Politics of Stabilization." In R. E. Feinberg and V. Kallab (eds.), *Adjustment Crisis in the Third World*. New Burnswick, N.J.: Transaction.

OECD (Organization for Economic Cooperation and Development). 1990. "Transition from the Command to Market Economy." Manuscript summary of a meeting held at the Vienna Institute for Comparative Economic Studies. Paris: OECD.

Porozumienia Okrągłego Stołu. 1989. Warsaw: NSSZ Solidarność.

Przeworski, Adam. 1991. *Democracy and the Market: Political and Economic Reforms in Eastern Europe and Latin America*. Cambridge: Cambridge University Press.

Rychard, Andrzej. 1991a. "Politics and Society after the Breakthrough: The Source and Threats to Political Legitimacy in Post-Communist Poland." In G. Sanford (ed.) *Democratization in Poland*. London: Macmillan.

1991b. "Limits to the Economic Changes in the Post-Communist Poland: Sociological Analysis." In S. Gomulka and C. Lin (eds.), *Limits to the Economic Transformation in the Post-Soviet Systems*. Oxford: Oxford University Press.

Rychard, Andrzej, and Sulek, Antoni (eds.). 1988. *Legitymacja: Klasyczne teorie i polskie doświadczenia*. Warsaw: Polskie Towarzystwo Socjologiczne.

Sadowski, Zdzisław, Iwanek, Maciej, and Najdek, Jozef. 1990. "An Overview of the Process of Change in Poland." Paper presented at Conference on East European Reforms towards Market Economy and the OECD, Vienna, 14–16 March.

Słupiński, Zbigniew M. 1990. "Poland: Law on Privatization of State-Owned Enterprises." Manuscript.

Staniszkis, Jadwiga. 1984. *Poland's Self-Limiting Revolution*. Princeton, N.J.: Princeton University Press.

Stark, David. 1990. "Privatization in Hungary: From Plan to Market or from Plan to Clan?" *Eastern European Politics and Societies* 4: 351–93.

Tarkowski, Jacek. 1989. "Old and New Patterns of Corruption in Poland and the USSR." *Telos* 80: 51–63.

Vanhanen, Tatu. 1990. *The Process of Democratization: A Comparative Study of 147 States, 1980–1988*. New York: Crane, Russak.

World Bank. 1990. *Poland: Economic Management for a New Era*. Washington, D.C.: World Bank.

Conclusions

Recipes for disaster seem quite clear. In recent years, whenever governments have pursued expansionist economic programs, the result has been inflation, a fiscal crisis, and a balance-of-payments crisis. Whenever democratic governments followed neo-liberal tenets, the outcome has been stagnation, increased poverty, political discontent, and the debilitation of democracy. Peru under Alan García, Portugal during the first phase, and Greece under PASOK, as well as France during the first two years of socialist rule, provide evidence that a combination of economic stimulation with fiscal indiscipline generates economic crisis in the highly internationalized contemporary world. Argentina and Brazil, where several attempts at stabilization failed, but also Poland and Bolivia, where stabilization was successful, show that pursuit of the elusive criterion "efficiency" can be counterproductive politically and even economically.

The traditional posture that rejects all attempts to stabilize, deregulate, and open up the economy because of the social costs inherent in such programs is untenable once an overprotected, overregulated, oligopolistic economy enters the spiral of fiscal crisis. Procrastination, socially more tolerable and politically safer, can only aggravate the crisis and prolong the deprivation. In turn, programs based on the promise of immediate improvement end in disaster.

Yet there is ample evidence that pursuit of the neo-liberal ideological blueprint fares no better. When stability and efficiency become goals in themselves, government policies under democratic conditions turn out to be economically either ineffective or counterproductive and politically explosive. Stabilization attempts either fail or induce recessions so profound that they depress investment, undermine the prospects of future growth, and generate social costs that make the continuation of reforms politically unpalatable under democratic conditions. Moreover, the technocratic style in which these policies are often formulated and implemented tends to undermine the consolidation of democratic institutions.

Hence, perhaps paradoxically, our conclusions add up to a case for left-wing governments to pursue a market-oriented program: a pragmatic and "social democratic" approach. But the recipe for success is, unfortunately, less clear, because there have been few successful experiments.

If success means resuming growth under democratic conditions, the evidence for successful recipes turns out to be much thinner than for disasters. The case that established at least the possibility of success as we define it is Spain, which underwent a painful period of industrial reconversion and irreversibly consolidated democratic institutions. This experience is paralleled by Portugal after 1983 and perhaps by Uruguay, to which we have paid insufficient attention. Chile is growing under democratic conditions, but the reform process, undertaken by an exceptionally repressive military regime, was long, and its economic and social costs were enormous. South Korea underwent successful stabilization in 1981 with some slowdown in growth, but it has been growing at a relatively rapid pace since (and had been before). Mexico, with its peculiar political regime, has been more attentive to social costs and may be on the brink of resumed growth, though not yet under democratic institutions. Finally, among the Eastern European countries, Hungary, which decided to proceed prudently, building market institutions and a social welfare system before plunging into the liberalization stage, may show success. But these cases are so varied that it is not easy to determine to what extent their success has been due to policies and to what extent to circumstances. Spain did not face the need to stabilize, and the rates of inflation in Portugal, South Korea, Mexico, and Hungary have been quite moderate by the standards of Argentina, Bolivia, Brazil, Poland, or Yugoslavia. Foreign debt was an overriding consideration in the cases of Argentina, Bolivia, Brazil, Mexico, Hungary, Poland, and Yugoslavia but not in Southern Europe. And the scope of reforms differed from country to country, measures aimed at stabilization, liberalization, and industrial reconversion having been combined differently.

Hence, we do not pretend to have established the conditions for success; there is just not enough historical experience to permit a solid empirical evaluation of the approach we propose.[1] Let us summarize and evaluate the evidence with regard to our three main hypotheses: (1) that stabilization and liberalization are not sufficient to generate growth unless reforms are targeted to redress the fiscal crisis and to generate public savings, (2) that without a social policy that protects at least those whose subsistence is threatened by the reforms, the political conditions for the continuation of reforms become eroded, and (3) that the technocratic style of policy making weakens nascent democratic institutions.

Before we examine these hypotheses, a comment is required concerning stabilization policies. Bresser Pereira argues in his chapter that these policies often fail because they do not redress the "fundamentals" and also because they misdiagnose the causes of inflation and induce unnecessary social costs. This analysis is now widely shared. On the one hand, as Di Tella (1991: 397) emphasized, trying to stop inflation purely by controlling nominal quantities is absurd: Without first correcting fundamentals, which include above all the fiscal crisis of the state, heterodox policies simply postpone fiscal adjustment. On the other hand, inflation is often inertial. And, as Bruno (1991: 2) observes in the introduction to a volume entitled *Lessons of Economic Stabilization and Its Aftermath,* given the inertial character of inflation "the orthodox cure is necessary but not sufficient. The correction of fundamentals does not by itself remove inflationary inertia. . . . Supplementary direct intervention in the nominal process, such as a temporary freeze of wages, prices, and the exchange rate, can substantially reduce the initial cost of disinflation." Correcting the fundamentals includes restructuring the flows of government expenditures and revenues and reducing the stocks of foreign and domestic debt. Breaking the spiral of inflation calls for policies targeted at nominal quantities, including policies dealing with incomes. Without correcting the fundamentals, stabilization policies are likely to be ineffective; without heterodox policies, they will be also inefficient: Relying exclusively on reduced demand to break inflation engenders unnecessarily high social costs.

To examine the effect of market-oriented reforms on growth, we need to distinguish three questions: (1) Why do stabilization and liberalization (of foreign trade and domestic competition) induce recessions? (2) Why do some stabilization programs undermine future growth? (3) Are stability and efficiency sufficient for a resumption of growth?

Stabilization programs tend to induce profound recessions even when they are not accompanied by liberalization. The reason is at least twofold: (1) Stabilization is usually achieved by reducing demand, and (2) interest rates tend to soar beyond the targeted level during stabilization. The mechanism that leads to excessive interest rates depends on the anchor being used (Blanchard, Dornbusch, Krugman, Layard, and Summers 1991), but one common effect is that successful stabilization makes holding money more attractive, and the increased demand for money cannot be met by increasing the money supply without rekindling inflation. In turn, reducing price subsidies and subsidies to industries, reducing import tariffs, and taking domestic anti-monopoly measures sharply lower rates of return and cause unemployment of capital and labor (Przeworski 1991: ch. 4). Among the cases of successful stabilization,[2] unemployment increased sharply in Bolivia after 1985;[3] it climbed from 9.7 percent in 1974 to 16.8 percent in 1976 in Chile, from 5.1 percent in 1984 to 7.1 percent in 1986 in Israel, and from zero in 1989 to over 10 percent in 1991 in Poland. In South Korea, the rate of utilization of capacity fell from 77.5 percent in 1980 to 69.4 percent in 1983.

High interest rates may be transitory, but their effect lasts beyond the stabilization period. As Fischer (1991: 404–5) pointed out, "Investment will not resume until real interest rates reach a reasonable level, and prolonged periods of high real interest rates create financial crises and bankruptcies even for firms that would be viable at reasonable levels of interest rate." Or, in Frenkel's (1991: 403) words, "stabilization efforts are often associated with extremely high real rates of interest, which discourage investment and hamper growth." Indeed, to consider again the cases of successful stabilization, in Bolivia private investment declined from the already minuscule level of 3.8 percent of GDP in 1984 to 2.7 percent in 1985 and 2.5 percent four years later; in Chile, it fell from 8.7 percent of GDP in 1974 to 3.9 percent in 1975, and it surpassed the prestabilization level only three years later; in Israel, gross investment (private and public) fell by 10.6 percent in 1985, recuperated a year later, and began to decline again by 1988. Only in Mexico did private investment continue to grow at a rapid pace throughout the stabilization period.

The second reason stabilization programs often undermine the prospects for future growth has been highlighted by Tanzi (1989): The expenditure cuts inherent in the attempt to cope with the fiscal crisis tend not to discriminate between government consumption and public investment. Indeed, investment projects are often politically easier to cut than government services or public employment. Both investment in the public infrastructure and measures to induce private investment are reduced, thus reducing future supply. The evidence from successful stabilization experiments is uniform: In Bolivia, public investment declined from 8.4 percent of GDP in 1984 to about 3.0 percent after 1985; in Chile, public investment fell from 12.5 percent of GDP in 1974 to 4.8 percent in 1983 and rose again to 7.1 percent by 1985;[4] in Mexico, public investment declined by 13.4 percent as early as 1987 and continued to decline afterward; in Eastern Europe, except in Hungary, public investment simply collapsed.

Neither the observation that stabilization entails a recession nor even that stabilization programs often undermine conditions for future growth is now controversial; indeed, the voices we have cited emanate from the World Bank and the IMF. Where we depart from the neo-liberal consensus is with regard to the point central in Bresser Pereira's analysis: when we argue that market-oriented reforms are not sufficient to generate conditions for growth.

Admittedly, the empirical evidence is inconclusive. In Bolivia overall GDP declined during the year following stabilization and then grew anemically, while per capita GDP continued to fall through 1990. In Chile GDP tumbled by 12.9 percent in 1975; growth resumed until the great crash of 1982, when it fell by 14.1 percent, and growth resumed again after 1985. In Israel GDP (business sector only) actually grew during stabilization but became stagnant three years later. In Mexico signs of recovery are evident, but per capita growth continues to be anemic. In South Korea growth slowed down but continued to be high by comparative standards. And all over Eastern Europe GDP continues to decline. Systematic reviews of evidence generate mixed conclusions. Williamson (1990: 406) showed that among ten Latin American countries that had pursued "full or partial" reform, four were growing in 1988–9 and six were stagnant or declining; among eleven countries that did not pursue reforms or undertook them only recently, one was growing and ten were stagnant or declining – a positive but not an overwhelming correlation. Blanchard et al. (1991: 61) reported that "looking at the post-stabilization performance of countries that have stabilized, one concludes that in most cases, economic growth has returned only gradually and unimpressively." Scattered data concerning private consumption show the same thing. Clearly, these patterns lend themselves to differing assessments, particularly when they are juxtaposed to the experience of countries that continue to suffer from a fiscal crisis and high rates of inflation. Yet the issue here is not whether countries that underwent successful stabilization perform better or worse than countries where stabilization attempts have failed. The question is whether or not a successful stabilization, when combined with other market-oriented reforms, is sufficient to generate growth. And since the experiments are continuing, one can always argue that one day it will be.

Given the paucity of evidence, it is useful to review theoretical arguments. The neo-liberal assumption that underlies the program of market-oriented reforms is that once stability and efficiency are achieved, growth will follow. Yet, perhaps surprisingly, this neo-liberal posture has shaky foundations even in neo-classical economic theory.

Neo-classical economic theory has little to say about growth. Its preoccupations are mainly static. And anyone who has read Schumpeter knows that static efficiency is a poor criterion of welfare. Indeed, several studies show that the Soviet economy was in the static sense more efficient than that of the United States: It was more efficient precisely because it generated little technical innovation. Dynamic economies are not efficient in the static sense: They use a number of techniques, with different cost–benefit ratios. In turn, the issue of whether or not a competitive market generates dynamic efficiency is already more complex. The theory of economic growth that emerged from neo-classical economics, the Solow–Swan model of exogenous growth, argued that competitive equilibrium is efficient but leads to stagnation of income in the absence of exogenous population growth and exogenous technical change. Recent models do provide an endogenous explanation of economic growth, but in these theories the competitive equilibrium is no longer efficient (Lucas 1988; Barro 1990; Becker, Murphy, and Tamura 1990; Romer 1990).[5] Some state intervention, including public investment, is optimal for growth. Barro (1990) shows that the present utility of future consumption or – equivalently under a Cobb–Douglas production function – the rate of growth is maximized when the share of the public productive sector in the output equals the marginal elasticity of public capital.[6] Findlay (1990) presents a similar result with regard to public employment.[7]

We need not get mired in the discussion of neo-classical economics to conclude that the present state of this theory does not support the conclusion that stability and competition are sufficient to generate growth. Whether one takes the theory of incomplete markets, with their informational asymmetries, or the theory of endogenous growth, with constant returns to a single factor and dynamic externalities, or the theory of non-Walrasian trade, one will discover (still neo-classical) arguments that state intervention is necessary for growth. True, these theories do not justify a blanket advocacy of state intervention; they are measured in their assessment of the appropriate role of the state, and they are specific in their recommendations (Grossman 1990). Moreover, they raise a fundamental institutional question: how to organize the state institutions so that they will intervene when appropriate and not intervene when not. Yet all these theories see the role of the state in generating economic growth as essential. The neo-liberal posture does not rest on any solid theoretical basis: To cite Stiglitz (1991: 12), ''Adam Smith's invisible hand may be more like the Emperor's new clothes: invisible because it is not there.''

Hence, in spite of the paucity of recent evidence, we consider that our first point is well supported: Stability and efficiency are not sufficient for growth.

Yet even if stabilization–liberalization programs are designed with a view to resumed growth, and even if the state adopts an appropriate development strategy, the period between stabilization and the resumption of growth is inevitably long. Edwards and Edwards (1991: 219) estimate eight to ten years as the lag to be expected. In the meantime, per capita consumption will decline or stagnate, and some incomes will be pushed below the threshold of absolute poverty. Hence, the question is whether or not such reforms will be continued as a verdict of the democratic process.

Our evidence is extremely limited. We have one case, Spain, where social expenditures were considerably extended as industrial reconversion proceeded; one, Poland, where they were drastically cut as the country simultaneously undertook stabilization and liberalization; and some intermediate ones, notably Bolivia, which developed, with foreign assistance, a narrowly targeted program of employment for the miners who lost jobs as a result of closing the mines, and Mexico, which developed a program of supporting the food expenditures of the groups most adversely affected by the stabilization. The distinctive features of Spain are that social policy was broad in scope – it comprised health, education, and income maintenance, and it entailed qualitative changes in the systems of self-government and delivery – and that this policy was accompanied by active intervention in the labor market. Poland provides the clearest contrast: The preexisting system of social services disintegrated, social expenditures were drastically reduced, survival was left principally to charity, and labor policy was limited to compensation. The political effect was that in Spain the Socialist Party, which led the reform process, was able to win three consecutive elections, and in Bolivia parties supporting the continuation of reforms won a majority in the 1989 presidential elections, whereas in Poland parties advocating that reforms be continued won about 20 percent of the vote in the parliamentary elections of October 1991. Yet since the initial conditions and the challenges facing these three countries were quite different, it is hard to treat even these cases as paired comparisons.

Spanish social policy was sufficiently extensive to be conceptualized by the government and perceived by the population as progressing toward "social citizenship": a guarantee of reasonably adequate and equal welfare protection for all members of the political community. This policy was financed by a significant increase in fiscal revenues, originating in progressive taxation and distributed through a decentralized system of regional self-government. As Maravall demonstrates, this experience of social citizenship was distinctly tied in Spain to the consolidation of political democracy: In spite of widespread unemployment, people there have learned that political democracy brings social rights. As a result, one striking feature of Spanish public-opinion data is the gradual dissociation between evaluations of the economic situation and of political institutions.

Such a broad social policy as Spain's may be infeasible in countries where the fiscal crisis is acute. In spite of the fact that welfare services in these countries are already far from sufficient, they may have to be reduced selectively. But from the purely economic point of view, such reductions will again undermine the capacity to grow. A central lesson of endogenous growth theories – and, indeed, one of the few robust statistical findings concerning the determinants of growth – is the importance of education, whether measured in terms of school enrollment rates or such stock indexes as the literacy rate (Meyer, Hannan, Rubinson, and Thomas 1979; Marsh 1988; Barro 1989; Levine and Renelt 1991; Persson and Tabellini 1991). Primary education for women has a particularly high return in terms of per capita growth (World Bank 1991). And while no similar statistical studies seem to be available with regard to health expenditures, the 1991 *World Development Report* (ibid., pp. 53–5) cites extensive evidence about the productivity-increasing effects of health programs. Hence, stabilizations that occur at the cost of reducing expenditures on education and health are likely to be counterproductive with regard to growth.[8]

Short of guaranteeing social citizenship to everyone regardless of his or her status in the labor market, there are three ways to secure basic incomes. One is to maintain full employment, another is to assure everyone of a minimum income, and the last is to insure against unemployment. Command economies rely on the first method; market economies, on various combinations of the three, often with incomplete coverage. The net of welfare services has always been rudimentary and fragmentary in the less developed market economies, and it disintegrated altogether, along with central planning, in the command economies.

Economic reforms cause unemployment – a new phenomenon for the command economies and an increasingly widespread one where markets had previously allocated jobs. When unemployment rises, basic income protection becomes the paramount concern of segments of the population several times larger than the segment of those actually unemployed at any particular moment. Active labor and income-insurance policies are thus to some extent substitutes, for without a net of social protection and without income insurance, loss of employment means loss of livelihood. This is a cost no one can tolerate even in the short run.

In the face of mounting unemployment, an active labor policy is thus essential to reduce not only the economic but also the social costs of reforms. The neo-liberal posture is based on the assumption that once the economy is deregulated and privatized and thereby the conditions for competition are created, markets will emerge and their operation will cause resources to be reallocated across sectors and activities. But, first, markets do not "emerge" out of competition; they must be created by policy. Even if unemployment is only frictional or structural, an elaborate and costly system of institutions is required to orient the newly unemployed to new opportunities.[9] Without a well-functioning labor market, resources will not be reallocated across sectors. Second, even when the basic markets are present, the reallocation of resources that is needed to make some economies efficient may be just too massive to take place without the extensive involvement of the state. To take just one case, albeit extreme, if agriculture in Poland is to become as efficient as it is in Western Europe, the number of persons dependent on agriculture will have to be reduced by at least seven million – about 20 percent of the population. A transformation of this magnitude cannot take place overnight, and all the OECD countries massively support agriculture to avoid the social and political effects of the dislocation that exposing this sector to competition would entail.

To the extent that widespread unemployment persists for extended periods, some people find themselves without a livelihood, and many others live in constant fear.[10] And the people who experience or feel threatened by un-employment are most likely to oppose reforms. If their livelihood is not protected, at the least by narrowly targeted income-insurance policies, their resistance may assume explosive forms.

Admittedly, our evidence that the absence of social protection, whether in the form of broad social policy or targeted income insurance schemes, be-comes transformed into an effective political opposition against reforms is again very thin; it relies on the juxtaposition of Spain and Poland.[11] Yet the Polish case – the only country where we were able to study political dynamics at the micro level – seems most suggestive. In Poland unemployment turned people against reforms and overwhelmed all the beneficial effects about which they had been convinced.[12] If market-oriented reforms fail in Poland for political reasons – and this possibility is real – it will be because unemployment was introduced without a net of social protection. But we are aware that the causal chain that leads from individual discontent to organized reaction and from organized reaction to the abandonment of reforms is contingent and complex. Reforms may well continue against popular resistance, even under democratic institutions.

This point brings us to our third and final hypothesis: that a technocratic policy style weakens nascent democratic institutions.

Reforms – in fact, policy in general – can be developed and implemented in four distinct styles:

1. Convinced that immediate reform is needed, persuaded of the technical soundness of the economic blueprint, and equipped with decree powers, the executive may force reform measures on the society. This so-called *decretism* is so widespread that it seems almost inherent in the neo-liberal approach: An overwhelming proportion of legal acts concerning the economy in Argentina, Brazil, and Peru consist of presidential decrees. The decrees need not and often do not correspond to programs advocated by the victorious candidates in election campaigns; from Paz Estenssoro in Bolivia to Fujimori in Peru, recent years have witnessed several cases where victorious candidates embraced the content and style of reforms against which they had campaigned vigorously.

2. When the executive has no decree powers but enjoys a majority in the legislature, the same technocratic style appears as *mandatism*. As Margaret Thatcher often observed, she had told the people what she would do if elected; they voted for her, and she had a mandate to do what she thought appropriate. People would have a chance at the next election to decide whether or not that was what they wanted. This style is still technocratic, since beyond the electoral campaign it entails no consultation with opposing political forces in the parliament and no concertation with forces outside it, either at the stage of policy formulation or of implementation.

3. *Parliamentarism* is the policy style that can result either from a deliberate decision by the majority to consult and negotiate with opposing forces in the legislature or, frequently, from the fact that systems of proportional representation fail to generate majorities, making coalitions and compromises inevitable. While the government enjoys some autonomy, it consults and negotiates at various steps along the way, making public the policy options and the conflicting views. Political support is thus organized as policies are formulated and implemented; indeed, when no party has a majority, policies can be pursued only if the approval of some coalition is obtained.

4. Finally, *corporatism* – or perhaps better, *concertation* – is a policy style that extends consultation and negotiation beyond the parliamentary actors to unions, employers' associations, or other interest groups.

Our hypothesis is that policy styles matter. One should, however, distinguish three considerations.

First, consultation and concertation may serve to improve the technical quality of reform programs. We realize that this is an unorthodox view; the usual argument is that having to negotiate the economic program undermines its logical coherence. But this argument assumes that the program is coherent and free from mistakes to begin with, and we have already seen that this is a questionable assumption. Neither the logical consistency of any particular reform strategy nor the design of specific measures is obvious even to professional economists, and in fact when decisions are hidden from public scrutiny, many important ones are made in a haphazard way.[13] Moreover, professional economists advise opposition political parties and even unions; their voices can serve to warn of impending mistakes. We believe that the Hungarian reform strategy, which prepared for the social costs before they were incurred, is more likely to succeed than the Polish one, which did not, and the reason Hungarians opted for this strategy was that politicians and economists, within and outside the government, disagreed about the appropriate sequence and pace of reforms.

Second, discussion and negotiation may serve to build political bases of support for the particular reform strategy. If the program is forged in negotiations with diverse political forces, it will emerge in a form that will be easier for these forces to support. Such a program may retard the pace of reforms and may eliminate the element of surprise necessary for some stabilization measures, such as freezes, price deregulations, or capital levies. Yet, to argue one more time against prevailing opinion, such a program may be more, not less, credible, because it creates the political conditions for the continuation of reforms. Contrary to frequent announcements by technocrats that they will proceed regardless of the political pressures upon them, decrees are often simply ineffective precisely because economic agents suspect that the particular policies are politically unsustainable.

Finally, if one cares about democracy, one must take the political criterion as autonomous. But why is the policy style particularly important for the new, as distinct from established, democracies?[14] Regardless of their age, democracies persist whenever all the major political forces find that they can improve their situation if they channel their demands and their conflicts within the democratic institutions. The reason new democracies are more vulnerable is that institutional issues often remain unresolved for a long period after a particular democratic system has been installed (Przeworski 1991: ch. 2). Since the choice of institutions is often problematic and conflictual when a dictatorship falls, often the conflict about the institutional framework remains open (Poland), or some institutions are adopted as just an interim solution. To set an institutional framework in place, sometimes a previous democratic constitution is reinstated even if it did not work in the past (Argentina), a foreign constitution is copied, or a constitution is elaborated that is expected in advance not to evoke compliance (Brazil). These institutional frameworks are frequently inappropriate to the specific political and economic conditions. Moreover, as Hardin (1987) has argued, habituation plays an important role in inducing political actors to stay within the existing institutional framework: Constitutions are often "contracts by convention."

Policy styles matter because they have the effect of channeling political conflicts and of teaching political actors where the real locus of power is. The Polish experience is eloquent. Most decisions were made outside the framework of representative institutions, and people quickly learned that this is how they were being made. Repeated surveys showed that people did not see the locus of power in the properly constituted institutions. Consultation and negotiation among representative organizations within the framework of representative institutions are necessary to channel political conflicts. If decisions are made elsewhere, representative institutions wilt. They do not necessarily crumble; experience thus far demonstrates that regular elections can take place and civil rights can be observed even in systems in which the executive, suspended above the representative organizations and unchecked by other branches of the government, makes repeated recourse to decrees. But anyone concerned with the quality of democracy will see such a political system as greatly impoverished. And, again, the experiment is not yet over; the question remains open whether or not democratic institutions can survive when decrees announce miracles that fail and are followed by demands for further sacrifices.

Hence, we find that subjecting the reform strategy to the competitive interplay of political forces is superior on the three essential grounds: It improves policy, it builds support for the continuation of reforms, and it helps consolidate democratic institutions. We do not see a trade-off between public discussion and the soundness of economic plans. Yet our advocacy of this policy style must be tempered in several important ways.

First, even if a government is eager to consult and negotiate, it is by no means a given that it will find willing partners. The dominant strategy of the opposition may be to let the government make its mistakes so that it will become unpopular and lose elections. Sharing the responsibility for a socially costly program as a minor partner may turn out to be politically costly. The Portuguese Social Democrats were willing to bet on this strategy and experienced spectacular electoral success as a result, but the Peronist Party and unions in Argentina repeatedly rejected overtures from the Radical government. Moreover, excessive consensus is also threatening to democracy. Some political forces should monitor the government from an adversary position; it is essential for some political parties, motivated by the desire to win elections, to monitor the government's performance.

Second, since the combination of left-wing partisan control and institutionalized concertation with unions and employers' associations is generally found to generate superior economic performance in OECD countries, the question emerges whether this policy style would not also be more successful in the case of new democracies. But this question is largely irrelevant, since the organizational preconditions for this policy style are absent in the countries we have been considering. Having reviewed union membership in eighteen newly democratic countries, Grassi (1991) found that the largest degree of unionization among them was about 35 percent and that union density was positively related to wage militancy. Lechner (1985) and Przeworski (1991) discussed other reasons why concertation with extraparliamentary actors is not a feasible option in the less developed countries. Indeed, since in many new democracies employers' associations enjoy disproportionate political influence through informal channels, and since they tend to oppose vigorously some essential elements of reform – notably trade liberalization and tax increases – concertation may result in undermining reforms.

Another way to pose the issue of policy style is to ask whether a "strong" or a "weak" government is more likely to be successful in seeing reforms to the end. These are, however, ambiguous terms. Some governments that appear strong because they issue decrees without previously building political bases of support end up simply ineffective; the experience of Collor de Melo is the prime example. In turn, minority governments, forced to build coalitions before they can launch reform programs, may turn out to be highly successful; witness the Socialist–Social Democratic government in Portugal. To make these terms more precise, we must distinguish between constitutional constraints that bind all governments and the conjunctural outcomes of elections that determine the majority or minority status of particular holders of office. A government may be weak in the sense of not being constitutionally enabled to make some decisions (because it must go through the legislative process, because legislation is subject to judicial review, or because some decisions are reserved for autonomous institutions, such as the central bank), or the government may be weak politically, incapable of legislating without first persuading its own party or without building a coalition of several parties.

We have in fact argued in favor of institutional structures that compel governments to discuss and negotiate when formulating and implementing policies. We see decree power as ineffectual economically and dangerous politically, and we see both political and institutional constraints as tempering technocratic proclivities. Yet, as Maravall demonstrates, policy styles are not uniquely determined by the strength of the particular government, and, again given the paucity of successful cases, the empirical evidence appears inconclusive. Moreover, we do not question the fact that governments cannot spend all their time consulting and negotiating; they must have the power to govern.[15] Nor do we underestimate the danger of self-serving, narrowly based opposition to reforms. Several sectors of society, notably firms that enjoy oligopolistic rents, the bourgeoisie that resists fiscal pressure, employees in the public sector, low-skill workers in the private sector, various groups that traditionally enjoyed entrenched privileges, and, in Eastern Europe, peasants, may see their interests hurt as a result of reforms. Separately or in (often strange) alliances they resist reforms. Yet the idea that this resistance can be beaten to the punch, that reforms can be conducted so swiftly that these groups will not have time to organize and make their voices heard, that the program must be concluded before "political fatigue" sets in – this technocratic posture is infeasible, counterproductive with regard to the prospect of continued reform, and risky for democracy.

Indeed, a central reason why the opposition to reforms often assumes the form of defending short-term particular interests is that these reforms are not a product of political interplay among representative organizations on the terrain of the representative institutions. Proponents of reforms should not fear democratic institutions. Their fear is largely unfounded: While we still understand little about the microfoundations of individual postures on reform programs, there is overwhelming evidence that such programs enjoy widespread support when they are launched even if it is known that they will induce hardship. The Balcerowicz Plan in Poland, Collar Plan I in Brazil, the Cavallo Plan in Argentina, and even the Fujimori program in Peru enjoyed overwhelming support in public-opinion polls. If the representative system were allowed to process conflicts about reform, it is most likely that only reasonable differences of opinion and responsible conflicts of interest would emerge – not a threat to the idea of reform as such but only to the specific blueprint. By stifling public discussion, the specter of populist reaction serves mainly to defend particular groups of technocrats against alternative conceptions and competing teams.

With all the caveats due to the paucity of evidence, we are ready to summarize our analysis in a more prescriptive fashion, as a strategy. We support reforms aimed at stabilization, principally reduction of the fiscal crisis with all its attendant consequences, because we see such reforms as inevitable once an economy enters an inflationary spiral. Moreover, we believe that increased reliance on markets, national and international, to allocate resources is necessary to enhance efficiency in economies that are monopolistic, over-regulated, and overprotected.[16] We do not believe that such reforms can be pursued without a temporary decline in consumption, a rise in unemployment, or other social costs. Yet we have been critical of the standard neo-liberal recipes, since we believe that they are faulty in three fundamental ways: They induce economic stagnation, they incur unnecessarily large social costs, and they weaken nascent democratic institutions. This is why we seek to offer an alternative, social democratic, approach to market-oriented reforms.

This approach consists of three recommendations. First, a social policy must be elaborated and put in place before stabilization or liberalization is launched. Second, the entire reform package must be efficient in the sense of minimizing social costs and must be designed with a view to resumed growth. Finally, reform programs should be formulated and implemented as a result of a political interplay of representative organizations within the framework of the representative institutions.

A social policy designed to protect everyone from the most dire effects must be an intrinsic part of any reform strategy that seeks continued political support under democratic conditions. Spain underwent a decade of unemployment hovering around 16 percent and approaching 22 percent in 1985 while the government repeatedly won elections, thanks to broad political support that was to some extent due to the absence of credible political alternatives but was largely due to a considerable expansion of social policies: Social expenditure increased from 9.9 percent of GDP in 1975 to 17.8 percent in 1989. This expansion of social expenditures reduced the effects of reforms on the groups hurt most drastically by the process and convinced people that the extension of social citizenship was a credible promise of democracy.

Although the economic crisis in many countries is too acute to permit following the example of Spain in developing a universal welfare system, both labor institutions and income-protection schemes must be put in place as reforms that cause unemployment and reduce consumption are initiated. The institutions affecting labor must be appropriate to the distribution and duration of unemployment. In countries with a large informal sector, they must facilitate access to the formal labor market or to petty entrepreneurship. They must comprise an information system, perhaps a subsidized credit system to promote self-employment, and, where the housing market is thin, a relocation system. Income protection must be sufficient to cover basic needs and facilitate job search and retraining without creating incentives to remain idle.

The goal of economic reforms should be to recover the savings capacity of the state and to enable the state to pursue development-oriented policies.

The stabilization package must be highly attentive to effects on growth. It must therefore combine discriminating reductions of expenditure with measures designed to increase fiscal revenue. The expenditure cuts must discriminate between consumption and investment. In the spirit of Tanzi (1989), minimal public-investment targets should be exempt from cuts, and, following Blejer and Cheasty (1989), selective instruments that raise the rate of return on private investment should be preserved. Moreover, given overwhelming evidence about the productive role of education, educational expenditures and at least preventive health programs should be treated as intrinsic aspects of public investment.

To put it bluntly, stabilization should rely on a reduction of current consumption but not of investment, and this reduction should be targeted, via the tax system or a one-shot capital levy, on those who can afford it. This includes foreign creditors; in most countries, resumed growth is not feasible without a significant reduction of external as well as internal debt.

While public bureaucracies should be streamlined wherever they are bloated, and while public programs should be eliminated or reorganized when they are not efficient in delivering the most urgently needed services, the only way public saving can be mobilized is by increasing fiscal pressure through well-designed taxes – nota bene, a recent recommendation of the World Bank – and by reducing foreign debt payments. Tax reform that enforces compliance, broadens the income base, and significantly increases the effective rates of collection should be an intrinsic ingredient of the reform package. One reason is that tax reform will constitute evidence that the distribution of burdens is equitable, but the immediate economic purpose is to raise state revenues instead of cutting those expenditures that support future growth. We are unimpressed by arguments about the deadweight cost of taxation. Empirical evidence is at best mixed,[17] and the present tax rates in most new democracies are abominably low, much lower than in the OECD countries (Cheibub 1991). Most resistance to taxation reflects a problem of collective action on the part of the bourgeoisie: While there is evidence that a financially healthy state capable of pursuing consistent policies would induce higher rates of return to private investment, firms and their stockholders seek to escape their burden.[18] A recent study by the World Bank (1991: 82) shows that the rate of return to private investment projects rises from 10.7 percent when the fiscal deficit is greater than 8 percent of GDP to 14.3 percent when the deficit is less than 4 percent. Hence, there is room for a Pareto-improving increase of state revenues: The rate of private after-tax return can go up as the effective tax rate is raised. To cite Blejer and Cheasty (1989: 46), "A tax system which is uniform and predictable, and which is associated with prudent macroeconomic management, may make higher rates more acceptable than they would be in a tax system with many exemptions that is associated with a fiscal position perceived to be unsustainable in the longer run."[19]

The pace and substance of measures designed to enhance domestic and international competition is an issue on which we do not take a stand, in part because these decisions must result from the political process. Nevertheless, it is clear that the most rapid pace is not the optimal one economically or the most popular one politically.[20]

We have nothing original to say about the content of state intervention. It is generally recognized that the state should engage in infrastructural investment not supplied efficiently by private agents and that it should pursue measures that increase the rate of return to private projects. This role includes a selective industrial policy that would comprise preferential credit rates for high-technology industries, in which the market rate of return is much lower than the social rate; for projects that suffer from high costs of entry, substantial economies of scale, or steep learning curves; and projects that have potential spillovers across firms due to externalities and asymmetries of information between suppliers and buyers (Grossman 1990). The danger is real that the very capacity of the state to engage in productive activities and differentially to favor private projects will cause rent seeking. The question of how to organize state institutions so that they will engage in activities that are socially beneficial and abstain from responding to private interests remains central. Yet unless the state undertakes some investments directly and induces the private sector to undertake others, stabilization or liberalization will not lead to resumed growth.

Finally, reform programs must be processed through the representative institutions. We have argued that the democratic process can improve the technical quality of reform policies and furnish the basis for continued support for reform. Yet democracy is an autonomous value for which many people made sacrifices when they struggled against authoritarian regimes. The quality of the democratic process, perhaps less tangible than material welfare, affects the everyday life of individuals: It empowers them as members of a political community or deprives them of power. And if democracy is to be consolidated,

216 ECONOMIC REFORMS IN NEW DEMOCRACIES

that is, if all political forces are to learn to channel their demands and organize their conflicts within the framework of democratic institutions, these institutions must play a real role in shaping and implementing policies that influence living conditions.

Hence, our social democratic approach to market-oriented reforms calls for orienting reforms toward growth, protecting material welfare against the transitional costs of reforms, and making full use of democratic institutions in the formulation and implementation of reform policies. We realize that each of these recommendations involves costs. Industrial policies, social policies, and political compromises cost money,[21] and trade-offs are inevitable. We do not offer blueprints. The design of specific reform strategies must reflect local constraints, and the trade-offs must be determined by the democratic process. All we argue is that, to be successful, reforms must explicitly aim at growth, income security, and democracy.

Notes

1. Several already concluded or ongoing research projects seek to explain inductively the ''success'' of economic reforms. Clearly, the feasibility of such undertakings depends on the definition of the dependent variable. Remmer (1986) studied compliance with the targets set by IMF standby agreements in a sufficiently large sample to permit inductive inferences. But if the definition of the dependent variable is success seen as resumed growth, there is not enough historical experience to permit such inferences. Thus, for example, the debates about whether authoritarian or democratic regimes are more likely to undertake and persevere with reforms that engender growth are based on four cases of success – authoritarian Chile and South Korea, democratic Spain and Portugal – and innumerable cases of failure. This is why we did not try to set up a quasi-experimental research design: Controlled comparisons of case studies are not yet feasible if one takes growth under democracy as the *explenandum*.
2. Except for Eastern Europe and South Korea, all the data cited here are derived from articles in Bruno, Fischer, Helpman, Liviatan, and Meridor 1991. For Korea, see Rhee 1987. For Eastern Europe, see Przeworski's chapter above.
3. The exact figures are disputed; see Morales 1991.
4. Note that Edwards and Edwards (1991: 215) attribute the resumption of growth in Chile after 1985 to increased public investment.
5. The engine of growth in these models is nondecreasing returns to some accumulable factor of production – typically knowledge of some sort – plus externalities. If the returns to this factor can be captured by the market, there will be some monopoly power, as in Romer's (1990) model. If they are not, the competitive equilibrium will be inefficient, since the market will undersupply the factors that give rise to externalities. See Ehrlich 1990.
6. One of the most striking results of Barro's model is that private investment reaches

maximum at a level of public productive expenditures lower than the level that maximizes growth (and the present value of the utility of the future consumption stream); hence, a negative relation between taxes and private investment cannot be interpreted unambiguously as evidence of inefficiency.

7. Statistical studies concerning the effect of government expenditures on growth yield disparate results. They suffer from definitional, econometric, and specification problems. Data on the stock of public capital are hard to construct, and using flows (investment) forces reliance on cross-sectional analysis – a problem confronted by Barro (1989). Weede (1983) found a negative impact of government on growth by taking countries where government expenditures exceeded 20 percent of GDP – a flagrant truncation bias. In general, no study attempted to control for selection bias. Finally, Barro (1990) is the only study that tests an explicit model of growth. If the size of government productive expenditures optimal for growth is more than zero and less than one and if all countries behave optimally, then the two variables should not be statistically related in a linear model, and this is what Barro discovered. For a discussion of some of these issues, see Barro 1990.

8. More generally, to general surprise, recent statistical evidence demonstrates that growth is faster in countries that enjoy a more equal distribution of income. The 1991 *World Development Report* (World Bank 1991: 137) presents startling data to this effect, while Persson and Tabellini (1991) offer regression analyses for two distinct periods.

9. Edwards (1990) seems to be the only person who emphasizes the importance of an active labor policy as an intrinsic element of a reform package, arguing that institutions affecting labor should be created before stabilization and liberalization.

10. It is worth noting that the increases in unemployment that invariably accompany market-oriented reforms are not necessarily accompanied by a drop in the real wages of those who continue to be employed. Wage rates in the private sector rose sharply after stabilization in Great Britain under Thatcher, in Spain, and in Bolivia after 1985 and in Chile after 1975, while in all these countries the rate of unemployment hovered around a figure in double digits. Only in Eastern Europe did wage rates fall sharply as the economies stabilized. This is a puzzling phenomenon; see the discussion of Bolivia in Bruno et al. 1991. One explanation is that stabilization followed a drastic drop in wages; another is that the exchange rate was too high; a third is that unemployment had a highly structural character.

11. In an interesting study, Grassi (1991) found that in eighteen new democracies wage militancy was negatively related to government spending and had no relation to either unemployment or investment. Hence, it seems that workers are willing to trade social spending for private wages.

12. According to Morales (1991: 29), unemployment was also the central issue that preoccupied voters in the Bolivian electoral campaign of May 1989. Note that we are not arguing that the mere presence of unemployment will cause people to turn against the reforms and the governments that pursue them but only that this will occur if the unemployed have few prospects of finding other jobs and have no income security. In Spain, for example, 58 percent of employed workers voted for the PSOE in the elections of 1986, and so did 57 percent of the unemployed.

13. Zélia Cardoso, the former minister of finance in Brazil, recounts that to decide the amount of funds that were to be subject to a capital levy, she wrote three round numbers and pulled them out of a hat at a social gathering (Sabini 1991).

14. Ellen Comisso forced us to make this point explicit.

15. Moreover, institutional constraints operate effectively only if they are supported by political conditions; institutions do not function in a vacuum. Influenced by the political culture of the United States, some neo-liberal economists call for constitutional restraint as the solution to the issue of credibility. Bernholz (1991: 50), for example, argues that instead of "prematurely" developing a welfare state, Bolivia should constitutionally restrain the power of governments. In his view, "the discretionary power of the administration and of parliament have to be circumscribed. . . . An independent central bank that can refuse to extend credit to the government, constitutional limits on budget deficits and on maximum marginal tax rates, provisions against over- and hidden expropriation without adequate compensation, and an independent judiciary are some of the institutional requirements necessary. Any violation of these rules should be prosecuted in the courts, and changes in the corresponding constitutional rules should require, say, a two-thirds majority in parliament." This kind of program seems to be motivated by the idea that what we cannot get in the United States we can at least introduce in Bolivia. But this idea cannot work in either country.

16. Throughout we have said little about privatization because we think that it is largely motivated by the need to improve the state's short-term financial position rather than by long-term considerations of efficiency.

17. Contrary to frequent assertions, the statistical evidence that taxation lowers private investment is at best mixed. Saunders and Klau (1985) did not find any effects for the OECD countries; Swank (1991) did. Blejer and Cheasty did not find it for the less developed countries.

18. Ca. 1986, taxes on income, profits, and capital gains amounted to 4.9 percent of government revenue in Argentina and 67.4 percent in Japan. The average for Argentina, Bolivia, Brazil, Chile, Mexico, Peru, and Uruguay was 13.7 percent; for ten industrial market economies it was 40.0 percent (based on Teitel 1991: 138).

19. For micro evidence based on interviews with Argentine businessmen, see López 1991.

20. Let the present value of the future consumption stream of the median voter without any reforms be S. Let the present value of the future consumption of the median voter under a liberalization program in which no one loses a job unless he or she can instantaneously get another one (or become self-employed) be G. Finally, let the value of a program that generates market incomes higher than G but also a positive probability of unemployment, ϕ, be $R(\phi)$. Then it will normally be true that $G > S$, but G is the lower boundary that R must exceed for the government to be victorious electorally under standard stylized conditions. Given minimal assumptions about risk aversion, this inequality imposes a constraint on the pace of liberalization measured by the time path of unemployment.

21. To cite just one number, according to Morgan Stanley (*Financial Times*, 19

December 1990), the cost of social policies that would maintain minimal protection in Eastern Europe over the next five years is between $270 and $370 billion.

References

Barro, Robert J. 1989. "A Cross-Country Study of Growth, Saving, and Government." National Bureau of Economic Research Working Paper no. 2855. Cambridge, Mass.

——— 1990. "Government Spending in a Simple Model of Endogenous Growth." *Journal of Political Economy* 98: S103–S125.

Becker, Gary S., Murphy, Kevin M., and Tamura, Robert. 1990. "Human Capital, Fertility, and Economic Growth." *Journal of Political Economy* 98: 12–38.

Bernholz, Peter. 1991. "Comments." In Bruno, Fischer, Helpman, Liviatan, and Meridor (eds.) 1991.

Blanchard, Oliver, Dornbusch, Rüdiger, Krugman, Paul, Layard, Richard, and Summers, Lawrence. 1991. *Economic Reform in the East*. Cambridge, Mass.: MIT Press.

Blejer, Mario I., and Cheasty, Adrienne. 1989. "Fiscal Policy and Mobilization of Savings for Growth." In Mario I. Blejer and Ke-young Chu (eds.), *Fiscal Policy, Stabilization, and Growth in Developing Countries*. Washington, D.C.: IMF.

Bruno, Michael. 1991. "Introduction and Overview." In Bruno et al. (eds.) 1991.

Bruno, Michael, Fischer, S., Helpman, E., Liviatan, N., and Meridor, L. (eds.). 1991. *Lessons of Economic Stabilization and Its Aftermath*. Cambridge, Mass.: MIT Press.

Cheibub, José Antônio. 1991. "Taxation in Latin America: A Preliminary Report." Manuscript, Department of Political Science, University of Chicago, July.

Di Tella, Guido. 1991. Comment in the panel discussion. In Bruno et al. (eds.) 1991.

Edwards, Sebastian. 1990. "The Sequencing of Economic Reform: Analytical Issues and Lessons from Latin American Experiences." *World Economy* 13: 1–14.

Edwards, Sebastian, and Edwards, A. C. 1991. *Monetarism and Liberalization: The Chilean Experiment*. Cambridge, Mass.: Ballinger.

Ehrlich, Isaac. 1990. "The Problem of Development: Introduction." *Journal of Political Economy* 98: S1–S11.

Findlay, Ronald. 1990. "The New Political Economy: Its Explanatory Power for the LDCs." *Economics and Politics* 2: 193–221.

Fischer, Stanley. 1991. Comment in the panel discussion. In Bruno et al. (eds.) 1991.

Frenkel, Jacob. 1991. Comment in the panel discussion. In Bruno et al. (eds.) 1991.

Grassi, David. 1991. "Economic and Organizational Determinants of Wage Restraint in New Democracies." Manuscript, University of Chicago.

Grossman, Gene M. 1990. "Promoting New Industrial Activities: A Survey of Recent Arguments and Evidence." *OECD Economic Studies*, no. 14 (Spring).

Hardin, Russell. 1987. "Why a Constitution?" Manuscript, University of Chicago.

Lechner, Norbert. 1985. "Pacto social nos processos de democratização: A experiencia Latino-Americana." *Novos Estudos* 13.

Levine, Ross, and Renelt, David. 1991. "A Sensitivity Analysis of Cross-Country Growth Regressions." World Bank Working Paper WPS 609. Washington, D.C.

López, Juan. 1991. "Political Determinants of Private Investment in Argentina: Field Work Impressions." Manuscript, University of Chicago.

Lucas, Robert E., Jr. 1988. "On the Mechanics of Economic Development." *Journal of Monetary Economics* 22: 3–42.

Marsh, Robert M. 1988. "Sociological Explanations of Economic Growth." *Studies in Comparative International Research* 13: 41–76.

Meyer, John W., Hannan, Michael T., Rubinson, Richard, and Thomas, George M. 1979. "National Economic Development, 1950–70: Social and Political Factors." In John W. Meyer and Michael T. Hannan (eds.), *National Development and the World System*. Chicago: University of Chicago Press.

Morales, Juan Antonio. 1991. "The Transition from Stabilization to Sustained Growth in Bolivia." In Bruno et al. (eds.) 1991.

Persson, Torsten, and Tabellini, Guido. 1991. "Is Inequality Harmful for Growth? Theory and Evidence." Working Paper no. 91–155. Department of Economics, University of California at Berkeley.

Przeworski, Adam. 1991. *Democracy and the Market: Political and Economic Reforms in Eastern Europe and Latin America*. Cambridge: Cambridge University Press.

Remmer, Karen L. 1986. "The Politics of Economic Stabilization: IMF Standby Programs in Latin America, 1954–1984." *Comparative Politics* 19, 1 (October).

Rhee, Sungsup. 1987. "Policy Reforms of the Eighties and Industrial Adjustments in Korean Economy." Korea Development Institute Working Paper no 8708. Seoul.

Romer, Paul M. 1990. "Endogenous Technical Change." *Journal of Political Economy* 98: S71–S103.

Sabini, Fernando. 1991. *Zélia, Uma Paixão*. Rio de Janeiro: Editora Record.

Saunders, Peter, and Klau, Friedrich. 1985. *The Role of the Public Sector: Causes and Consequences*. OECD Economic Studies 4. Paris: OECD.

Stiglitz, Joseph A. 1991. "Whither Socialism? Perspectives from the Economics of Information." Manuscript, Yale University.

Swank, Duane H. 1992. "Politics and the Structural Dependence of the State in Capitalist Democracies." *American Political Science Review* 86.

Teitel, Simon. 1991. "Comments." In Bruno et al. (eds.) 1991.

Weede, Erich. 1983. "The Impact of Democracy on Economic Growth: Some Evidence from Cross-National Analysis." *Kyklos* 36: 21–39.

Williamson, John. 1990. "The Progress of Policy Reform in Latin America." In Williamson (ed.), *Latin American Adjustment: How Much Has Happened?* Washington, D.C.: Institute of International Economics.

World Bank. 1991. *World Development Report 1991*. Washington, D.C.: World Bank.

Author index

Subject index